]

THE STORM WHISPERER is a book that needs a shoutout and I want to be one of the loudest. Dolly combines her deep commitment to her Scripture foundation together with her clinical training without compromising either. Whether you are a struggler or one who serves them, I highly recommend this book. Her use of the book of John to share insights on emotional and spiritual recovery is superb. As I reviewed the manuscript, I kept thinking *Dolly, get this in print as soon as possible so I can recommend it to dozens of my colleagues* . . . On a personal note, as Co-Founder of Adult & Teen Challenge, I believe strongly in keeping Jesus at the center of our calling to treat addiction. After reading this Biblically, yet clinically sound manuscript I say, "Thank you, Dolly." Every faith-based recovery worker needs to read this!

Rev. Don Wilkerson
Co-Founder of Adult & Teen Challenge

With intentional grace and expanded wisdom, Dolly Thomas brings simplicity and clarity to those struggling with mental health issues. Through her gentle writing, she encourages readers to lean in to the God who heals, comforts, and brings a peace that truly passes all understanding. If you need help or if you help others, this book is for you.

Dr. Gary W. Blackard
President/CEO Adult & Teen Challenge

In *The Storm Whisperer,* Dr. Dolly Thomas offers valuable insight into Jesus' approach to healing the brokenhearted. Her book identifies Biblical truths and explains how to use these powerful tools to combat emotional and relational dysfunction. Dolly's personal challenges after the tragic death of her father during early adolescence propelled her in the direction of Christian psychological counseling. I wholeheartedly recommend this book as a helpful addition to personal, spiritual growth and development.

Rev. Tim R. Barker
South Texas Assemblies of God District Superintendent

Dr. Dolly Thomas insightfully reveals the answer to our world's growing mental health crisis. Drawing from a wealth of practical experience and spiritual depth, she uses Scripture to identify and unpack key facets of the way Jesus brought healing to the broken and hurting. Through guided reflection and practical steps, the reader will be better equipped to walk in wholeness. This book is a gem that we hope will be read and treasured.

Jim and Kathie Hobson
National Directors of The Ultimate Journey

This is not just another book on mental health, but a gateway for freedom and wholeness as Dr. Dolly leads you through a personal narrative of pain, grief, rejection, revelation, and renewal through the Gospel of John. These chapters will captivate your heart and challenge your soul as she encapsulates each story in a personal and powerful way.

Rev. Paul Strong
Legacy Church—Stafford, Texas

Wow! What an incredible journey Dolly takes us on in this vital work. Her experiences of tragedy and hope bring inspiration and determination to walk closer with Christ and learn how to rise from the ashes of our own disappointments and setbacks. Dolly's insight into the principles gleaned from the Gospel of John is practical and needed in a world where everything seems to be falling apart. You will want to apply these principles to your life and give this book to all your friends and family.

Rev. Greg W. Keylon, President
Rev. Dan T. Strickland, Former President
Living Free; www.LivingFree.org

Too often people live their lives outside in, overly influenced by the world around us. Dr. Dolly Thomas identifies crucial choices that lead to overcoming emotional storms and becoming mentally stable and shows us how to live inside out, by faith.

Rev. Doug Clay
General Superintendent Assemblies of God

THE STORM WHISPERER

Letting Jesus calm your troubled mind and lead you to mental wellness

Dr. DOLLY THOMAS

COPYRIGHT PAGE

The Storm Whisperer
Letting Jesus calm your troubled mind and lead you to mental wellness

Published by CHARA Publishing House
ISBN 9798837 198243

Cover Design: 90designs.com; Photo Image: Diana Rackow; Consultant: Rick Marschall
Editor, Type-setter: Barbara E. Haley

Disclaimer: In order to maintain anonymity when discussing clients, I have changed all names and identifying details to protect the privacy of individuals.

Printed in the United States of America

In Memorandum

In Memory of Eapen G. Varghese

My artist dad, childhood hero, and the one who still inspires me to love creation and be creative. Thirty-four years closer to seeing you in heaven!

In Memory of Ardell Fleck Reimer

I love you and miss your friendship. You always believed in me. It's finally done!

Dedication

This book is written in honor of my parents, Eapen and Rachel Varghese, especially my mom, who raised me in the Lord and gave me a solid foundation in the principles of God's Word. I am indebted to her sacrifice and to ceaseless prayers—I became who she prayed me to be. I honor my parents by marriage, Rajan and Leela Thomas, who raised George to love and serve God wholeheartedly. Our faithful prayer warriors, they have taught by example that always putting God first brings great blessing.

I write this book in honor of the incredible people God has given me the privilege of counseling and teaching over the years, through Transform Counseling, JBQ, First AG SA, Chi alpha, and Adult & Teen Challenge. All of you inspire me to keep living a Christ-serving, abundant life, and I thank God for your courage to choose life, find freedom, and live for Christ.

To our beloved pup, Paws. You and I shared an office, and you were a sweet writing buddy. I had no idea that during the writing of this book that you were dying of a stomach cancer that would take your life suddenly. We miss you and are so grateful to God for our memories with you.

I dedicate this book to my husband, George, and my children, Jadyn, Liana, Caris, and Luke. The five of you give me life, reason, and excitement every day, and it is a JOY to be your wife/mom. From pickleball to daily jogs to karate to game nights to road trips, there are no better people to do life with than all of you. Thank you for your patience as I spent long hours writing. LY4L.

For my Lord and Savior, who gave me breath and saved me from fire to declare Your salvation from eternal fire, I am nothing without You. This book is Yours. My life is Yours. All THIS is for Your glory, Lord.

He stilled the storm to a whisper;

the waves of the sea were hushed.

Psalm 107:29

I have come that they may have life,

and that they may have it more abundantly.

John 10:10 (NKJV)

TABLE OF CONTENTS

FOREWORD

I recently purchased a new classical guitar that came with a warranty, care instructions, and detailed information on how this 6-string was built. It plays at its best if it is stored in the recommended temperature and humidity range, wiped down after play, and handled in a specific way. Alternately, if steel strings are placed on the guitar, if it comes into contact with material containing certain chemicals, or if it is subjected to drastic temperature changes, the guitar can warp, break, and not operate as intended. My recent purchase reminds me how God created us as spiritual beings – with a body and a mind. Our Creator was gracious enough to also provide care instructions and include a warranty that guarantees help at all times—His very presence!

In the United States, one in five adults experience mental illness each year. The most common conditions are anxiety and depression. But it's the ripple effect of mental illness that is alarming—increased likelihood of cardiovascular and metabolic diseases, substance use disorder, unemployment, and dropping out of high school. A humanistic mindset says that a human, independent from God, with determination, knowledge, and medication, can possibly manage addiction and learn limited functionality with mental illness. But a Christ-dependent mindset highlights the hope, victory, healing, and testimony that ensues when God intervenes in our impossible situations.

While serving with the ministry of Adult & Teen Challenge over the last few decades, I have been privileged to witness the salvation of thousands of students who once struggled with addiction. Beyond that, I've witnessed their healing from mental illness and emotional trauma. I attribute these miracles to the power of Jesus Christ, healthy relationships within the body of Christ, and obedience to the Word of God. In each situation, the student's mess became his or her message.

My unwavering conclusion is that there is restoration and eternal hope for anyone struggling with mental, relational, and emotional storms. When we acknowledge our dependence on Him, the storm we are going through will either settle down or Jesus will captain the boat we are sailing in through the storm!

Dolly gets this! She has written an excellent resource that will resound with the reader and provide hands-on instruction on how the Word of God applies to caring for our spirit, mind, and emotions. Each principle presented in *The Storm Whisperer* is taken directly from the Holy Scriptures. Dolly's personal experiences and formal training accentuate, illustrate, and explain how the creation intimately responds to its Creator and receives joy, peace, and an abundant life in return.

I highly recommend this resource for anyone going through or helping someone navigate a storm.

Dr. George Thomas—President/CEO
Adult & Teen Challenge of Texas

ACKNOWLEDGEMENTS

To my dear friends and family who have prayed me through the labor pains of this book, thank you. Writing is no easy feat, especially when you're juggling life. But just like the paralyzed man had friends of tremendous faith who brought him to Jesus to be healed, my faithful and faith-filled friends (you all know who you are) brought me and my need to our Jesus. That's why the book is finished. Thank You, Jesus, for the people in my corner. Each of you has truly blessed me.

When I finished my first draft of the book, I felt a sense of fulfillment, but I knew I was not done. I had obeyed God in writing, now I knew He intended for me to put it out there. I sought God for help to go the next steps, and He provided amazingly.

Many thanks to Diana Rackow for the excellent cover image and video.

I am so grateful for Sarah Bottarel's editorial expertise: for your attention to detail, thorough critique, and constant encouragement.

I am indebted to Barb Haley for her sincerity, passion, dedication, and discernment in preparing the book for distribution. Barb, you freely gave countless hours of your editorial and publishing expertise to invest in the ministry of this message. Thank you for mentoring me, and for your sacrificial labor of love. May God bless you even more.

With deep gratitude, I honor George, who spent hours combing through every word of this book and praying with me for God to use this for His glory. I love you!

To Mom, my sister Julie, and my brother Tobin—thank you for letting me share our story.

Introduction

"Mom, I can't breathe." I moaned weakly, coughing for breath. The overpowering odor of smoke and blood filled my airways. Drowsy and disoriented, I wiped my face, horrified to see blood on my hands.

I scanned my surroundings, and to my shock and horror, realized we had crashed into a tree and our car was on fire. Bright orange flames from the engine of our Ford Fairmont pierced the starry night sky.

"Dad, Dad! Wake up!" I desperately tried to rouse him as he lay unconscious, but he would not respond.

"Mom! Please!" I continued with futile attempts, but she, too, had been knocked unconscious.

"Julie! Tobin! WAKE UP!"

My seven-year-old brother, seated between my parents in the front without a seat belt, leaned limply against the dashboard. My nine-year-old sister, seated beside me in the back seat, started to awaken. Terror-stricken, with burns on her left arm, she moaned in pain and struggled to breathe.

The car shifted unsteadily in the embankment. Dad's beloved video camera was dangerously close to falling out a shattered window. "Dad, your camera!"

I tried to rescue it but pulled my hand back quickly as the flames closed in on us. The doors of the sedan were jammed shut; attempting to climb out of the broken window, with shards everywhere, seemed useless.

Finally, I looked toward the moonlit heavens and whispered from the depth of my eleven-year-old soul, "Oh, God, please help us!"

In what seemed like just a moment later, people made their way down to our car through the wooded ditch. Risking their lives to save ours, they pulled us from the car: my brother, my sister, and then me. Finally, they were able to drag my father out of the vehicle. We found out later he was able to regain moments of consciousness and asked about each one of us by name, wondering if we had gotten out.

However, my mom was stuck. The vicious fire raged on, and by this time, her seatbelt had melted shut. Jack, one of our brave rescuers, told us years after the accident that he thought she was a "goner." Though they tried all they could, there was no way they could get her out. Exhausted and defeated, they were forced to leave her there to burn.

But God.

I remember looking down into the ditch from the side of the highway, watching our heroes pull my father out, waiting for them to come back with Mom. Out of nowhere, someone on a motorcycle drove up. Without hesitation, he walked into the fire-filled ditch and carried my mom out in his arms. By this time the ambulance had arrived, and he put her on a stretcher. No one caught his name. Then, just as suddenly as he had come, he drove off into the night. Minutes later, the Ford exploded.

Mayhem ensued, and I had no presence of mind to ponder what had just happened—or the fact that had God heard my prayer. That the Creator of the universe actually heard me, a young immigrant girl, and brought people to rescue my family from tragedy. That the Commander of the armies of heaven summoned one of His heavenly beings to cross from heaven to earth, take on human form, and pull my mom out of a fire.

The miraculous night also marked the most devastating one of my life. My father, my best friend, was life-flighted from the accident scene and died soon after reaching the trauma hospital. Cardiac hemorrhaging took his life.

My beloved mom remained in critical condition for days, suffering a broken leg and third-degree burns on a third of her body. She was in a hospital bed for a year and endured countless surgeries and skin grafts to save her left arm from amputation.

My precious sister, Julie, had to recover from her burn and a broken rib. My darling brother, Tobin, had a broken jaw and leg, while I had cuts on my face and damage to my teeth.

But our physical pain paled in comparison to the emotional distress each of us suffered in our own way.

For me, the months following the accident were dotted with recurring nightmares involving fire and car accidents, coupled with heartache and yearning for someone who would never come back. Life would never be the same at home.

We were thrashed by a storm that broke our joy, peace, and security. Though ferocious waves of sadness and discord crashed upon our home, my mom held onto an anchor that would never fail or disappoint. Just like she couldn't exist without air, she depended on God to guide her. Jesus came to her rescue, and He did the same for my siblings and me.

I marvel at the fact that God can take our worst moments in life and bring good out of them. Like He did for countless saints in the Bible, He has done for me.

While lying in a hospital room after the accident, my siblings and I constantly asked about the condition of our parents. We learned Dad was taken to a trauma unit and Mom was in critical condition in a burn unit. Everyone dodged our questions about Dad. Finally, Regi Aunty, a social worker who attended our church, came to my hospital bed with the news.

"Dolly, your father died," she stated bluntly.

Disbelief and searing pain filled me as my skin grew warm and my eyes burned with tears.

As I cried, she went to my sister's bed and gave her the same dreaded report. My sister erupted in heartbreaking sobs.

My brother, wondering what was happening, just kept asking, "What, guys? What's the matter?" I will never forget what happened in the next few moments. As Regi Aunty announced that my brother's hero and mentor—Dad—had gone from earth to heaven, Tobin let out a shrilling scream.

At the sound of his distraught voice, God did something for me. He took the focus off my loss and caused me to feel deeply for my baby brother. What would life be like for him, growing up without his dad? How would he handle the pain?

Of course the loss for my sister, my mom, and me was earth shattering in different ways, but I began to wonder how this little boy would handle Dad's death. I didn't realize it until many years later, but in that supernatural moment, I believe God birthed in me a compassion for people enduring pain and suffering.

In a manner only God could do, the Lord didn't erase my pain but gave me purpose for it.

I was called to help the brokenhearted.

The Storm Within

A well-dressed professional lady in her late twenties walked into my counseling office with a shy smile. Handing me her intake paperwork, she positioned herself nervously on the couch. I saw uncertainty in her eyes. She was about to disclose her life story. Would I judge her? And more importantly, could I help her?

She had battled depression and anxiety for so long it had crippled her ability to make decisions, pursue dreams, or hear God's voice. She loved God genuinely but felt deeply insecure and bruised by the fact that *everyone* around her was married and progressing with life, while she remained stuck.

As I got to know and understand Lyla, it became clear that none of her accomplishments mattered to her and the joy of her current blessings waned because she didn't have a husband—the one thing in life that she believed would define her worth and self-concept.

Lacking this one thing triggered attention to every deeply held flaw she perceived in herself. In the next several sessions, she explained how she felt inferior, ugly, undesirable, and incapable. Her childhood insecurities had resurfaced, negating her adult successes.

One day I asked her to write down and then state aloud how she saw herself. These words proceeded: "You're ugly. You're fat. You don't measure up. You are not good at anything. You are worthless."

"Would you ever say those words to anyone else?" I asked gently. "I'd like for you to call me those names."

Abashed, the kind lady insisted that she would never speak so harshly to another. Surprised by the intensity of her self-disgust, she commented on how abusive it all sounded when she said it out loud. Yet her inner voice bullied her constantly as she waited for her prayers to be answered, with longing in her soul. These thoughts led to bouts of depression, suicidal ideation, lack of motivation, and overwhelming anxiety about her future.

Can you relate to Lyla's story? Do you, too, wrestle with self-disgust and discouragement? Many people are tired of battling age-old voices and feel stuck in their own private world of life-controlling depression and anxiety. The statistics are upsetting; rates of depression, anxiety, and suicide are rising at alarming rates.

Dependence and substance abuse is also on the rise. Addiction, a hybrid of medical and psychological issues, might seem like it fits in a category of its own since it involves a unique set of neurological conditions. However, if you peel back the layers, you will find that thoughts leading to addiction are extremely similar to thoughts underlying anxiety and depression. With dismal success rates for "curing" addiction, is there even any hope?

Addiction . . . anxiety . . . depression: each represents a storm in our minds that needs calming.

Jesus understands storms. In Mark 4:35-39, Jesus and His disciples were on a boat in the dark of night when a furious squall arose. Waves splashed over the sides; water pooled in the bottom of the boat. Jesus, who had fallen asleep on a cushion in the stern, didn't stir.

The disciples woke Him. "Don't You care if we drown?"

Jesus stood and addressed the storm. "Quiet, be still!" In essence, "You're scaring my friends. That's enough."

And like an obedient,well-trained child, the wind and waves returned to their place. The disciples calmed, relieved to know Jesus was completely in control. After all, Jesus is the Storm Whisperer.

Our minds can resemble this stormy sea; we're influenced by the elements around us. New ideologies confuse us, changing circumstances lead to insecurity, our bodies age and make us more vulnerable to certain issues, and the people with whom we surround ourselves affect us like atmospheric patterns impact the weather.

Trauma and losses from childhood, like the loss my family weathered, change the trajectory of our future. Before we know it, a storm brews in our minds, and if we're not mindful, it can develop into full blown depression or anxiety and completely overtake us.

The storms in our minds need calming. People attempt to calm these storms in different ways. Some externalize and take out their pain on others. Some internalize and take their feelings out on themselves. Some act out and aggress. Others escape and numb.

But the reason underneath the surface of these different symptoms, found deep within the cerebral cortex and even deeper inside every soul, is a struggle to believe the truth and adopt certain mindsets.

Are you searching for truth that will overcome your storm? There's only one person who has the answers to all of life's difficulties. His name is Jesus. Psalm 107:29 states His superiority over any storm: "He stilled the storm to a whisper; the waves of the sea were hushed."

If you struggle to find peace amid the squalls of your life, this resource is written for you. This book is intended for anyone wanting to prevent and treat mental illness—specifically, anxiety, depression and addiction—using a non-pharmaceutical approach. For the record, I use the term "mental illness" very generically. I'm not defining it as a disease like a sickness one contracts. Rather, I use the phrase to describe different emotional and psychological issues that perturb humankind.

Jesus Cares About You

Jesus has always gone after the *one*. His ministry is personal and individualized, not cookie cutter and predictable. He came into a broken and lost world where sin has ravaged and wreaked havoc for thousands of years. He focused on one person at a time. One person whose transformed life then had the power to touch others and spark a revolution. Because every life matters, regardless of one's gender, age, ethnicity, or religion, every life has potential and purpose. Every life is the apple of God's eye. And for every life, God sent His Son to be the way to an abundant life—not just a meager, meaningless existence. He gives people significant lives.

Jesus, alone, can lead us to an abundant life by healing our minds and transforming our mindsets.

The Gospel of John records how Jesus ministered to special individuals in each of its twenty-one chapters. He attended to their whole person, perceiving the needs and answering the questions underlying people's words.

Jesus cut to the heart. Not to destroy or judge, but to set free and break people from their habits and hang-ups . . . *our* habits and hang-ups. He had a way of gently turning people upside down.

Jesus sees the storm brewing inside the soul cavity of each person. After all, He is our Creator and He knows us better than we know ourselves. He has perfect insight into how to calm our mental storms.

The way Jesus addressed fears, insecurities, loss, self-esteem, and soul wounds in Biblical times serves as great medicine for us today.

Jesus is the answer to all psychological problems and relationship issues. He still performs ministry to heal the whole person. He rescues countless individuals from the pit of emotional turmoil and relational struggles. This book weaves together Biblical insights with findings from science to help us understand how to live wholly healed.

Is the Bible Enough?

Are you skeptical that principles from the Bible and a drug-free approach can treat mental illness and addiction?

I can relate. Twenty years ago, when I was in graduate school learning about all the different symptoms of mental illness, I was growing in my faith. God had called me to help His children in suffering, but I was not sure which path to take. I loved God and genuinely believed the Scriptures, but I believed that science and medicine had greater insight than my Christian faith on how to heal a broken heart and fix broken relationships (though I would not have openly admitted it). So I put my efforts into learning how to approach life problems from a clinical perspective.

At the time, I didn't realize that God's power through His Word could fully combat the thoughts underlying mental illness. I saw myself as powerless in fighting against them.

I now believe the Bible gives us every tool needed to defend ourselves against mental illness and ward off its symptoms.

When I was finishing up my degree, I took a mission trip to India. While there, a missionary introduced me to Biblical counseling and a whole new world of books, research, and programs that taught people how to overcome mental illness from a Biblical perspective. I became a student of the Bible and of counseling from the Word of God.

God used my husband's first ministry appointment and my first clinical research appointment to demonstrate God's power to transform lives.

While in Connecticut, George visited a Teen Challenge (TC) center near our home and was immediately struck by the transformation of the young man who had given him a tour of the facility. He told me, "Dol, you're not going to believe this place. This guy was completely strung out on drugs and is now set free by Jesus."

Shortly after, George became a full-time volunteer for TC in New Haven. While he volunteered, I visited the center and was also smitten by the work. With neither of us having a background of addiction, I guess you could say that George and I got addicted to the *ministry of the saints* mentioned in 1 Corinthians 16:15 (BSB).

What hooked me was the contrast. The patients I saw at my hospital, affiliated with Yale, and the students George served at TC presented with similar symptoms of addiction and mental illness, but the approach to treat them couldn't have been more distinct.

While George worked with students using the simple gospel, my patients, diagnosed with bipolar disorder, depression, and borderline personality disorder, were offered cutting-edge treatments and medications. As I worked with my patients day after day, I saw minimal improvement. Although they learned coping skills and attained some level of comfort, I saw little lasting change over the weeks. The patterns of their symptoms and relationships remained largely stagnant.

On the flip side, the students at Teen Challenge were metamorphosing week by week; even their countenances were changing. It was like *Extreme Makeover*: Ex-Addict Edition.

What was TC doing to change people so dramatically? They prayed with someone to be saved, taught them the Word of God, and showed them how to live it out. Could it be that simple?

Most of the staff had only a high school diploma and some Bible school. TC used a Biblically-centered curriculum, not necessarily scientifically based. I couldn't believe what I was witnessing. At Yale, I sat in trainings and staff meetings with extremely learned, world-renowned researchers who could offer the best and brightest the world had available. But it simply was not enough to heal the mind and break people from the bondage of addiction and mental illness. Nothing compared to the power of the Word of God to restore, resuscitate, and revitalize people's lives and set them on a new course.

God was patient with me as I struggled to reconcile the two types of treatment. He broke my pride and opened my eyes and my hungry heart. After all, the reason I went into the field of clinical psychology in the first place was because God had given me a genuine compassion for the hurting and the brokenhearted. I wanted do His work in the best way possible, so I followed the course He set directly before me.

God showed me that even the best of what the world has to offer pales in comparison to the power of simple precepts of the Bible to change people. Nothing is as powerful as the Word of God to heal people's minds.

Did the God-Inspired Changes Last?

A 2019 national study found that 78 percent of Adult & Teen Challenge graduates surveyed continued to live upstanding lives even two years post-graduation, an astounding rate compared to the 5-10 percent of secular recovery programs. A program based on evangelism and discipleship was proven again to be far superior to healing the mental issues of a recovering addict.[1]

I resolved that whatever I was going to do as a licensed psychologist, I would do under the authority of Scripture, in deference to the principles of God's Word to set the captive free.

The Bible is full of examples and stories and concepts that inspire and guide people to mental freedom and abundant mental life. How could it not? After all, God is the Creator of the human mind. God knows what sets us off, what distracts us, and what puts us on a path headed toward destruction.

And the magnificent news is that He knows the flip side, too. He knows what brings us to freedom and wholeness—the blueprint to mental health. God is Creator. Therefore, no theories compare to His knowledge and understanding. Research will never discover anything He doesn't already know. Why not consult the source, the ultimate physician, the Great Healer?

I realized that in order to serve people desperate for life transformation, I had to fully immerse myself into the study of God's Word and become a servant of the gospel.

A Completely "Other" Approach

In John 10:10, Jesus warned that "The thief comes only to steal and kill and destroy." Jesus came so we "may have life, and have it to the full." He referred to the enemy of our souls who wants not only our eternal destruction but also our subpar living on earth.

Jesus explained that God sent Him to earth in the form of a human to fulfill God's great mission of making a way for people to have abundant life. The Greek word for "full" or "abundant" is *perissos* which refers to "extraordinary, uncommon, more remarkable, and more excellent."[2]

Jesus offers a much better alternative to the devil's attempts to steal and destroy our lives. Yielding to Christ gives us an amazing, more-than-we-can-imagine, super advantageous life.

Did you catch that?

The life Jesus offers is better than the best thing out there. It's above and beyond the latest trends and the best-selling self-help books and life hacks. It's better than what the most recent and best researched finding psychology has to offer.

Jesus is completely *other!* What do I mean by that?

The thought life and mental health Jesus offers surpasses any existing category. Jesus came to give us a full life. That doesn't mean it will be problem or stress-free, or a life devoid of pain. On the contrary. He uses pain as a vehicle to grow us. Every setback becomes a setup to show His power and grace. "My grace is sufficient for you, for my power is made perfect in weakness" (2 Cor. 12:9). Our weaknesses, losses, and pains become the very avenue by which Christ gives us an exceedingly abundant full life. What is our role? Developing an "exceedingly abundant" thought life.

What does that mean in practical terms? The exceedingly abundant thought life is, simply put, *other* than the thought life of this world. It transcends cultural and current trends. Though not always contrary to the world, Jesus' principles for a healthy thought life do contradict how the world tells us to think and live.

We live in a time when anything goes. You can be your own person, you can create your own definitions for words, and you can espouse your personal opinions and call them truth. Everything seems relative—modern culture embraces no absolute truths.

On the contrary, God's grounding principles for our thought life are based on absolutes and non-negotiables. Scary at times? Yes. But surprisingly, most people who once lived their lives to the extreme, find submitting to sensible rules and restrictions very comforting.

Our Adult & Teen Challenge (ATC) students are a prime example. Many come from a lifestyle of utter lawlessness, and although the rules of the twelve-month program are initially jolting and even confining, those who choose life find great security and comfort in the guidelines. In fact, the guidelines actually become anchors and guideposts.

This book focuses on thought patterns that lend to a victorious life. Much has been written on the power of positive thinking from a secular psychological perspective. There are great concepts and effective coping skills to learn. However, like I experienced at Yale, skills devoid of the power of God can only go so far. Only a "completely other" or an "exceedingly abundant" approach can truly overcome the depths of mental and emotional destruction in which people can find themselves.

THE GOSPEL OF JOHN

When I counsel people for the first time, I often encourage them to read through the Gospel of John to acquaint or reacquaint them with the person and perspective of Jesus. The twenty-one chapters of John serve as a springboard for the principles of mental health presented in this book. This study does not provide an exhaustive Bible study on the Gospel of John; there are many great resources for that. Instead, we will focus on a concept from each chapter that will lead you to freedom in your mind and mental wellness.

As mentioned earlier, in each chapter of John, Jesus ministered to an individual or group of people with a life-changing truth to calm their storms. Whether He was confronting people, correcting them, or curing them, He always ministered to the whole person. We will explore His interaction with His brothers, His disciples, Mary and Martha, the Jewish leaders, and many others. We will touch on precepts for "soul hygiene" and cultivating an abundant thought life.

This book highlights twenty-one choices one can make. I encourage you to read the corresponding chapter of John before you read and respond to each chapter of *The Storm Whisperer.*

You can read a chapter a day or chunks. Each chapter contains response sections on **Truths to Live By** and **Lies to Refute**. Commit these to your life like medicine to prevent or treat emotional disturbances. You will have the opportunity to follow practical suggestions in the **Take It to Heart** section. Take your time working through the concepts to increase your probability of lasting change. The tools found in each chapter will reinforce and incorporate liberating truths in your daily life.

Incorporating these principles into your life will inoculate you from future attacks on your emotional health by creating a mental fortress to protect you when the troubles of life come, as Jesus promised they would in John 16:33. "In this world you will have trouble. But take heart! I have overcome the world."

One does not need to be a Christian to glean truth from this book, but be fairly-warned that this writing is founded upon the Bible because no textbook or self-help book or article can stand in comparison to the abundant life that flows from it.

Unfortunately, I cannot guarantee results. True change always involves a combination of your effort with God's power. That's how miracles happen—your part and God's part. By faith, if you practice these suggestions consistently, change will happen, and I believe God will help you move forward.

A behavior repeated consistently over time can lead to new life patterns. Brain scans indicate nerve maps actually change through the repetition of new behaviors and thoughts.[3] Of course, you still have to exercise the power of decision and continue the habit that you have worked hard to form.

Create a time and space to engage with the material of this text. Consider distinguishing the location in some way so you can attribute it to a place of healing, self-reflection, and victory. Find a time that works best for you when you are not too tired and can be free of distractions. This journey is so important. Proverbs 4:23 cautions, "Guard your heart with all diligence, for from it flow springs of life" (BSB).

SECTION 2

21 CHOICES FOR ABUNDANT MENTAL WELLNESS

Choose To Worship Wisely

Read: John 1

The doctor's words stunned me. "We need to give you magnesium sulfate to stop the contractions. Without it, you could both die."

Our firstborn daughter wasn't due for five weeks, but my worsening preeclampsia trumped my dreams of experiencing natural, drug-free labor. All those weeks of labor coaching, all the preparation seemed to be in vain. God had different plans.

I was faced with an unwelcome choice. I could keep fighting what was happening to my body on the chance the baby and I could make it through and enjoy a natural delivery. Or I could give up control and trust God in His sovereignty. The choice tormented me. How could I let go while still gripped with fear? Nevertheless, the choice remained and demanded an answer. I asked God to help me let go.

In an amazing turn of events, just a few hours later, our miracle baby Jadyn was born at 4 pounds 3 ounces, 16 inches long. When George and I held our tiny arrival in our hands, I was awestruck and humbled that God had entrusted us with the responsibility and power to shape this important life and influence her future.

Have you ever been given a gift that is both beautiful and scary?

When God created us, He gave us the gift of choice. This gift offers freedom but can alternately lead to a lifetime of bondage. It has great power to influence our future but can also impact our present mood. Some think we might be better off without it, but if God had not given us choice, we would never have been *true* followers of Christ. To follow requires a choice.

Choice is one of those gifts that comes with two sides, like a pool in your backyard that offers hours of entertainment but is a great chore to maintain. My children have wrestled with deep truths in their journey of faith and have all asked at different points in their lives: Why did God create us with the ability to choose? Why couldn't He have made us just love Him and do what is right and follow His path? Wouldn't that have been so much easier? All of us could seemingly go to heaven and live happy lives. Why did Adam get the free will to choose from that tree of knowledge of good and evil?"

The reality is that the choice God gave us sets us apart.

God designed Adam and made Eve to be his helper. He could have created them without free will, without the ability to choose. He could have programmed them like robots, controlling every aspect of their personality and decisions and will. He could have designed people to live in the same manner as the rest of creation, unable to determine what their days would look like, living at the mercy of their instincts and surroundings. Instead, God gave us a piece of Himself, making us in His image, with the ability to think and choose.

Without choice—or free will, our world and history would have been very different. The same would be true in heaven had angels not been given choice. God seeks those who willingly choose to find Him.

The KJV dictionary defines choice as "the voluntary act of selecting or separating from two things that which is more preferred; or the determination of the mind in preferring one thing over another."[4]

The history of choice began at the inception of time. Genesis 2 details how God allowed Adam to choose names for the rest of His creation. He invited Adam to pick a suitable helper from among them, but no suitable helper was found. So the Lord created Eve to be Adam's counterpart and entrusted them both with the gift of choice.

We face countless choices every day. We choose what we wear, we choose our mood, we choose to serve, we choose to follow, we choose to respect our leaders and ourselves, we choose to react out of anger or to have self-control. We even choose who we love—"we don't *fall* in love as we fall into a ditch" (to quote Pastor Wayne Clark.) Rather, we choose to keep thinking about a person and to let an attraction grow into something more.

Of course, many things cannot be controlled, but with everything that happens, we can choose how we respond. Every counseling issue under the sun can be "fixed," or treated, by making new choices–to perceive differently, to feel differently, and to act differently.

Treating the Whole Body

When someone comes in for counseling, I explain my worldview as a counselor. I point out that no one is entirely unbiased and that no matter how neutral I try to be, my belief systems and values will spill over. As a Christian who practices counseling and psychology, I believe God created us as three-dimensional beings—body, mind/soul, and spirit. Although the thrust of counseling is soul care and usually deals with the mind or the soul, addressing the spirit and body must happen in order for holistic healing to take place.

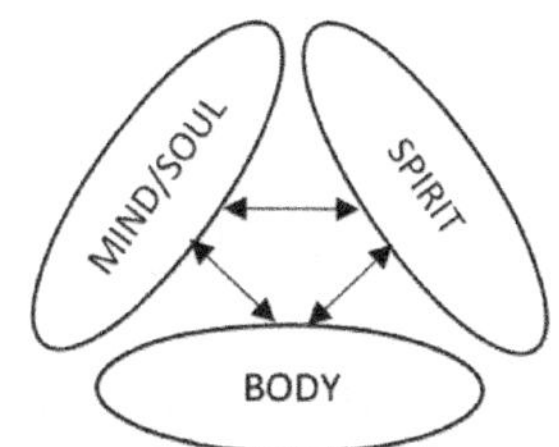

These three aspects of the person co-exist and affect each other.

Starving your spirit will affect the way your body and mind feel and behave; feeding your spirit will nourish the other aspects of your being. The same goes for your body. Treat it well, and you position your mind to function clearly and your soul to flourish, as well as your spirit to be able to connect with God.

In dealing with mental health, it is impossible to affect true and lasting change without addressing all aspects of who we are. Although there has been a recent trend to include spiritual discussion and exploration in secular psychology, I believe the spiritual element should be paramount, not ancillary. Getting to the heart of a person and affecting change requires a renewed spirit, and this must happen before any other lasting work can begin.

The Most Important Choice

There is no choice more significant than who we will worship. Tim Keller said once, "Everyone worships something. The only choice you get is what to worship."[5] Every chance my husband George gets to minister to our ATC students, he teaches that addiction is a worship disorder, a truth Mark Shaw expounds upon in *Heart of Addiction*.[6]

> We all worship something. The problem is that many of us choose to worship things that can't truly satisfy, can't heal, and won't answer our prayers and fulfill our deepest longings. No matter how hard we try, money, sex, drugs, sports, people, or status cannot complete us, define us, or take away our pain. We may look to them, but they will always fall short. Only God can fulfill. Only God has the power to give us purpose and heal our hurts.

THE OBJECT OF OUR WORSHIP

John 1 begins with an introduction to the person of Jesus. He existed in the beginning. He is the Word; He is God. All things were made through Him. In Him is life. He who became flesh is the light of men. Jesus dwelt among people, but came from the Father. He's full of grace and truth. We meet Him as an ethereal being, completely extraordinary. But as we get to know Him better, we recognize that He came to earth for a reason . . . to make the Father known.

In the first chapter of John, we are also confronted with tension. Although Christ came with grace and truth, He was not received or recognized by the world. To those who *did* receive Him, however, He gave power to become the children of God.

Jesus presented a foundational principle for our journey to mental wellness and storm-calming. When the disciples followed Him, Jesus asked, "What do you want?" (John 1:38).

The Greek word for seek is *zeteo*, which means to crave, demand, to aim at or strive after, to endeavor, and to worship.[7] Jesus had an amazing way of asking profound questions in simple ways. He realized the disciples wanted to know where He was staying, but He delved deeper, challenging them about the true motive of their hearts. "What do you really want by following Me? Who do you really worship?"

Some of the first questions I might ask a client or a student at ATC are: Why are you here? Why are you seeking help? In essence, what do you seek? What do you really want from this process?

After reviewing years of counseling notes, I have concluded that clients present with similar problems, though the particulars and complexities differ. Common issues include broken relationships, loss of purpose, and intolerable pain. The clients feel out of control or overwhelmed by emotions and surrounding symptoms. People usually want the same things: answers, relief, restoration of peace, and a return of joy. They want to understand themselves and regain a sense of control to manage their life.

Pause and think about a difficult relationship, a frustration, or a disappointment you are facing. Ask yourself Jesus' questions: What do I really want? Who or what do I really worship? Is it the idea of peace and security in my home, having money or my needs met? Do I worship my spouse or child and place preeminent importance on them? Do I worship the respect and praise of others, friendships, and attention that validate my sense of worth? Do I worship convenience, orderliness, or my own self-seeking preferences?

Paul David Tripp, in his book *Age of Opportunity: A Biblical Guide to Parenting Teens,*[8] suggests that objects, concepts, or people we worship represent idols in our lives. I agree that we discover what we really worship when it's stripped away or hindered in some way. We tend to worship what gives us confidence, joy, and security.

Jesus, knowing our propensity to worship everything around us, teaches us to worship the God who designed us and died for us—to leave all else behind because nothing else will satisfy. If we get our worship right, then our spirit will be whole. That leads to health in our mind and soul.

Accept the Invitation to Belong and Be Whole

Jesus invited His disciples to follow Him: "Come and see what it's like to live a life that totally worships Me and trusts Me, even when you don't understand. Come and see that I have more for you than you can ever imagine and more than the world can ever offer. Come and see–you are invited to the greatest adventure of your lifetime!"

In Matthew 11:28, He said, "Come to me, all you who are weary and burdened, and I will give you rest." Come and you will find rest for your souls. Come and you will see wonders, even heaven opening and angels of God ascending and descending (John 1:51).

As an Indian immigrant growing up in white suburban New Jersey, I craved to fit in, to be part of the majority culture. Unfortunately, this seemed unattainable. When I was in the fourth grade, a neighborhood classmate invited me to her birthday party. I was shocked and elated. It never dawned on me that her kind parents most likely took pity on me and forced her to invite me.

Excited, I walked to her house for the party. Once there, though, hardly anyone spoke to me, not even the birthday girl. While a horror film played on the television, the birthday girl invited the other girls one by one to join her in another room. I was never called. I figured it was something private between her and her friends, and although I tried to shrug it off, I felt left out and out of place. Shortly afterward, I left the party, feeling alone and dejected and worse than if I'd not been invited in the first place.

Uninvited. This feeling resurfaced during childhood and later in life. Maybe you've experienced its different forms: feeling not as cool as others, not being in the know, missing out on opportunities and experiences others seemed to share, and feeling inferior to certain people. Maybe you've felt like a social outsider because everyone else's life seems to be marching forward, and your life just doesn't seem to measure up. You have been waiting for a prayer to be answered that would allow you to catch up with the social clock, the expectations placed on you by the world to be married or have children or to have things. Or perhaps you do have that job or that dream family, but this feeling of loneliness creeps up from time to time, making you feel like you're on the fringe, not important to your world.

By stark contrast, God, the Creator of the universe, has His heavenly arms opened wide to you with an eternal bidding, the greatest invitation you could ever receive, to come unto Him.

This invitation is not forced and has no strings attached. He beckons you and me to a life of worshiping Him. He invites us to come and see what a life following Him would be like.

"Come and see," He says. He's inviting us to come and see how feeding our eternal innermost being with His Word and with His Presence will strengthen and nurture us in ways nothing else can.

Psalm 34:8 says, "Taste and see that the Lord is good; blessed is the one who takes refuge in him."

Jesus invites us to try Him out. To see how He can take our hurt, our baggage, and our issues and work things out for us while we worship Him. When we trust in Him, God works everything out for our good. Sounds like quite the deal, and it may not make sense. But by taking Him up on His invitation, we say in essence, "Lord, I'm trusting You with what is bigger than me. I belong to You, and since You're my Father, You will help me."

Now Choose Life

Joshua, a mighty leader of God, made a farewell address before the assembled tribes of Israel in Joshua 24. In this prophetic speech, God used Joshua's mouth to remind the people how He had fought and provided for them. He recounted victories and the fulfillment of promises.

God had shown the Israelites unexplainable grace, giving them things they did not earn or deserve; this was His unmerited favor. In Joshua 24:14, Joshua challenged them:

> Now fear the Lord and serve him with all faithfulness. Throw away the gods your ancestors worshiped beyond the Euphrates River and in Egypt, and serve the Lord. But if serving the Lord seems undesirable to you, then choose for yourselves this day whom you will serve, whether the gods your ancestors served beyond the Euphrates, or the gods of the Amorites, in whose land you are living. But as for me and my household, we will serve the Lord.

The Israelites had been delivered from bondage in Egypt. Now, under Joshua's leadership, they had settled near the Amorite people. The Amorites worshiped whatever they wanted—much like the world today in its worship of celebrities, music artists, drugs, alcohol, fame, sexual pleasure, lovers, jobs, and money. Joshua, knowing his time of departure was imminent, challenged the people he had faithfully served all his adult life. "Who are you going to follow when I am gone? The gods from your past or the gods you see around you?"

"Now choose life!" he implored them. To worship the one true God is to choose life. But this decision comes with a price—you cannot serve God simultaneously with other things.

True Worship Cannot Be Shared

I remember visiting northern India once where decorated Hindu shrines and temples dotted street corners. I noticed one shrine had a shelf with a picture of Jesus surrounded by other "gods." All were decked out with florals and sweet treats. It was a striking picture of how we try to keep God on the throne along with other things. To think we can worship God while we worship people or while we worship drugs or anything else is to be deceived.

To be free, we must choose. To be whole, we must declare our allegiance to God alone. Many ATC students come into the program claiming they have loved God their whole life. The truth, however, is that while they may have had a love for God, they were not worshiping Him exclusively or wholeheartedly. A half-hearted love is the same, if not worse, than having no love at all.

In Revelation, Jesus admonished the church in Laodicea for being lukewarm, for being halfway in, halfway out. "I know your deeds, that you are neither cold nor hot. I wish you were either one or the other! So, because you are lukewarm–neither hot nor cold–I am about to spit you out of my mouth" (Rev. 3:15-16).

Our worship of God must be pure, complete, and wholehearted. Only He can handle the immense responsibility of meeting our physical, emotional, mental, and spiritual needs. If we place complete faith and trust in a person—a spouse, child, parent, friend—we will eventually destroy the person. God did not create humans to bear this kind of weight.

Imagine David the shepherd boy preparing to go before Goliath. King Saul placed his own armor on David's shoulders, a massive coat of metal plates and a bronze helmet for his head. David took a few steps, then removed the gear. He couldn't function under this burdensome weight he was not designed to wear. Now picture the weight of your needs as that heavy armor. Only God can bear such weight without failing. He alone is worthy to receive our attention, our faith, and our worship.

In 1 Samuel 5:3-4, we read that the Philistines (enemies of God's people) stole the ark of God and placed it in the temple of their god Dagon.

> And when they of Ashdod arose early on the morrow, behold, Dagon was fallen upon his face to the earth before the ark of the Lord. And they took Dagon, and set him in his place again. And when they arose early on the morrow, behold, Dagon was fallen upon his face to the ground before the ark of the Lord; and the head of Dagon and both the palms of his hands were cut off upon the threshold; only the stump of Dagon was left to him. (KJV)

The Lord was not willing to share His throne. He is greater than any other thing or concept we can imagine.

How Do We Worship?

When created, we were hard-wired with a need to worship, so it is actually a natural thing to worship God. However, because so many of us have spent our lives worshiping created things instead, we have to retrain our minds to worship our Maker.

Think about something or someone you really love and enjoy. It could be an activity, a person, or an object. They bring great pleasure, calm your fears, and make you feel comfortable in their presence. You find yourself thinking about this thing or person often, and you can't wait to be with them again. Or it could be an activity to which you are naturally drawn and gifted in performing.

Worshiping God is all of that. It involves a desire for God, an infatuation with His presence, and a desire to put Him first. We might describe it as an insatiable hunger for more of God. The Psalmist understood this when he wrote: As the deer pants for streams of water, so my soul pants for you, my God" (Ps. 42:1).

To worship is to ascribe to someone or something what it is worth, so when we worship God, we are telling Him how worthy He is. In John 4:24, Jesus tells us we must worship God "in the Spirit and in truth"—with desire and longing in spirit, but also with an understanding of the Truth of who He is and how to approach Him.

The Holy Spirit opens our eyes to the goodness of God and stirs us to rejoice in His power and majesty. To worship Him in truth, we must let the Word of God teach us how to approach God and show us His nature. The Word must be the bedrock for our worship of God, or else we are prone to worship Him incorrectly. A person who truly worships God cannot do so without a true dependence on the Word of God. It doesn't matter how loud we sing or how emotional we get when we're singing a song of praise to the Lord if our life isn't also marked by a clear desire to be in the Word of God consistently.

A Life Healed by Worshiping God

The principles in this chapter are true, and they work. I have seen people transformed simply by learning to properly appropriate their worship to God. Witness the story of an ATC student whose life was changed because she made great choices. Step by step, she chose to worship God and belong to His family.

Vida could have chosen to stay stuck in her world of despair, enslaved by the drugs that enticed her when she was young. But when she seemed to have nowhere to go, she made a choice. The truth is, even when you are at rock bottom, you still have choice. Someone told her about ATC of Texas, and she came.

Throughout the program, I had the privilege of watching this courageous woman make choices. When she first came in, she carried a huge weight. Although most of us would never really choose to pick up such a weight, it had become a bag of comfort to her. She chose to pick up this bag of anxiety, fear, paranoia, rejection, even meanness at times, because that's what she knew; that's what her childhood was like. When people rejected her, she found control by being mean and unapproachable. That's not who she really was deep down inside, but the mask of meanness made her feel safe and in control.

What she didn't realize is that when we continue to choose some things, we actually forfeit the freedom of choice. We get enslaved as we entangle ourselves in a pattern and trap. We position ourselves poorly and make decisions that actually hurt us.

While in the program, Vida chose to look at herself and get everything she could get from her education, counseling, and advising. But it wasn't always easy. Somehow, she found herself reverting back to old ways as she progressed through the program. When she was triggered, she went back to old choices and comfortable patterns rather than embracing the new person she was becoming.

I remember the day in my office when she was faced with the choice of being transferred to a sister campus or walking away from ATC due to disciplinary issues. I wanted so badly for her to choose well, for her to choose life, for her to choose Christ, even if it seemed harder at first. At times when I'm counseling, I might look calm like a serene duck on the surface, but underneath I'm furiously paddling–I'm asking for the Spirit of God to intervene and help someone choose well. Only He can change a person's mind and help her make a choice that will positively impact the trajectory of her future.

She chose to go to the other campus—the best choice she could have made. She felt at peace because she knew she had just afforded herself the chance to make a new beginning. God opened the door, but she had to choose to walk through it.

A few weeks later, she told me she felt a mental fortitude that she hadn't felt in a long time. What was the secret? Besides the amazing leaders and serenity around her, the secret was really her choice—to seek God, pursue Him with all her heart, look to Him, trust Him, delve into Scripture, and draw close to Jesus. And to recognize that she had been set apart to serve God.

It was Vida's choice to view ATC as holy ground, a special place God gave vision to because of the obedience of one man, David Wilkerson, and the faithfulness of countless servants along the way—a vision that brought life to thousands of people and is still doing so today. And in this place of miracles, she chose to be willing to be corrected, to be steered, and to help others.

It all began with worship and accepting the great invitation to belong and be whole. Her life is now completely transformed, she is restored to her family, has good friends, and knows peace and purpose. Today, Vida serves on staff at ATC, influencing many others to know Jesus and to find freedom for life.

Will you accept the great invitation?

Sometimes it's hard to worship when you don't feel like it. I'm not suggesting you ignore your feelings but that you trust that God will help your feelings line up with His truth as you worship Him.

Choose to trump your feelings with a sacrifice of praise. In moments of pain, God invites you to come to Him and simply worship. There is no greater antidote to pain than expressing our love for God for all He is and all He has done. There is nothing that can combat the fiery darts of depression and anxiety like worship, praising, and adoring God for all He is. There is nothing that can overcome the pull and temptations of addiction like a heart of worship!

The first step in calming any storm in your mind is to attend to your spirit and to get your worship right. Jesus sees your heart. What do you seek? Put your faith in Jesus Christ, the one who gave His life for you. Pray this simple prayer: "Lord Jesus, I choose to worship You and put You first. I need Your help in life."

Create a space to engage with what God is teaching you through the mental health principles of the gospel of John, outlined in this book. Carve out a nook in your closet, like in the movie *The War Room*. Let it be a place of little distraction where you can linger in the presence of God.

Whatever you desire today, know that trusting Him to meet your needs and placing Him on the throne of your life, while removing all competitors, is the first step in the pathway to healing, restoration, and peace.

Recap and Engage

Truths to Calm Mental Storms: When I trust and commit to worship God, He will take care of what I cannot handle and give me peace.

Lies to Refute: Who or what I worship does not matter.

Take It To Heart: What is it *you* want most in your life?

Have you made the decision yet to worship Jesus?

If not, today is the day of salvation. Your choice to worship and follow Christ will be the most important decision you will ever make. Declare your allegiance to God and make Him your Lord:

1. Admit that you are a sinner who needs to be saved. "For all have sinned and fall short of the glory of God" (Rom. 3:23).
2. Choose to believe that God sent His Son to die and be raised to life to save you (John 3:16, Acts 16:31).
3. Confess that He is Lord and let Him have authority over your life (Rom. 10:9).

Prayer: *Lord Jesus, I confess that I am a sinner. I have no hope for heaven apart from You, and I need You to have abundant life and peace. I believe You died on the cross to save me from my sins. I choose to worship You, and I trust You to help me live for you!*

Lord, help me to make up my mind to worship You with the free will You have given me. Thank You for the invitation to know You! I believe my mental healing begins by aligning my spirit with Yours. Thank You for coming to earth, living a sinless life, dying for my sin, and rising again so that I can be whole. In Jesus' name, amen.

CHOOSE TO HONOR YOUR BODY

Read: John 2

In 2020, we uprooted our lives from San Antonio to Houston. With only a few main pieces of furniture and wall art to stage the house, walking through the house was deeply calming.

I have come to the humbling reality that much of what I own is unnecessary. It convicted me as I thought of unpacking in our new house. Will I really need to empty out every box? How will I evaluate what to keep and what not to keep? What would the Lord want me to do with all that I own?

What if I worked on simplifying the "stuff" in my mind? How much of what I think about is unnecessary and not edifying?

John 2:14-17 records a story of Jesus having a very intense and seemingly uncharacteristic reaction to the "stuff" that was in a house—in this case, the house of God. In the temple gates, Jesus found men selling animals and exchanging money. Jesus made a whip of cords and drove all from the area, crying out, "Stop turning my Father's house into a market!" Matthew 21:12-17 records Jesus saying, "My house will be called a house of prayer, but you are making it a den of robbers."

Like bookends to his public ministry, the cleansing of the temple marked both the first and the last great public acts of Jesus' ministry (John 2 and Matt 21:12-17). It showed His paramount concern for the holiness and integrity of God's house. He did not want anything to profane the temple or the church, and He did not want anyone to use it for personal gain or glory. His zeal stemmed from a deep love for righteousness and a genuine respect for the presence of God. There was a holy way to worship, a way to approach the presence of God, and He was making it evident that they had fallen terribly short. There was a way to care for His temple. And to feign worship or to have an outward appearance of holiness was deeply offensive to our Savior.

The History of God's Care for the Temple

Jesus' concern for the sanctity of the temple is woven throughout the Word. In the Old Testament, God gave precise instructions to the Israelites for building a tabernacle to be a meeting place between the Israelites and Almighty God. Its distinct elements had to be made out of specific metals, fabrics, and colors. At its completion, the Creator of the Universe stepped out of heaven to dwell with His people in this man-made, God-inspired place. "Then the cloud covered the tent of meeting, and the glory of the Lord filled the tabernacle" (Ex. 40:34). What awe and wonder!

Knowing the Israelites would move many times, God gave instructions for transporting Tabernacle pieces, namely the ark of the covenant. This gold-covered, wooden box contained the stone tablets upon which the Ten Commandments were written and possibly a jar of manna and Aaron's rod. Disregard for how the ark was transported was punishable by death. The Lord gave exclusive charge of the Tabernacle and its belongings to the priestly tribe of the Levites and instructed that only they could carry it around and set it up. "Anyone else who approaches it is to be put to death" (Num. 1:51).

Four hundred and eighty years after their departure from Egypt, King David had a desire to build a permanent temple for the Lord. God allowed David's son Solomon to fulfill this dream. Built around the 10th century B.C. in seven years, the temple was a pinnacle of beauty and order, incorporating the main elements of the Tabernacle (1 Kings 6-7). With different rooms in the temple, there was an outer court leading all the way to the innermost room known as the Most Holy Place, which only the High Priest could enter once a year with the blood of a sacrificed animal.

God's strict commands about the temple, its articles, and its uses were not to be taken lightly. He made this clear in 2 Samuel 6 when, under David's leadership, someone carrying the ark attempted to stabilize it, touching it in an unauthorized way. "The Lord's anger burned against Uzzah because of his irreverent act; therefore God struck him down, and he died there beside the ark of God" (2 Sam.

6:7). The Lord's discipline of Uzzah was confusing even to King David because it seemed harsh, but God was making a point that His temple and its articles were to be revered because He was to be feared. The Lord showed zeal for His own house and everything belonging to it!

This first temple was purposed to be a place of prayer. Because the Israelites forsook their covenant with the Lord, the temple was destroyed in 587 B.C. It was rebuilt seventy-two years later, under the guidance of Zerubbabel (Ezra 3:12), and refurbished during the reign of Herod the Great. A magnificent edifice, the new temple to which Jesus' crowd referred in John 2, took 46 years to build. This temple would be destroyed once again in 70 A.D. during the Jews' revolt against the Romans.

The temple of God has a fascinating history, but the intention has never changed. It was to be a holy place of worship of the one true God—sacred and set apart.

It's no wonder Jesus was deeply offended when the temple was cheapened to a shameless bazaar where greedy people tried to make money off of others' need to atone for their sins. The meeting place for God's glory turned into a marketplace for people's personal gain.

Jesus Redefines the Holy Temple

When the religious authorities questioned Jesus about His authority to "cleanse" the temple, Jesus introduced them to a new concept, saying, "Destroy this temple, and I will raise it again in three days" (John 2:19).

The authorities did not understand. Historically, the temple was only a building. "But the temple he had spoken of was his body. After he was raised from the dead, his disciples recalled what he had said. Then they believed the scripture and the words that Jesus had spoken" (John 2:21-22). No longer was there a need for a building because God Himself had come down to the earth through Christ, and His body was literally the meeting place of God with man on earth.

Later, in John 20:22, Jesus breathed on His disciples and invited them to "receive the Holy Spirit." This signified a new miracle. The body of the believer could actually become a meeting place between God and man. God now dwelt within man through His Holy Spirit.

Paul expounded on this truth when he addressed the early church of the Corinthians. He said, "Do you not know that your body is a temple of the Holy Spirit who is in you, whom you have from God, and that you are not your own? For you have been bought with a price: therefore glorify God in your body" (1 Cor. 6:19-20).

God could have chosen to replace the Old Testament temple with the New Testament church to be His dwelling place. But the Lord instead chose *people* who freely follow Him to be His temple on earth. Everywhere we go, as faith-filled, Christ-abiding believers, we carry the presence of God with us. Just like God blessed the house of Obed-Edom when the ark of the covenant landed there (2 Sam. 6:11), He blesses the places we touch because of His presence within us.

Let that sink in! As a follower of Christ, I carry within my body the presence of God.

Your Body Is To Be Honored

Recognizing the value God placed on the first tabernacle and the first temple, we can appreciate how critical it is to respect the temple. However, do we look at our bodies with the regard the Lord put into the original temple? Maybe, like me, you're feeling convicted. Perhaps you've abused your temple with a pattern of horrible foods or you've corrupted it by giving others freedom to do as they wish to your body.

Maybe you had no choice. As a child, there were people who had little regard for your body—even those who should have been trustworthy. Have you been abused, neglected, and hurt? I can't imagine how much that saddens the Lord who fashioned your body.

Notice again what offended Jesus about the misuse of the temple that He thrashed in John 2:14-15. People turned the holy ground into a meat market for their own greedy purposes. I believe Jesus' reaction in the temple symbolized the way He feels about what ungodly people do to human beings. Selling them, exchanging people for one another in relationship after relationship, and turning even children into "meat" to be abused and mistreated. This disgusts God! It's not His will for our relationships! Yet He allows bad things to happen and uses our hardest experiences; more on that in later chapters.

ZEAL FOR YOUR HOUSE—FOOD, SLEEP, AND EXERCISE

In the last chapter, we discussed how storm-calming and mental wellness begin with the spirit being made whole through choosing to worship God first and foremost.

The second aspect we must address is caring for our bodies. When I explore this with those I serve in counseling, it's usually an uncomfortable conversation that goes something like this:

"Tell me about how you eat, like what did you have for your meals yesterday?"

My client might have been bearing his soul just seconds before about all kinds of negative thoughts and life experiences, but he starts to squirm with this question—like I'm getting too personal or he's about to get judged.

"I'm not here to judge you; I just want to explore ways your diet and lifestyle habits might be contributing to your experiences. And I want to give you some tools to see if subtle changes will help."

Usually, my clients will not expect to have a conversation about diet when they come in for mental wellness, but I explain that every part of us affects the other; even what we put into our bodies affects our mental health. Food affects mood. So I ask them to take an inventory of what they eat, and how they feel before and after they eat it. Completing a food diary is an excellent exercise to help us become self-aware of how our eating contributes to our emotions. Write down what you eat over a 3-5 day period, including beverages and snacks, and record your emotions and your energy level with each thing you consume. This allows you to observe trends.

Let me address food intake and how it affects our mental wellness. A diet high in carbohydrates and unhealthy fat actually contributes to anxiety and depression.[9] In fact, a poor diet is almost always involved in mental illness.

Our gut, often referred to as our "second brain," is a major source of neurotransmitter production in the body. These neurotransmitters, or biochemical substances, directly affect our mental state and mood.

Carbohydrates, anything your body can quickly convert to sugar, are mood depressing and stimulating, while protein is mood stabilizing. If you are prone to anxiety or depression, it behooves you to consume protein consistently to help keep your mind strong, to improve your concentration, and to stabilize your mood.

Every body is different. You and I can eat the same foods and do the same exercises, but our bodies will process them differently. We will look and feel differently afterward.

However, there are principles to follow in taking care of our temples. Foods should be nutrient-rich and fresh. They should reflect the colors of the rainbow and include a combination of raw and cooked foods. Toxic and inflammatory foods should be avoided. These include refined sugars (cakes, cookies, crackers) and anything that is dead (overcooked) or overprocessed (packaged). Great foods to build a firm foundation for mental wellness include berries, eggs, root vegetables/fresh greens, whole grain (especially oats), and healthy sources of protein.

Making small steps in these areas can have a significant effect on our mental storms. For example, if I know I'm going to have a stressful week, I plan ahead with healthy foods on hand. Be proactive and kind to yourself: remove every food item from your house that is toxic to your mental health and tempts you when you feel cranky or depleted.

Limiting (eliminating) caffeine and sugar can improve your mood. Individuals with severe anxiety who implement these steps to cleanse their temples sleep better and their overall mood and energy levels improve. I help clients learn to work on this at a manageable pace.

People with chronic digestive problems tend to be anxious and depressed. Probiotics or fermented foods like kefir, yogurt, and kimchi can lower the stress response by regulating GABA, the relaxation neurotransmitter.

Chronic inflammation can occur as a result of poor diet, physical inactivity, obesity, smoking, increased gut permeability, lack of sleep, and vitamin D deficiency. Those with chronic inflammation are at greater risk for depression, anxiety, and other cognitive issues, including Alzheimer's disease.

In addition to needing proper nutrients, our bodies are designed by God to need rest. Broken sleep, shift work, and insufficient sleep are all detrimental to our overall health. The pressures of life as well as the allures of TV and Internet beckon us and preclude us from getting the rest we need. Most experts recommend seven to eight hours of sleep as optimal for adults. In addition to nightly sleep, a weekly day of rest is commanded (not suggested) by God to protect us, provide for us, and distinguish us as His people.

Exercise promotes social connections (while mental illness grows in isolation), workouts provide structure and routine, and exercise is good for the brain. The Mayo Clinic and the *Journal of Clinical Psychiatry* describe exercise as a neglected intervention for mental wellness.[10] A workout a day keeps the psych doctor away![11]

The reasons why exercise has such a positive effect on one's mood are unclear, but it's generally thought that aerobic activity increases blood circulation to the brain, reduces our stress reactivity, and influences the limbic system that plays a part in our mood, fear responses, and motivation.

I have witnessed the improvements to mood that occur when patients begin to incorporate sustained physical activity. Personally, my daily jogs are my mental health treat, and I use the time to think, pray, mull over ideas, and ironically, to relax. It's kept me through very stressful seasons of life, and I'm glad for the habit.

Jesus Drove Them All Out

Jesus drove out everything offensive to God's design for the temple; therein lies a principle for mental wholeness. Let's apply that to our minds and spiritual life. If Jesus sat next to you, would He be offended by the images or sounds going into your temple?

Studies link depression with social media, even up to 66 percent increased rate of depression for users who spend the most time engaging.[12] Your social media addiction could be costing you your happiness and peace of mind.

We haven't talked about substances yet, but any mood-altering, mind-numbing drug can be used as a way to avoid pain or substitute a sense of pleasure. Simply put, illicit drugs steal, kill, and destroy. They change people's personalities and motivation and make people do things they would never imagine doing otherwise.

Drive out anything that separates you from God. The Bible says, "If your right eye causes you to sin, gouge it out and throw it away. It is better for you to lose one part of your body than for your whole body to be thrown into hell. And if your right hand causes you to sin, cut it off and throw it away. It is better for you to lose one part of your body than for your whole body to depart into hell" (Matt. 5:29-31 BSB).

What about the thoughts that reign in your mind? Belittling, self-degrading thoughts come from a long history of neglect or abuse to your person, usually initiated by others and then perpetuated by ourselves.

Are your thoughts inviting to the Lord? Would He make Himself at home with how you think about yourself? Drive every cobweb of unrighteousness from your mind. Do you protect your thought life by intentionally refusing to think about anything that might distract you, lead you astray, or offend God?

To wrap it up, we've talked about the temple and how God sees it as important because it was designed to be a sacred space, a meeting place between Him and His people. When we come to believe in Jesus, He makes His home in us; it is now our job to attend to this house with great care.

Our temples beg attention. We are finite human beings on a time clock. As children of God, our bodies no longer belong to us. "You are not your own; you were bought at a price. Therefore honor God with your bodies" (1 Cor. 6:19-20). We honor God by the choices we make with our bodies and by removing any impurities from them.

Of course, concern for our bodies is not of paramount importance, as 1 Timothy 4:8 makes clear. "For physical training is of some value, but godliness has value for all things, holding promise for both the present life and life to come." Godliness means to refuse ungodly habits that take up our thought life, so as to make room for good thoughts to grow. Follow these principles for physical health to set yourself up for an abundant mental life.

Recap and Engage

Truths to Calm Mental Storms: Healing our mind requires taking care of our body.

Lies to Refute: It doesn't matter what I do with my body.

Take It to Heart: Keep a food diary to evaluate what you are eating and how your food makes you feel. This week, prepare yourself to succeed in caring for your body by taking out one processed item every day and replacing it with healthy protein or vegetables.

Studies have proven that a starvation diet is unhealthy and has a negative impact on health, mood, and personality. Simple steps to care for your body will go a long way.

Consider what shifts you can make to get more rest.

Find a friend to work out with or find an activity that you can do with a family member to encourage exercise as a unit.

Deal with a habit you need to drive out from your life because it's causing you to sin or be distracted or even depressed.

Prayer: *Lord, thank You for today's study on the temple. Forgive me for ways I have disregarded my body. Help me make changes so I can step into freedom. Lord, thank You for being gentle with me as we work together to calm the storms in my heart. In Jesus' name, amen.*

Choose to Receive the Father's Love

Read: John 3

Jenna's story broke my heart. Neglected by her young mother, she experienced her first sexual assault as a little girl. As a teenager, Jenna unsurprisingly succumbed to a lifestyle of drugs and promiscuity. Desperate for love, she was wooed by a man who feigned security and promised to meet her needs. But he used her. He became her pimp and the next decade was marked by pain, assault, addiction, crime, and every kind of abuse imaginable.

In God's mercy, someone told her about Adult & Teen Challenge, and she checked herself into a program. I remember her tired, somber eyes which betrayed the pain she tried to hide. How could any coping skill or group or talk therapy help her? Nothing could promise hope.

But then there was Jesus—ready to reach out to Jenna in the middle of her brokenness and heal her. He knew she didn't just need some new set of skills. Jenna needed a completely fresh start in life, a whole new mindset. And Jesus was just the One who could offer that.

Jenna opened her heart to Him, she began to worship Him, and her life slowly started to change. She began to eat properly and sleep and find rest for her soul. But the hardest thing for her to come to grips with was the idea that someone actually loved her. Growing up, no one truly loved her, yet the truth that the Creator God loved her was setting her free, one day at a time.

A New Approach

I love that Jesus, as the Wonderful Counselor, always knew a person's need without asking. He was keen on reading between the lines of the presenting problem, the need for which people sought Him. In John 3, the Savior ministered to a Jewish leader who didn't even realize he needed fixing.

In the same way, He knows what keeps you awake at night, what causes you friction in your closest relationships, and deeper yet, what makes you question the goodness of God.

Do you ever blame God for your emotional struggles?

Many atheists stop believing in God because they are actually mad at Him. Disappointed that life didn't turn out the way they hoped, they reject this God who would allow evil or sickness to prevail. It's easier to believe He does not exist, than to reconcile that a good God would allow such pain.

The Lord meets us in our questions and doubts, even our cynicism. In John 3, He reveals His true nature as a God of love. The loving God, who created the world, saw it in its desperately fallen state and had a plan to save humankind from the result of sin.

This chapter opens with the account of a prominent leader named Nicodemus setting up a clandestine meeting with Jesus. The word on the street was that the methods and miracles this teacher, Jesus, performed were out of this world, and Nicodemus wanted answers. Little did he realize that Jesus was about to do for him what He had just done to the temple– turn his world right side up with truth.

A Hole Made Whole

In his book *Experiencing Father's Embrace*, Jack Frost details how his harsh father had not expressed love to him as a child. This left a deep longing in his heart throughout his adult years. Even though Jack became successful in ministry, for decades he experienced a vacancy that came from not feeling loved. This affected the way he related to his wife and children. Jack was impeded in receiving the love of God, his heavenly Father and in giving love.

When our pain is so profound, it's tempting to remain stuck in a victim mentality that believes life is not fair and that bad things always happen to us. In reality, many people in our broken world grow up in dysfunctional homes where love is not safely and consistently expressed. Millions of people are stunted emotionally and interpersonally because they do not know true love from the security of their own home.

Can you relate to this pain? I can in some ways. I was blessed to have a loving father and mother, but when Dad died just before my 12th birthday, it left a hole for me. I knew he and my mom loved me, but the emotions and events surrounding his loss were so intense, and the fact that I would never hear his voice or touch his presence on earth created a vacuum. My questions and doubts started to cloud my perspective on God. Did God really love me? Why would He let such a horrible tragedy happen? My mind twisted people's expectations of me, and I started to believe a lie that I was most lovable when I performed or made people happy. At some point, this twisted thinking trickled into my view of God, that I needed to curry His favor and love by my good deeds.

I had a God-sized hole, a void that no relationship or accomplishment or wealth could fix. Countless people walk around with this cavernous gap and they don't realize that all their earning and striving stems from trying to fill it. Only Jesus' whole can fix the hole. Only His ministry of wholeness to body, soul and spirit can tend to the wounds of the heart and truly heal. Everything else will fall short. Jesus understands the depth of our pain and provides a totally different approach to how we can be healed from hurts. No, not five tips for emotional success, or seven steps to mental health. As we read in John 3, His prescription was radical and required a spiritual makeover, a complete restart.

Hit the Restart

I think it's interesting that half of my computer troubles can be solved by hitting the restart button first. Your internet isn't connecting? Hit the restart! The app is not loading? Hit the restart. There's something magical about shutting something down and giving it a reboot.

Jesus' famous encounter with Nicodemus gives us a spiritual truth which is a great backdrop for emotional healing: a supernatural reboot is the first step to freedom. He told him, "I tell you the truth, no one can see the Kingdom of God unless he is born again."

What does it really mean to be born again? The Greek word *anothen* denotes either "again" or "from above".[13] To be born again means that a person's whole nature is made new. Doubtful and possibly cynical, Nicodemus questioned if it was possible for someone to start over.

Jesus then explained that to enter the Kingdom of God, we need to be born of water and born of the Spirit. Nicodemus had been taught the Jewish Law since childhood and most likely recognized the Scripture Jesus referred in Isaiah 44:3: "For I will pour water on the thirsty land, and streams on the dry ground; I will pour my Spirit on your offspring, and my blessing on your descendants." Jesus was explaining the two types of baptism to Nicodemus: the present-day baptism by water and the future baptism in the Holy Spirit.

Yet, the educated man, who thought he had it all figured out, was perplexed and asked himself, "How can this be? Is it possible for God to really transform? Is it possible for me to start over?" The truth Jesus introduced would have rocked this religious man's world.

The twenty-one verses of Jesus' discourse with Nicodemus is just the highlight reel, yet the message is clear. He came to reverse and replace the institutions of Jewish religion, to show their incompleteness and flaws. In the same way, He offers us a reversal and replacement of our childhood institutions, our incomplete and flawed systems with which we grew up. Whether our parents were perfect or horrific or absent, Jesus' presence will supplant their function and give us new life. You can literally start over with God!

He Makes All Things New

Do you understand the impact of a restart? No matter what has happened to you, or what your current situation is like—whether you caused your pain or not—God offers you a do-over. A restart. A new beginning. A new life!

If your typical way of interacting with others is mean, impatient, and untrusting, the Lord says, "You can start over, My child . . . with My help." If you were utterly abandoned or abused as a child, the Lord invites you to receive His great love for you and begin anew.

Does this sound too good to be true? It was difficult for Nicodemus to take it all in. To openly believe it would require taking a stance, siding with the Truth and walking in the light.

Jesus taught that God can make a person completely new. Do you relate to Nicodemus' struggle to believe this truth? By accepting Jesus as your Savior, by believing that God sent His Son into the world to save the world, you, too, can be born again. You can become a new creation. "Therefore, if anyone is in Christ, he is a new creation. The old has passed away; behold, the new has come" (2 Cor. 5:17 ESV). Washed in the blood, you are regenerated and made new. "But because of his great love for us, God, who is rich in mercy, made us alive with Christ even when we were dead in transgressions—it is by grace you have been saved" (Eph. 2:4-5).

You can start over into a new family—your brothers and sisters in Christ. Regardless of how your family of origin behaved, you have the chance for a new beginning. Regardless of your tendencies, your lifestyle choices, and even your addictions, God can actually make you brand spanking new. You are not stuck. You don't have to be what you have always been.

God's Love for You

Do you struggle to believe that God can actually love you? The fact that Jesus said that God loved the world would have been another strike to Nicodemus' theology. Jews believed that God loved Israel, yet Jesus made it clear that His love extends to all. God's love is not limited. He doesn't love you only when you do what's right, He doesn't love you only when you feel it or when things are going well for you. He loves you. Period. And because of His great love, He gave His Son to save you and me.

Think about what it means that God gave us His Son. He is on your side. He came to the cross and endured death to bring the lost world back to Himself. "All this is from God, who reconciled us to himself through Christ and gave us the ministry of reconciliation: that God was reconciling the world to himself in Christ, not counting men's sins against them. And he has committed to us the message of reconciliation" (2 Cor. 5:18-19). Jesus' ministry on earth was an expression of the Father's love.

Jesus explained, "For this is how God loved the world: He gave his one and only Son, so that everyone who believes in him will not perish but have eternal life" (John 3:16 NLT).

God sent Jesus so that everyone could live joyfully forever. No matter your background or bank account or life experiences, you can have an abundant, eternal life when you believe in Jesus. Why? Because God lovingly sent His Son to save the world, not condemn the world.

As a religious leader, Nicodemus knew God pronounced judgment on those who did not keep His commands. Jesus graciously explained that God, knowing people could not possibly keep His commands, made another way. He sent His Son.

The fact that Jesus referred to Himself as Son probably offended Nicodemus' theology. People in his day didn't refer to God as Father. He was Jehovah Jireh, Raphe, Nissi, and Roi. According to Jewish understanding at the time, God was Father not to the whole world, but to the nation of Israel because of His special relationship with them.

When Jesus came, He challenged this theology and stated that now, through Him as the Son of God, people could know God as Father. In John 5, when the religious teachers accused Jesus of working on the Sabbath, Jesus stated, in essence, "If my Father works every day, then I can work on any day, too" (John 5:17, author's paraphrase). The Jews sought to kill Jesus because He said "that God was his Father, making himself equal with God" (John 5:18 KJV).

Amazingly, Jesus did not keep this relationship with the Father to Himself. Quite the contrary!

With assertions like, "He who has seen Me has seen the Father" (John 14:9 NKJV) and "I and the Father are one" (John 10:30), Jesus beckoned His followers into an intimate relationship with the God they feared. He was not a faraway God, but a God who wanted to be known.

I love what Jesus told Mary right after His resurrection. "I am ascending to my Father and your Father, to my God and your God"

(John 20:17). Jesus, through His life and sacrifice, allows us to know God as our Father, and to make Him our personal God.

Paul exhorted the Galatians: "Because you are sons, God has sent the Spirit of his Son into our hearts, crying, 'Abba, Father!' So you are no longer a slave, but a son, and if a son, then an heir through God" (Gal. 4:6-7 ESV).

Through Jesus, we can commune with God the Father; we are heirs to the kingdom of heaven. John 3:35 gives us insight into the relationship between God the Father and the Son. "The Father loves the Son and has placed everything in his hands."

If the Father loves the Son, then the Father loves those who believe in the Son and calls us all His sons and daughters. That's epic!

Let's pause here to take this in. You have a Father who loves you. You are no longer an orphan, no longer a slave, no longer a piece of driftwood just passing through aimlessly. You are LOVED!

Simply by believing in Jesus, you enter into a love relationship as pure as the relationship between the Godhead. It doesn't matter if you didn't have parents who loved you or thought about you; God says, "I made you. I see you. I know you. And I love you."

The Effects of Broken Attachment

Experiencing abandonment of parents can be crushing to the core. Only God's love can minister to the storm of insecurity and the lack of attachment that ensues.

Many people who are deprived of love and attention from their first caregivers are vulnerable to the symptoms of Reactive Attachment Disorder (RAD). Signs usually manifest between the ages of 0-5 years, and may include withdrawal, sadness, not seeking comfort, failure to smile, and watching others but not engaging in social interaction. Another hallmark symptom is failure to ask for help, or learned helplessness. When a child's fundamental needs for affection and nurture aren't met, it affects her ability to attach to others as she grows up. It becomes hard to trust. Even without a full blown case of RAD, many people struggle to attach.

This phenomenon became highly popularized by the research of John Bowlby, spawned by his work with homeless children. He stressed that an infant having a close bond with his mother would set him up for healthy relationships as an adult.[14] Harry Harlow's 1950s and 1960s fascinating studies on rhesus monkeys further suggested the importance of a mother bond. He found that in times of stress and fear, monkeys separated from their birth mothers would run to a cloth-covered wire monkey (resembling a mother), as opposed to a cold, wire monkey attached to a milk bottle.[15]

In the 1970s, Mary Ainsworth elaborated on this research in her critical work with children; this led her to describe different styles by which infants attach to their mothers. When caregivers respond consistently, quickly, and lovingly, children learn they can depend on people responsible for their care.[16]

My own work over the last twenty years with people in private practice and through ATC echoes these findings. Having a supportive bond with a caregiver from your earliest years protects you, but when you lack this for different reasons, you are more prone to struggle. When you don't have people in your corner to affirm you, love you, and assure you, you find it difficult to trust people and to trust God. Even when those with unhealthy caregiver relationships enter into a relationship with Christ, they struggle to truly accept that God loves them.

Many people know God loves them but still feel alone, anxious, depressed, fearful, and insecure. The truth they know seems disconnected from the reality they feel. If that's you, you're not alone.

God's Love Heals

Healing comes by faith, and faith comes by hearing God's Word (Rom. 10:17, author's paraphrase). "Can a mother forget the baby at her breast and have no compassion on the child she has borne? Though she may forget, I will not forget you!" (Isa. 49:15). "When my father and mother forsake me, then the Lord will take me up" (Ps. 27:10 KJV).

God is telling you that despite the love you may have lacked, He can fill the gap. You are His. Growing up without my dad, the verse "A father to the fatherless, a defender of widows, is God in his holy dwelling" (Ps. 68:5) was especially comforting to my family.

When Jesus told Nicodemus that God the Father loved the world just as He loved His Son, Jesus was saying that God's love is limitless and unstoppable. His love is able to break through any barrier and cut straight to the heart of any wound. Nothing is too hard for God, not reactive attachment disorder, or broken bonds, or caregiver wounds.

In the **Take It To Hear**t section of this chapter, I outline a process I have used multiple times in counseling to help people heal from wounds from the past. Please take time to tend to your soul. The concept of healing early wounds by addressing your childhood self was taught to me first by a discipleship ministry curriculum we use at Adult & Teen Challenge of Texas called "The Ultimate Journey."[17] I highly recommend their resources, similar to cognitive processing therapy, for soul healing from broken attachments and other childhood traumas.

I can't think of a truth more grounding than knowing that I am loved by a Heavenly Father. Nothing I go through in this life can shake me when I am solidly planted in His love.

> No, in all these things we are more than conquerors through him who loved us. For I am convinced that neither death nor life, neither angels nor demons, neither the present nor the future, nor any powers, neither height nor depth, nor anything else in all creation, will be able to separate us from the love of God that is in Christ Jesus our Lord. (Rom. 8:37-39)

When you and I believe in God's love, we are protected from every thought that would lead to depression and anxiety. Isaiah proclaims it boldly: "'Though the mountains be shaken and the hills be removed, yet my unfailing love for you will not be shaken nor my covenant of peace be removed,' says the Lord, who has compassion on you" (Isa. 54:10). Because God's love for us is unshakeable and cannot be removed, we can walk in confidence, knowing that we are loved.

God the Father's love does not have to be earned. He already gave it; all we have to do is believe in it and receive it. "But God demonstrates his own love for us in this: While we were still sinners, Christ died for us" (Rom. 5:8).

We are loved completely and wholly because Jesus paid the price for us. Just as He ministered to Nicodemus and addressed the curiosity of his mind and the longing in his heart to know more of God, Jesus meets us today. He says, "Son or Daughter, you are loved. You are My child. I came to let you know that it doesn't matter if others failed to treat you with love. You *are* loved and wanted because you are Mine. Are you skeptical? I've already proven My love. I died for you to have life and live forever with Me. All you have to do is believe."

What a wonderful, free gift. What healing to our soul to know that we are loved!

Friend, let me pray a prayer over you which the apostle Paul penned, "I pray that you, being rooted and established in love, may have power, together with all the Lord's holy people, to grasp how wide and long and high and deep is the love of Christ, and to know this love that surpasses knowledge—that you may be filled to the measure of all the fullness of God (Eph. 3:17b-19). Choose to receive His love today.

Recap and Engage

Truths to Calm Mental Storms: God went to great lengths for you!

Lies to Refute: I am unlovable.

Take It To Heart: If you feel unloved, complete the following exercise in a quiet space. You may find it comforting to have a trusted friend, pastor, or counselor support you through this exercise. Don't rush.

Tell or write about a time in childhood when you felt unloved. What happened? Who was there? How did you feel? Allow your mind to go back to that day. This may be hard, so be gentle with yourself and allow yourself to feel whatever you need to feel.

Now picture Jesus walking onto the scene. What does He do and say? In our triumphs and tragedies, Jesus is there to defend us.

Put your hand on your heart and declare the love of God over yourself as a child. Let yourself feel what you need to feel as you tell your soul that Jesus loves you and will never forget you.

Read John 3:16 with your name in it and sit in awe of the fact that our God ministers like this to the whole world, including to the ones who may have hurt you, forgotten you, or caused you to feel unloved.

Forgive anyone you need to forgive and release them from the pain they caused you. By doing so, you set yourself free as well. Thank God for ministering to the love wounds in your soul. Worship Him.

When you are ready, repeat these steps for other memories that still come to you from time to time and make you feel unloved.

Prayer: *Lord, thank You that no matter what I got or didn't get in childhood, You are my Healer, and You love me with an everlasting love. I choose to believe in You and receive Your love; help any unbelief. Help me to walk in Your love today. In Jesus' name, amen.*

CHOOSE TO BELIEVE YOUR WORTH

Read: John 4

"Why can't you do anything right?" the man yelled. "You are a disgrace. Get out!"

Photine whimpered, fumbling to gather her meager portion of food. It was almost noon, the sweltering air hung heavy with the desert heat. Pungent smells from the market wafted into the shack.

She needed to travel to the well, an hour-long journey that was bearable for most women because they could walk in the cool of the morning and enjoy one another's company. But not Photine. She had made too many mistakes.

She covered her head with a chiffon shawl and walked toward the countryside, turning her anger toward herself. *Why do I keep going back to that man? What is wrong with me?*

Lost in her shame, she didn't notice the unfamiliar man sitting near the well until it was too late to turn away. Photine sighed as she began to draw water. Just what she needed . . . another person to spit on her.

FROM WORTHLESSNESS TO WORTH

Named Photine by Eastern Orthodox and Catholic traditions, this Samaritan woman's story is captured in John 4.[18] Interestingly, this conversation between Jesus and the sinful, ostracized woman was the longest recorded conversation between Jesus and another person in Scripture. Not with some important religious figure. Not even with Peter or one of His famous disciples. Rather, it was with a woman hiding behind a shadowy past, broken by life.

Tired from His physical journey, Jesus stopped by the famous Jacob's well in Samaria. This was more than just a rest stop; Jesus was on His Father's mission—a divine appointment to minister to someone who was tired of life. Though most Jews avoided this road, Jesus knew He must go there to make a woman whole and through her life, save a village.

Jesus, though physically tired, focused on Photine's emotional and relational fatigue. He may have been physically thirsty, but He perceived a spiritual thirst this woman didn't even realize she had.

Not limiting Himself to social mores, Jesus broke a few rules talking with this Samaritan woman. First, men of that day did not talk with women outside of their family. Second, Jews despised and avoided Samaritans. Third, Photine's past and lifestyle opposed Jewish religious and cultural expectations for marriage.

But Jesus didn't seem to mind. He didn't just *notice* Photine; He went out of His way to talk with her. That one encounter with Jesus changed everything.

Take that in for a moment. Jesus didn't see the messed-up lady others saw. He knew she was created with purpose, and He wanted to restore her to a place of value.

Knowing religious customs, Photine was shocked when Jesus addressed her and asked for a favor. With a rude retort, she questioned His worth—"Do you think that you're better than Jacob?"

It's so true that *hurting people* hurt people.

Photine's lack of self-worth primed her to question Jesus' worth and answer unkindly. When Jesus explained that the water He could provide would forever quench her thirst, she desired what He offered.

Then Jesus cut to the heart. He went straight to her dysfunction: her relationships and failed marriages.

Thrown off by Jesus' ability to see into her, Photine attempted to sidetrack the conversation with a political/religious question. But Jesus perceived her spiritual thirst and said that the One who desired to be truly worshiped in Spirit and in truth was He, the One talking with her.

Photine gasped. Had the Messiah just revealed Himself to her? Could He really be the One everyone had waited for? He knew everything she'd ever done, and yet He came and talked to *her*. Suddenly, she knew for sure. He was the One!

In a single instant, the lady left behind what she came to get because she had been given life, living water, understanding, purpose, and worth. All in one encounter with Jesus. Photine became a messenger for Christ and told the entire Samaritan village that the Messiah had come. They were amazed by her witness. Later, they, too, met Him and believed for themselves.

She was transformed from worthlessness to worth. From being rejected to being sought out by others. All because of Jesus.

Jesus Calms the Relationship Storm

As we delve into Photine's story, we discover that she probably wrestled with dysfunctional relationships. Emotional difficulties either *cause* relationship issues or *result* from them. Because of sadness, loneliness, fear, and worry, we may be vulnerable to letting people into our inner circles who may not be the best for us. When we let them in, their patterns can influence and even destroy us. Tension in relationships can exacerbate depression and anxiety. This perpetuates the merry-go-round.

Photine had five husbands and was at the time living with a man who was not her husband. We can assume her relationships were dysfunctional and codependent. She had six attempts at love; the community kept score. The fact that she was coming to the well after the sixth hour implies she did not get along well with the women of the town and was rejected by their company.

Jesus went straight to the core issue and addressed her codependency.

In healthy relationships, we rely on one another for support. There is give and take. I help you, you help me; I share with you, you share with me. It's a dance that's not perfectly balanced at all times, but in healthy relationships, there is rhythm and harmony. In the relationship between parent and child, siblings, spouses, or friends, we depend on each other to help meet different needs. However, no one person was ever designed to meet *all* of our needs.

Codependency is a behavior learned over years in which one takes responsibility for another's feelings or actions. Usually, there is a "giver" and "taker" in codependent relationships. The giver gets her sense of worth from being able to meet the other person's needs, while the taker gets his worth from having someone to meet his needs.

I say her and his, respectively, but it's not always that the man plays the taker and the woman plays the giver. These roles are not confined to the sexes and can occur in relationships between parent-child, spouses, siblings, romantic partners, and friendships. Additionally, a person can be a taker in one relationship and a giver in another.

In a codependent relationship, neither the giver nor taker are really at peace with themselves. The giver feels worthy if he has pleased others, often putting other people's needs ahead of his because he fears rejection. The taker finds her worth when others satisfy her; when they don't, she feels rejected and crumbles emotionally. This pattern becomes addictive, where both parties are fed by the other person meeting their needs and fueling their worth.

I worked with a mom named Candice whose son became addicted to drugs in his teen years. Her daughter, by contrast, was successful and high-functioning, achieving well in her academics and career.

From the time they were young, the difference between the siblings was noticeable. Mom tried to stroke Brother's ego. She felt guilty for any way in which she unknowingly discouraged him; this drove her to try to help Brother keep up with Sister. Mom bought him nice cars and clothes and encouraged him, even though he was going down a destructive path.

Candice tried her best to set limits and say no to her son's demanding requests, but he kept her hooked by questioning her love and allegiance.

In this relationship, Candice became the giver, getting her sense of worth as a mother fed by pleasing and placating the young man and making sure he was okay. The son became the taker, feeling loved and valuable only when he got what he wanted. Both needed each other, but continuing in this cycle was slowly destroying each of them.

Candice finally decided to change and set firm boundaries. Setting up firm boundaries is one of the healthiest and most healing things you can do for a relationship. Like Cloud and Townsend describe in their popular *Boundaries* series, a boundary is a marker you erect to indicate to others what is okay with you and what is not okay.[19]

Lack of boundaries can lead to dysfunctional, codependent relationships. When we have allowed others to walk all over us in the past, we have a hard time knowing what's okay and what's not okay. Habitually saying yes when we really mean no creates resentment and builds stress. This leads to conflict in a relationship. Eventually, it can lead to a breakdown of trust and intimacy and even result in the death of the relationship if not properly addressed.

In the case of the Samaritan woman, going through husband after husband, we can assume a low self worth made her vulnerable to dysfunctional relationships. Add to that the fact that single women did not fare well in this culture and were likely to end up in poverty. In the end, it is of little wonder that she repeatedly remarried—even when she had to lower her standards.

The real issue was that she was sinful and lonely and needed a Savior.

By this time, the other women in her world had ostracized her, so she had no other way to meet her emotional and relational needs. Her sense of worth came from the attention these men gave her, and she compromised her own morals and values to have someone "love" her. She was trapped.

Do you relate to this?

Maybe you've been stuck in a pattern of relationships that stems from your childhood and the way you treated your parents or they treated you. Maybe it was your job to keep them happy. Or maybe you got into dating relationships early on in which you felt better when others went out of their way to please you. Consequently, you learned to believe, incorrectly, that that's what satisfying relationships should feel and look like.

Unfortunately, I have had my share of dysfunctional relationships, and I consider myself a recovering people-pleaser. I know what it's like to feel motivated to make others happy and live for their approval.

But God has taught me over the years that to live for man's *well done* jeopardizes the Father's "Well done, good and faithful servant." Galatians 1:10 says, "Am I now trying to win the approval of human beings, or of God? If I am trying to please people, I am not a servant of Christ." That's about as clear as you can get. You can't do both–live to please God and people.

To move out of codependent relationships, we must receive Christ's love to such fullness that it overflows through us to others (Eph. 3:19, author's paraphrase). It's not about what *they* think or want or what *I* think or want; it's about looking at what God says I need and what I am to be, then interacting with others accordingly.

So, in Candice's case, she needed to say, "God, I want to please you. Fill me with Your love for me and others, and help me set boundaries."

In that process, Candice learned to tell when she was doing things because she was afraid her son would be mad versus when she really felt like God was asking her to do something. More often than not, she noticed she needed to stop saying yes and be more careful to guard her heart. Then, when she did something, she knew it wasn't because someone had manipulated her. She had done it genuinely and because God led her.

A big part of moving out of codependency is learning to let our sense of worth come from God Himself and not depending on people.

Gracey, a student at ATC, was vulnerable to codependency from a young age, as her parents expected her to do everything right and to be the easy, understanding child. Unfortunately, this mindset led her to try to please boys as she got older, and she was introduced to and got hooked on drugs.

As long as Gracey could make everyone happy, she was fine. However, if someone got mad at her, her day was ruined. She hated that feeling so much it drove her to abuse drugs. Healing came only when she learned to value and seek God's approval.

Gracey learned to ask herself, "Why does it matter so much if my friend is happy with me?" She learned to realize that others might be reacting disapprovingly as a result of their own issues, and that she needed to rest and set her eyes on pleasing God.

WORTH AND MISSION

Jesus saw Photine's addiction to relationships and set out on a mission to heal the core issue of her mind and heart, a lack of self-worth. To God, it didn't matter who judged her, made fun of her, or stamped her with a label that said she would be alone and rejected forever. God sent Jesus to redeem her value.

Without using words, Jesus relayed to her: "You are worthy, my dear child, because you are Mine." He literally went out of His way, broke some cultural rules, and entered into this conversation because He wanted to resurrect her sense of worth.

Take note of a few things that show the worth He ascribed to this rejected woman. He lingered with expectation, sitting down at the spot where He knew she would come to draw water. He sent His disciples off to get food because He had more important food to nurture His soul. His food was to do God's work. His work was to heal this broken soul.

Jesus knew who Photine was and who she was going to be. Jesus showed Photine worth by the way He engaged with her. Although she became argumentative and defensive, Jesus cared more about winning a changed heart than winning an argument.

Each time she questioned Him, He revealed more of Himself. First, He explained He could give living water, then He showed His prophetic ability to see into her past, and finally, He disclosed that the time had come for true worship because He was the Messiah. Through this process, her worth deepened as she came to believe in Him (John 4, author's paraphrase).

There is no way for you and I to know our worth without knowing our Savior. Our self-concept is not defined the way the world tells us it is—by our talents, accomplishments, looks, or wealth. Rather, our self-worth is defined by the fact that we have been created with a purpose. There is a divine reason for why we exist. Giving our worship to and serving the Lord is what gives us value and lasts for eternity.

Our worth also increases as we come to know Christ more and allow Him to define us. The more time we spend with Him, the more secure we become in our identity in Him.

God gave Photine value by giving her a new assignment, part of why He created her. Her worth would come from doing God's work. Becoming a soul winner would fill and satisfy her in ways that none of the men she knew could. Her spiritual thirst was quenched by becoming a giver of living water to others.

Jesus made clear that His own worth came not from changing a life or doing good things, but doing the Father's will and pleasing Him.

That's where I can rest my worth. It doesn't matter who likes me or who likes how I lead or how I perform. My worth—our worth—comes from simply being obedient to God, doing what He's called us to do, and living a life of worship and humility. What a profound contrast to what the world teaches.

Do you struggle with your worth today? Will you rest in the fact that God notices you and wants you to receive the worth that comes from believing in Him and doing His mission? The results are not up to you.

Do you struggle in your relationships today? At the root of dysfunctional interconnections is a desire to find your worth from people by means of their approval. People will never fully satisfy you because they fall short. You will always feel like you're not measuring up. Examine your relationships and make changes to guard your sense of worth.

Friend, you are worthy because you are a child of God! As His child, you have been commissioned to live at this time in history and impact souls in your family, community, and world. You have such significance. You are here on purpose. Your life has eternal value, and I pray that you find deep security in knowing this and living it out!

RECAP AND ENGAGE

Truths to Calm Mental Storms: I have worth as a child of the Most High God! I need to be honest in my relationships.

Lies to Refute: I am not worthy. I have no value. My needs don't matter in relationships.

Take It to Heart: Journal time! Take a few moments to evaluate your relationships. Is there anyone with whom you experience repeated struggles? Maybe you find yourself afraid to say no, or you tend to walk on eggshells around them. What changes do you need to make to honor God? Are you saying yes because you're trying to please someone else, or are you trying to please God? Take baby steps, and I encourage you to read *Boundaries*, by Cloud and Townsend, for deeper exploration.

If you struggle with self-worth, confess that to the Lord, and let the fact that you are His son/daughter whom He sees, loves, cares for, and commissions, sink deep into your heart. Consider a time when others ridiculed your worth. Imagine Jesus speaking words of truth and affirmation over your soul. Forgive anyone who needs to be forgiven. Write a letter to yourself, reminding yourself of your worth. Remember, your worth is not based on your performance and we're not trying to puff up your ego and make you feel good about yourself. Your worth comes from your identity as a child of God.

Prayer: *Lord, thank You for going out of Your way to show me my worth. Thank You for my worth as Your child, that I'm here on earth to do Your will. Heal me of my broken relationships and give me courage to change. In Jesus' name, amen.*

Choose to Believe You Can

Read: John 5

Elephants are amazing creatures that boast of God's attention to the tiniest details, seen in every fold and wrinkle of their skin. When in India, I saw my first elephant, ridden by a wiry man, one fraction of the beast's size.

Elephants are not naturally docile and must be tamed by breaking their will at an early age. Tied to a stake, they are not permitted to move. As they grow older and stronger, trainers strengthen the rope. One day the giant animals give up. Once their will is broken, elephants comply and can do great tasks. In the process, they learn helplessness and develop the mindset that they are powerless to break free.

Lara, an ATC student, grew up without a father. She experienced sexual abuse from a young age and dabbled in drugs as a teenager to numb her mind from her pain. There was no one she could trust. One day, she met an older man who said all the right things, bought her gifts, and promised her a future. Lara didn't realize he was conditioning her, weakening her will, and luring her into a lifestyle of bondage.

"I felt loved for the first time," Lara explained. With time, she let down her guard. Eventually, the man asked Lara to do something illegal. It broke her heart, but it was too late. She was hooked on the meth he gave liberally, and she needed to comply with his whims and requests if she wanted to survive. What she once considered free, she now had to earn. She was stuck and couldn't get out—helpless.

Learning to Be Helpless

Lara's story is a classic example of how people get caught in the sex industry, lured into addiction, and enslaved into human trafficking. They become stuck in a mindset and feel like they cannot escape.

John 5 opens with the story of a man paralyzed for thirty-eight years who had learned helplessness. When most people experience repeated failure in an area, they learn powerlessness and stop trying to succeed. "It's not worth it to keep trying," people reason. They believe they will probably always fail and can never change.

The concept of learned helplessness explains issues some children experience. Children who cry out for help but never receive aid display symptoms of learned helplessness: quitting easily, failure to seek help, poor self-esteem, passivity, poor motivation, and lack of effort.[20]

This is especially evident with institutionalized and marginalized children who don't have consistent caregivers to challenge them to keep trying. They grow into adults who believe nothing they do can change their destiny. It's no wonder addiction and mental illness prevail in those individuals who are not helped, especially those who have never been introduced to a God who offers hope.

Depression and other mental disorders understandably arise from learned helplessness. If you believe nothing will make a difference, no matter what you do or how hard you try, you will feel depressed. When one feels he has no control over the events of his life, he will fail to execute and will even try to numb himself from that feeling.

If you struggled in school, you may have developed learned helplessness in some areas. Why bother trying at math when there's no way you're going to be good at it? Why bother with sports when everyone makes fun of you? This mindset cripples and stunts.

Research about the power of self-perception has led to much discussion about fixed and growth mindsets in schools. A fixed mindset says I can only be what I am good at now. This limits what you will try because you are afraid to fail. On the other hand, a growth mindset allows you to make mistakes and even look foolish because you understand you are a work in progress and can grow.

Jesus embraced a growth mindset with His ministry. Defying norms and breaking barriers, Jesus was not limited by who the world said He was, or by what the world thought He could or could not do.

The paralyzed man Jesus met was depressed and defeated. Can you imagine being a *regular* somewhere for thirty-eight years? As such, everyone knows your name and story. Changing your identity or outgrowing your labels would be almost impossible. This man was as permanent a fixture at the Pool of Bethesda as the five colonnades that surrounded it. He reeked of the place and the place reeked of him.

Do You Want to Get Well?

In typical Jesus fashion, the Savior went out of His way to encounter this defeated man. Yes, Jesus was in Jerusalem to celebrate a holy festival, but more importantly, He had a divine appointment to transform this man's life. That's the way God loves and saves. He walks the extra mile to seek the lost. Jesus approached the man with a poignant question, "Do you want to get well?"

At first glance, that might seem like an obvious, even insulting question. Why wouldn't someone want to get better? Isn't that why he parked at this particular pool, notorious for its healing powers, for so long? Why would anyone today want to stay in his or her affliction?

The question begs a response. People stay stuck because it's easier. Change requires effort and the results are uncertain; whereas, current pain is a known variable. It hasn't killed us yet, so why change?

We pessimistically reason that we cannot escape our fate; bad things always happen because there's something wrong with us. Psychologists like one of my college professors, Dr. Martin Seligman, have found a pessimistic explanatory style to be closely associated with depression.[21]

The paralyzed man blamed others; no one helped him into the water. His mindset epitomized learned helplessness. He believed he would never have anyone to help him. He obviously couldn't do it himself, so he assumed he would always be stuck.

It's likely this man was eager to get into the pool when he first arrived. Maybe a friend dropped him off and said this could be his answer. That hint of hope kept him trying. The popular crowd-funded TV series *The Chosen* illustrates the lame man's story masterfully and shows how a lack of success over time caused this man to give up.

Jesus always got to the core issue. Addressing the paralytic's thoughts, He showed that changing how we think changes everything. His sincere question subtly addressed the man's heart condition.

As David Guzik puts it, "Jesus knew that not every sick person wants to be healed and that some are so discouraged that they have put away all hope of being healed. Jesus dealt with a man who may have had his heart withered as well as his legs. Jesus therefore attempted to build the faith of this man."[22]

The Greek word for the phrase "do you want" is *thelo,* which means to be resolved, determined, purposed, and to have desire or a wish or delight in something.[23] Jesus wanted to know if this man was *determined* to get better. Did he want healing enough to do whatever it took to get better? Was getting well his true intention?

I've talked to many counselees who come to marriage counseling in a last ditch effort to do anything to save the marriage before the divorce. Although people are genuine when they invest in themselves to get help, they may not realize that they are just going through motions in wishful thinking that something might change. The process of counseling and healing your mind and restoring your relationships takes *resolve*, a made-up mind that says I am going to stick with this process even when it's tough because the hope of results is much sweeter than what I'm stuck in now. Jesus was asking the man, "Will you make up your mind to be healed?"

The Greek word translated into "get well" is *hygies*, which means to be sound in body and restored to health.[24] Jesus asked the lame man if he wanted to be wholly healed, not partially. He commanded him to get up, using the Greek word *egeioro* which means to be aroused from sleep, from death, and "figuratively, from obscurity, inactivity, ruins, nonexistence."[25] When this man picked up his mat, he was raised to a full life; he probably skipped for joy as he picked up his old crutch and left his yesterdays behind.

In this account recorded in John 5, we witness a miracle. The Son of God touched not just the body, but the mind and the spirit. With his first question, "Do you want to get well?" Jesus challenged the paralyzed man's motives, desires, and mindset. He sought to open the man's eyes to reveal his *mental* storm of giving up and accepting defeat. When Jesus healed the man's body, He restored his physical temple to complete health, superseding all devastating effects the crippling disease had caused.

Later, we learn that Jesus found the man and warned him to stop sinning, lest a worse thing come upon him. Jesus was concerned for the man's spiritual condition and wanted to make sure his worship was properly oriented. After his healing, the man was suddenly accepted and wanted. This might have tempted him to worship people's approval over God's, but Jesus warned the revived man to keep his eyes on the One who transformed him.

Becoming wholly healthy is multifaceted, and to live abundantly, one must be in full communion with the Lord through praising Him and guarding a mentality of growth.

Overcoming a Mindset of Defeat

I remember an ATC student named Jack, who came in stating that he couldn't read and therefore, could not do the educational requirements of the program. Half the battle was getting Jack to see that he could accomplish something. It started with simply trying. Finishing his first assignment was a great victory. Little by little, Jack kept at it, and not only did he fulfill the academic standards and graduate ATC, he also earned his GED! We celebrated his achievement *and* his choice to believe in himself.

Start now to overcome your mindset of learned helplessness. Understand that the healing of the mind does not happen overnight. When you understand how your previous failures can set you up to expect defeat, you are on the way to victory.

I wish I could assure you that "*knowing* is half the battle" like action figure G.I. Joe would say. But it's not enough to just say the right things or repeat affirmations or even *know* the truth! Just as the lame man had to get up and walk, you must walk out your victory.

A Thought Exchange

The first step in changing thought patterns is to replace negative thoughts with true thoughts. Let's take the example of losing excessive weight. Often behind binge eating is not just a mindset that food is comforting but also the thought that I can never be healthy. "I was never good at it, and so I am not meant to be."

Suggestion: when you realize you are limiting yourself, write down *why* you won't be able to take action. Then analyze and challenge your thoughts. Who told you those lies? Who put a ceiling on what you can accomplish? Who teased you? Do you want to keep listening to their evaluation about who you are and what you can do, or do you choose to believe you can be helped?

Again, it comes down to the gift of choice. You may be helpless in your own strength, but the truth is that you have a Helper, someone who answers prayers and wants to help you live abundantly. My grandfather used to declare Psalm 46:1 every time he prayed, "God is our refuge and strength, a very present help in trouble." Jesus describes the Holy Spirit as our Helper. "And I will ask the Father, and he will give you another Helper, to be with you forever" (John 14:16 ESV). Don't stay stuck in your helplessness; you have a helper who longs to pull you out and take you to the next level.

Relying on yourself and refusing to be helped is a matter of pride. It's looking to yourself for results and security. Confess your pride and acknowledge that although you have tried and failed on your own, Jesus can help you experience His victory. Don't give up—whether it be a goal of being physically healthy or improving your relationships. Don't stop praying. Get back in the game. The almighty God is on your side!

Change Your Behaviors

It is not enough to change your mindsets; you must also change your behavior. There's been great discussion in the field of psychology about whether attitude impacts behavior or behavior impacts attitude. Do our beliefs tell us how to act or do our actions dictate our beliefs? What do you think?

How we act can powerfully impact our belief system; the reverse is also true—our beliefs can dictate our behaviors. Let me give you an example of action affecting attitudes.

I know many college students who have grown up in church, but move away from God when they go off to college. They do not keep their convictions about abstaining from pre-marital sex, and instead choose to live for pleasure and making others happy. Naturally, they feel guilty about not staying true to their Christian upbringing. And over time, they experience cognitive dissonance, a feeling of discomfort that comes when their behavior does not line up with their personal beliefs. To avoid this discomfort, many subconsciously change their beliefs. They reason one of two things: it's not that big of a deal—either not that important to God (changing their interpretation of the Bible) or no longer important to them (changing their personal convictions). Once their beliefs are changed, their behavior produces less guilt and cognitive discord.

Alternatively, they could determine to put a stop to behavior that is inconsistent with their beliefs and start living according to their convictions.

This is a compelling example of how behavior can really alter beliefs, and in this case, even a basic faith in God. Behavior powerfully influences whether we hold to our beliefs or change our beliefs to relieve the discomfort of cognitive dissonance.

In the case of learned helplessness, or believing that nothing in life will ever change, our behavior affects our attitude.

For example, consider a woman who wants to lose twenty pounds for health reasons. At first, she might be excited about working toward her goal. But day after day, when she realizes she is not taking steps toward her goal, she feels guilty. To reduce the guilt, she subconsciously decides the goal is not worth the pain or is not necessarily important. So she gives up her initial hope to lose weight.

Can you relate to this? Regardless of the desired change, when we recognize that we are not even trying, our thinking shifts. We wonder if the change we believe we should make is truly important. Why even bother? We get discouraged and tell ourselves we're never going to achieve our goal, so why put up with the constant guilt? Why not just decide to forego the goal and live with the consequences?

The first step toward overcoming this learned helplessness is to intentionally embrace the idea of change. We do this in our minds when we determine to behave consistently with our new beliefs. Taking a mini-step toward that goal motivates us to take another step. And another.

I love the practice of affirmations for others and myself, but it's not enough to say we are conquerors or that we can accomplish great things. It's time to start living it!

Get Your Grit On

We usually give up when what we are trying to accomplish does not come easily. This is when our decision to keep going and take action comes into play. This takes grit.

Grit is a concept that has become a buzzword in psychology in recent years. In the Bible, the Greek word for grit is *hypomone*, meaning steadfastness, constancy, and endurance.[26] Patient endurance characterizes a person not swayed from his deliberate purpose and loyalty to faith and piety, even amid the greatest trials and sufferings.

Angela Duckworth, a professor at the University of Pennsylvania, left a consulting job to begin teaching. She observed that it was the grittiest students, not the smartest ones, who were most successful. The students who plugged on and remained passionate about their goals achieved the most. When Dr. Duckworth studied students at West Point Academy, in the national Spelling Bee, at underprivileged schools, etc., she again found that students who showed the most grit were most likely to succeed.

What is grit? Dr. Duckworth defines it as "perseverance and passion for very long-term goals." It's not about intensity or a burst of effort, like working hard for one weekend; it's consistently working hard over time. Grit is not a sprint; it's a marathon.[27]

I ran track in high school and loved to run, though I often came in last place in my races. In my early 20s, I decided to run a marathon and raise money for special-needs kids. In the process, I discovered that while training played a large part and talent a small part, it was the mental component that kept me running to the finish line. With the help of supportive friends, I was committed to finishing despite my pain. God helped me to have grit instead of giving up.

Our failures provide opportunity to develop grit. Each obstacle we face presents us with a choice to either give up or to embrace the obstacle and allow it to shape our character. We can dwell on our past failures or we can look to the God who helps us. We can stay stuck or we can choose grit and let our weaknesses reflect the strength of God. Paul explains in 2 Corinthians 12:10, "For when I am weak, then I am strong." The power of God shines especially well in those areas in which we are weak. When I'm not naturally able in some area to do something, and God does it through me, He gets the glory.

In what area of your life do you need a mental reframe? Have you struggled with sin in a particular area and feel like you can never overcome it, so you have given up trying? Do you feel helpless to face an addiction that keeps beating you? Do you feel like there's no point in trying in those relationships or even in prayer? Do you put limits on what you can do or become or on a small scale, refuse to even attempt something because you don't think you can be as good as others? Are any of these mindsets underlying your current depression or anxiety?

Jesus taught people to focus on Him rather than comparing themselves to others or allowing others' expectations to restrict them. He reminded them that they were not stuck by their parents' actions or defined by their past.

Jesus' life-changing encounter with the paralyzed man foreshadowed Paul's declaration:"I can do all things through Christ who strengthens me" (Phil. 4:13 NKJV). You don't need to remain in helplessness. You *can* change, grow, heal, and reach your goals.

Do you want to get well? Pick up your mat and walk!

RECAP AND ENGAGE

Truths to Calm Mental Storms: You can achieve your goals with a determination to be gritty because your future is worth it!

Lies to Refute: I can never change. I will always fail in that area.

Take It to Heart: Name something you've put off or that you don't try to do because you think you can't be good at it or you won't succeed. Write down why you limit yourself. To whom do you compare yourself? Who made fun of you or told you that you wouldn't make it? Forgive them, confess to God that you have believed lies, and begin to speak truth over yourself. Take a baby step today in the direction of your goal and share it with someone you trust who can keep you accountable to keep going.

Prayer: *Lord, thank You that when I feel helpless and hopeless, You are always there for me. Help me move beyond helplessness into victory and develop in me a gritty character, for Your glory. In Jesus' name, amen.*

Choose to Trust

Read: John 6

The young man extended his hand. "Do you trust me?"

She considered the options. Plunge to her death? Be captured by her pursuers? Or trust this person she just met? Without a second to spare, she said yes.

That trust saved her from capture. I love this scene from the Disney movie *Aladdin* portraying Aladdin's authentic heart and Jasmine's willingness to put her faith and life into someone else's hands.

Do you find it easy or hard to trust? Trust bonds people and puts a soul at rest. The lack of it robs millions of sleep; it's the heart of why we don't feel at peace.

Not being able to trust people often leads to not trusting God. Trust was shattered when Adam and Eve chose not to trust God and sin entered the world in Genesis 3. Though God had never failed them, they put their trust in a serpent. They chose the words of the created over the Creator. They forsook peace for the false promise of more. This led to a future plagued with trustless relationships.

But God had a plan. He sent His Son Jesus to save the world, aware that He would experience unbroken trust again. Through religious rules and scarred relationships, people's minds had been deceived. They made God out to be a task-master, difficult to please. They feared God but found it hard to trust and love without abandon.

Jesus came to fix that broken trust and invites us into a lifetime of trust. Even if the promised "magic carpet ride" of life doesn't make sense, we are invited to let go and trust.

In John 6, Jesus performed many miracles. He fed a vast crowd and walked on water to rescue His disciples from a brewing storm. In each scenario, His disciples faced an impossible situation. As Jesus helped them, He revealed the heart of Christianity—trust. "The work of God is this: to believe in the one he has sent" (John 6:29).

Was trust easy for the first followers? Jesus displayed His power right in front of them. However, God did not move in the way they expected. They had to learn to trust in Jesus as a man who claimed to be God's Son—to trust in a person *and* trust in God. The apostles would realize after His resurrection that Jesus fulfilled hundreds of the Old Testament prophecies, and His life would make sense. But at the moment, they were required to take a leap of faith. Would they trust God? Would they trust man?

God Is Worthy of Our Trust

Throughout John 6, Jesus invited the disciples into a deeper level of trust. First, He taught them God is trustworthy to meet basic needs. The disciples needed to feed a crowd of 5000 men, not including the women and children. Jesus knew how His Father would provide, yet He tested the *trust-ability* of His disciples. The disciples were completely dumbfounded and in a frenzy to figure out what to do.

Finally Andrew found one boy willing to share his lunch. We don't know his name, but I love this little hero. A growing boy isn't quick to share something he really likes, especially if he's hungry. But this lad shared, I believe, because he trusted. He trusted Jesus had something better and could provide. What an example!

Jesus' disciples doubted. How in the world would these two loaves and five small fish make a dent in their massive problem? Amazingly, God is never limited by the resources we have or lack. The extent to which He moves in our lives is only limited by our faith. Things only become impossible when we don't believe He can do what He says He can. Things only become hard when we aren't willing to give Him what we have because we're afraid or we want to stay in control.

Jesus accepted the fish and loaves and directed the disciples to have the people sit in groups, a small detail Luke records (Luke 9:14) to show us the ability of God to bring order to any chaos. The God of order can restore order to any difficult situation.

Jesus thanked God for His provision publicly to show that this miracle came directly from God the Father. He also recognized that the Father already had the answer before the people could see it.

Think about the burden the men felt to provide for their families. To sit down at that time didn't make sense. Yet they obeyed, and in that obedience, they saw God do the supernatural.

Trust always involves obedience and going against the natural. We must stop attempting to find a solution and let go. Trust says, "God, even if it goes against what I think or know, I'm going to do what You say. I believe You know more and have a better way."

A Lesson in Trust

Trust waits on God, even when it doesn't make sense. From the moment Abraham of the Old Testament was called to leave his father's land and to go to a land he did not know, he had to trust God's voice (Gen. 12). Later, Abraham and his wife Sarah struggled to conceive but were given a promise and a choice to trust God for their promised child. With every promise comes a choice. Will I trust God to follow through? Will I obey when I can't yet see?

The couple crumbled under the pressure. Who can blame them? They had waited thirteen years. How many times they would have second guessed themselves. Did we really hear from God? You can imagine how they talked themselves into plan B with Hagar the maid having the baby, rather than waiting on God's perfect plan A. Yet, Romans 4 tells us Abraham believed God, and it was credited to him as righteousness. God rewarded Abraham's trust.

Abraham walked out his trust and faith with dignity and obedience. All in all, they waited twenty-five years before their promised child arrived. By this time, Abraham's trust had deepened.

Later, God asked Abraham to sacrifice his son. When Isaac asked about the animal for the sacrifice, Abraham stated, "God will provide." Abraham waited for God's voice as he obediently prepared the altar and bound his son. Finally, when he drew the knife, the angel of the Lord shouted, "STOOOOOPP! Abraham, you've proven yourself. You trust in Me more than in what I have given you."

Trust involves putting our faith in God's ability rather than our own. Jesus showed the disciples that man's small offering, combined with a dose of God's miraculous power, brought great dividends. Trusting in God's abilities always multiplies our own resources.

In launching each new campus for Adult & Teen Challenge of Texas, we have had to trust God to provide. We didn't have connections and lacked resources. But we gave God what we had—our willingness, talent, time, and mustard seed-size faith. Like breaking the bread, God broke our fears, pride in our own ability, and mental barriers about what could and couldn't be done. We give God glory for what He's accomplishing now to save lives from addiction!

Practice Faith in Fear

Not only are we challenged to trust God with our needs, the Lord beckons us in John 6 to trust Him when we are afraid. After the miracle of the multiplied fish and loaves, Jesus slipped away alone. The disciples were headed to Capernaum in a boat, without Jesus, when a storm started brewing. Imagine their fear in the wind and mighty waves. Would their fishing boat hold up?

Unrecognizable to His friends from a distance, the Storm Whisperer appeared. Jesus approached the boat, walking on water. He invited them to trust Him and let Him in, saying, "It is I, don't be afraid" (John 6:20).

The disciples had to invite Jesus into the boat, into their place of fear and insecurity. Of course, they let Him in. But think about it. In order to let Him in, they had to stop navigating the crazy storm—stop looking at what their senses told them to do, drop their oars, and stop paddling. They had to stop trusting in their own methods and resources and trust this man who claimed to be the Son of God. And when they did, the boat immediately reached the shore. Another miracle!

Have you ever wondered why it's so hard to trust Jesus when we are afraid? Let's talk about your brain on fear.

In a situation of fear, our brains go into a fight, flight, or freeze mode. We prepare to protect ourselves. Our eyes send a message to the brain that something crazy is happening. The brain communicates with the rest of the body through the autonomic nervous system. Your body secretes different hormones like adrenaline and cortisol, and blood flow increases to the big muscles of your body to prepare you for fight or flight. This explains why some people feel unusually strong when they're extremely fearful but are not able to think through the consequences of their choices. Basically, your brain's ability for higher level reasoning is pushed aside as your mind focuses on staying alive.

In our moments of greatest fear, the Lord invites us to trust Him and welcome Him into our boat. Even when we can't control our bodily functions, we can activate our spirit to engage with the Lord.

How? We must practice trusting God when we are *not* afraid so our trust response will be automatic in the moment of fear.

When little problems come your way, practice believing God will come through. Declare His faithfulness to provide because He is loving and good. Practice remaining calm in tough times. State that God will get you through. Obey Him, even when it doesn't make sense.

For example, when you decide to trust God with your tithe when you don't have enough money to cover your expenses, to take time to pray and read your Bible when your schedule is packed, or to rest on the Sabbath when commitments scream at you to work, you are practicing trust in God.

Faith, the product of trust over time, is a muscle. God allows situations that test our faith—this is the only way to grow faith muscles. In self-defense classes, instructors simulate fearful situations so students develop muscle memory when fighting back.

We need to develop the skill to *think like we want to think* instead of freezing in our fear or faith. When faced with heartbreaking situations like death, loss, or shattered dreams, we may be tempted to forget God is trustworthy and struggle to believe He will help us. So, we must practice responding in faith before the feared situation comes.

Why Do We Have Trust Issues?

Many of us struggle to trust God because we have difficulty trusting people. Usually, trust issues stem from breaches of trust that start in childhood and continue into adulthood through broken relationships, betrayal, and people's accusations. When we put our hearts innocently into someone else's hands and they hurt us, trusting becomes difficult.

When training an animal, if rewarded immediately, the animal will repeat the behavior. By contrast, if punished when it has done something, the animal is conditioned to not repeat the behavior. Similarly, our early childhood experiences train us to trust or not trust.

God wired us to trust and to attach to our mothers and caregivers, but if they fall short or aren't present, we learn not to trust. Childhood trauma, whether abuse or neglect, opposes trust because attempts to trust are met with punishment.

Ridicule + Rejection + Wounding = Resistance to Trust

Sometimes we struggle to trust God because we like the feeling of being the captain of our own ship and calling the shots. We have an innate trust in ourselves. Even if we are untrustworthy to others, we still trust ourselves to have our own best interests at heart. Even if we are self-destructive, we have this flawed mentality: look out for yourself. No one else will.

Ironically, our own loyalty, fidelity, and follow-through—and lack thereof—limit our capacity to trust others.

Learning to Trust People

When we've experienced early ridicule, rejection, or wounding, we can become self-protective. We adopt a mindset of "others will hurt and fail me; therefore, I must protect myself because I'm the only who has done so." Living with this mindset, though understandable, is tiring and lonely. You know how flawed you are. If you can only trust yourself, you are setting yourself up for depression and dysfunction.

Like our faith muscle, we learn how to trust people by practicing trust and clarifying expectations. First, we must believe that some people are actually trustworthy and then give them a chance to prove their trustworthiness. Followers of Christ who are genuine in their walk with the Lord are usually the best candidates. In this process, we must remember that a trustworthy person won't be perfect. Christians fail at times. Only God's track record is flawless.

The healing of the mindset that no one can be trusted begins with forgiveness. If your birth parents were untrustworthy, forgive them for what they did; they may not have known their actions would scar you for life. Believe that you *can* learn to trust again. It's good to remind ourselves that God wired us with the ability to trust others.

Then, with God's help, find a few people who seem Christ-like in their character. They read the Word of God and show the fruit of the Holy Spirit, as listed in Galatians 5:22-23. Seek people who, like Jesus, are kind, loving, and joyful. Open yourself to them and pray for them and yourself while you do this. Know that they may let you down at times, so don't be surprised. Trusting people may not be easy because people fall short.

However, God will always be consistent and "predictable" in terms of His character. If we choose to believe in Him, we become His children. If we choose to believe that He is always trustworthy, that He will never disappoint us or fail us, then we can know that everything God allows is something He will use for good, as He states in Romans 8:28. Trusting people follows our choice to trust in God's character.

Overcoming Unbelief

I've had my own battle with trust. My issues sprang from the deep loss I experienced upon the death of my father. Our family loved God, and even as a child, I was devoted to Him. I couldn't understand why He would let my beloved dad die in a fiery car accident. Why would a good God allow my mom to suffer third-degree burns on a third of her body in the same accident that took my dad's life and injured my siblings and me? On the outside, I tried to understand and still go through the motions of my faith, but inside, I was in deep pain.

In college, I wrestled with anger toward God and questioned His character and judgment in allowing my father to be ripped out of my family. God let me wrestle with Him. Seems so funny for me to write that now. Who did I think I was to even think about wrestling with the great big God? But He met me where I was and let me question and doubt.

Thankfully, I surrounded myself with other believers, and they inspired me to keep reading God's Word and take my complaints to Him. Little by little, my faith grew as I learned to accept God's sovereignty over my life. He was the Author, not me. He was writing my story in the way He deemed best, and all I needed to do was trust Him to work it all out according to His plan for my life and family.

I wish I could say that trusting has been easy ever since, but it hasn't. It's a muscle that is constantly being tested and developed. Because of my loss, not only did I struggle to trust God, I also had difficulty trusting people and attaching myself to them because deep down, I was afraid to lose them. Sometimes, though, we don't want to see within ourselves, and we need a little help.

Years ago, a lady with a prophetic prayer ministry came to our church. She prayed nice encouraging prayers for others. But for me, she prayed something like, "Lord, help her unbelief."

I thought she had the wrong person. Surely, after serving the Lord in ministry for two decades, I wasn't still struggling with a lack of faith. But, later I realized it was true. Sometimes, even today, I struggle to believe God is good and to trust the people He's placed in my life. I find myself tempted to look out for myself, feeling like no one else will. I have to ask the Lord regularly like the man whose son was healed in the Bible, "Lord, I believe. Help my unbelief!" (Mark 9:24 NKJV).

We have to guard against unbelief, to challenge ourselves to intentionally trust God. He uses storms, large and small, to grow our trust muscles, preparing us for times of great fear. At some point, we learn to say, "God, whatever You allow, it's going to be okay because You are with me in this. As long as we are in it together, I can have peace. You will not fail me."

Trust Is Our Foundational Assignment

The "work of God is this: to believe in the one he has sent" (John 6:29). My most important task is to trust God, believe who He is, and put my faith in Him. More important than service and sacrifice is a life of faith. By calling Himself the bread of life (John 6:35), Jesus essentially said, "Trust Me to be who I am and to be your *enough*." He encourages us to believe that if we have Jesus, we have it all.

The Father wants us to trust in Jesus in order to receive everything we need on earth as well as eternal life (John 6:40). Trust Him even when it doesn't add up. People didn't like this teaching because it didn't make sense to them. Many fell away. Finally Jesus asked His disciples in essence, "Will you believe?"

Peter responded with faith, "Lord, to what other source can we go? We believe and know that You are the Holy One of God" (John 6:68-69, author's paraphrase).

We are faced with the same question. Will we trust Jesus? Will we trust God to be who He says He is? What would our life be like if we truly trusted? We'd enjoy peace, security, and joy. We would sleep well, as most sleep problems stem from worrying about life and from not trusting. We are working things out when we try to sleep rather than giving it all to God. What if instead of worrying, we said, "God I trust You have a solution. You will work it out. You are all I need. You will see me through."

Friend, I encourage you to *choose* to trust others and let trust be your default, rather than constantly questioning and worrying if someone cares, loves, or has your best interest at heart. Stop trying to look out for yourself and start trusting God to meet your needs and comfort you in your fear.

Healing comes one step at time. Take the steps today to trust and obey God and open your heart to trust others with healthy expectations.

RECAP AND ENGAGE

Truths to Calm Mental Storms: My God is trustworthy, and I choose to believe in His goodness. My ability to trust can be developed, and I can learn to trust people and have healthy expectations.

Lies to Refute: I can't trust God. I can't trust people.

Take It to Heart: Do you have trust issues stemming from childhood? Take time to forgive your birth parents and/or caregivers for how they fell short. What they did or failed to do does not define who you are today. God wants to release you so you can experience the fullness of life He has for you.

Prayer: *Lord thank You for being patient with me while I learn to trust. I do believe; help my unbelief. Thank You for showing me how important it is to trust You during times of fear. In Jesus' name, amen.*

Choose to Accept God's Timing

Read: John 7

I know resolutions get a bad rap, but I love setting goals and getting a fresh start in the new year. One year, I decided to try to become a timely person. Living in San Antonio for many years, we were surrounded by military families whose "on time" was fifteen minutes early. My definition of on time, by contrast, is arriving within the first five minutes of something starting. I'm a work in progress!

Interestingly, our kids are on time people—probably a survival skill. They keep us in check, help us get to church on time, and make sure we get to school on time. When our daughter Jadyn was little, she would stand beside our bed, totally dressed, breakfast eaten, backpack on back, and say, "Papa, wake up. Time for school."

Jesus Is On Time

God is never late. It might seem like He's delaying and not moving as fast as we wish, but He's always right on time.

John 7 records Jesus' ministry to His biological brothers and teaches us how to prevent and combat mental storms when we are given the opportunity to wait. In John 7:1-5, Jesus intentionally stayed away from Judea because the Jews were waiting to take His life. His brothers tried to convince Jesus to leave for Judea so His followers would see His miracles. They thought He wanted to become a public figure, and they wanted Him to go public with His trade secrets and reveal His plans to the world.

Think about that. These siblings had lived with Jesus most of their lives, but they did not really know Him or believe in Him. You and I can "live" with Jesus, attending church week after week, quoting Scriptures, and knowing what He says, but not really know Him.

The more we spend time seeking and listening to God, the more we become true followers. The more we are able to put aside our own agenda, the easier it is to trust God's timing for the events of our lives. The less we connect with God, the more important our personal agenda becomes, leaving us less concerned with God's timing.

Like Jesus' brothers, our sense of time can be off. Maybe you expected a promotion or it was time for you to be married. I remember feeling that way after being a bridesmaid for the eighth or ninth time. Maybe you have been praying for a baby, miracle, healing, job, or a family member to get saved. And you've thought, *God, any day now!*

We don't understand. It seems like God is delaying, but Jesus has an answer for this. He told His brothers, "So Jesus said to them, "My time has not yet come; but any time is right for you" (John 7:6 AMP).

For people, any time is right, but for God there is a *right* time.

It's such a simple thought, yet so profound. We base our sense of the *right* time on the social clock and compare ourselves to others. When it comes to trials and suffering, we sometimes put time limits on how long we should have to suffer, to wait, or even to pray.

God has a specific time for things, based on His sovereignty and the way He's masterminded the whole world, time and space, and your life. In John 7:7-8, Jesus explained that the world hated Him and thought of His works as evil, and that it wasn't the right time to disclose Himself to them, saying, "My time is not yet fully come."

THE FULLNESS OF TIME

One phrase Jesus repeated in the Gospels was "my time" or "the hour has not yet come." God has a sovereign plan. Time has to be fulfilled in history to set other things in motion. It says in Scripture: "But when the fullness of time had come, God sent forth his Son, born of woman, born under the law, to redeem those who were under the law, so that we might receive adoption as sons" (Gal. 4:4-5 ESV).

In the fullness of time. It had been 400 years since God's people had received a revelation from God. Can you imagine the flurry of angelic activity before the birth of the Savior as they waited to do His bidding? They would deliver messages to Mary, Joseph, and the shepherds. People on earth were ready, the stage was set, and hearts were hungry. Then, at the exact *right time,* God sent His Son into the world. God has an appointed time for all things.

Although His brothers did not understand, Jesus was content to stay "hidden" until the fullness of time and wait patiently for the Father's green light.

Since the Savior lived much of His life on earth in obscurity, we have few details of His early days except the events that surrounded His glorious birth, how the wise men visited Him after the age of two, and how His parents lost Him at the temple at the age of twelve. Then, at the right time, He came out of obscurity, revealed Himself to His cousin John, was baptized, and began His public ministry.

Jesus' days on earth were characterized by a submission to God's time. He also referred to a future time. Jesus predicted to His disciples that "a time is coming and in fact has come when you will be scattered, each to your own home. You will leave me all alone. Yet I am not alone, for my Father is with me" (John 16:32).

Jesus always trusted and submitted to God's timing because He knew it was sovereign, planned, and perfect. He knew everything was created "beautiful in its time" (Eccl. 3:11). He spoke about the right time because He knew that going outside of God's time would not lead to good results.

Waiting Is Hard

There are Biblical examples of people who did not wait on God's time. King Saul was asked to wait in Gilgal for the prophet Samuel to arrive to offer burnt offerings and see what to do in battle (1 Sam. 10:8). But Saul, tired of waiting, offered the sacrifice himself. This disobedience cost him the kingship.

Jesus understands that waiting is not easy, yet He lived His whole life on earth essentially waiting for the Father's right time. He waited for God's time to be born, to be dedicated, to be taught, to be baptized, to begin His public ministry, to begin to call disciples, and to teach His disciples. During the temptation of Jesus, the devil tried to tempt Him to move outside of God's time—to reveal His power—but Jesus would not give in.

What a powerful lesson. We don't like to wait. We crave action and results. Show me the numbers. Let me see the fruit, and now!

Why is waiting so hard? We feel powerless and bored, like we are wasting our time. Think about what happens when we are forced to wait. A workday that is productive feels quick. But when we are forced to wait, we become acutely aware of the passage of time, and it's unsettling.

While we wait, we feel like we are on hold and that real living won't happen until we reach a destination or achieve a goal we've set. Waiting for something is not real living. It's just in-between time.

I was challenged recently when my daughter was getting her driving permit at the Department of Motor Vehicles. I didn't realize until after we left that our cashier was watching us while we waited for three hours. God helped us stay patient during the process and gave us the chance to pray with and encourage this lady, who had just lost her mom. Real living actually happened while we were waiting; someone's life was touched, and Jesus shined.

Often, though, we don't like to wait because we feel unproductive—barren and empty. This reminds me of winter, when no fruit is visible like during the summer seasons of life. But think about trees in the winter season. Though they appear barren, God uses that time of waiting, of hiddenness, to strengthen the tree. In the winter a tree's roots go deeper and spread wider, searching for water. The wait, when we can't see any growth, is what allows the tree to remain sturdy and strong through its life's storms.

God is at work during the waiting times in our lives. Don't rush beyond it. Don't resent it. Don't think you need to make something happen for yourself. Choose to rest in God's timing and to see how God uses that time to grow deeper roots in your life.

There Is Great Purpose When God Makes You Wait

During the wait, God purifies our motives and teaches us patience. Sometimes we want to accomplish great things, but we have impure motives, like we want to make a great name for ourselves, or we want our comfort or convenience, or other people's admiration and approval. We want to enjoy life and have things come easily, but God did not intend for the Christian walk to make us happy. He intended for it to make us holy.

God teaches us patience in the waiting. What a long time Noah had to wait for that ark to be built! Can you imagine the man's patience and his character formation over a 100 to 120 year span? That's a long time to wait. He had to patiently endure the jeering from others and the uncertainty in his own mind.

During our wait, God wants to strengthen our character and make us people who trust in His goodness no matter what. Waiting on God's right time builds intimacy and dependency on God.

Waiting is hard because it has a way of opening up Pandora's box. It unearths things inside us that we don't even realize exist. But God knows. Like my client Lyla, I struggled during my own years of waiting to be married. Waves of insecurity, jealousy, doubt, comparison, and envy came at me and created such a squall in my mind that it became all-consuming. I couldn't enjoy the good things that were happening in my life. I had a choice to make.

Would I resolve to trust God and His timing for my life? Would I trust Psalm 84:11 that promises He does not withhold any good thing from His children? Or would I let the wait sweep over me and lead to depression and numbing from pain?

While I waited, God gave me the choice to see that He allowed the wait to make me look like Him and to grow my faith in Him. Nothing else would be as great a teacher in my life as the wait. Little by little, I gave Him my desires and trusted Him to work it all out in His time.

Jesus Moves to Action at the Right Time

In what way could God be using the season you're going through in life to grow you in ways you would not grow otherwise? Maybe it's an unanswered prayer, a business that is not yet succeeding, or a child who is not walking with God. Or maybe it's where you are in life. Just as Jesus waited for the Father's time, choose to wait gracefully for God's time in your life.

So far, we've seen that our timing may not be God's right time. Jesus waited on God the Father's *right* time. Now, we will see how He springs to action when the time is right.

In John 7:10-19, we read that Jesus eventually made His way down to Judea, a distance of about eighty miles. At first, He did not reveal Himself to the divided crowd. Some, amazed at Jesus' teaching and miracles, silently approved of Him but were too afraid to say anything for fear of the Jews and what might happen. Others saw Him as a liar, a deceiver. Jesus would eventually reveal Himself to that crowd midway during the festival. He started teaching in the temple courts where the lower caste people still hung out. He stated that His teaching came from God, and He sought the glory of the One who sent Him.

This might seem like an obvious point, but the fact is that at the God-ordained, sovereign time, Jesus chose to reveal Himself. The right time is always the Father's time, and the Father's time is always the right time. The crowd tried to seize Him, but they could not because His hour had not yet come. It wasn't time yet.

The disciples saw Jesus escape from the crowds at several points when people were trying to kill Him. He told them again and again that the hour had not yet come, but eventually, closer to His death, He stated numerous times that the time was finally right. The hour had come. The moment for which He was born was now approaching; He would have to face the cross.

In John 7:37-39, Jesus stood and said in a loud voice, "If anyone is thirsty, let him come to Me and drink. Whoever believes in Me, as the Scripture has said: 'Streams of living water will flow from within him.' He was speaking about the Spirit, whom those who believed in Him were later to receive. For the Spirit had not yet been given, because Jesus had not yet been glorified" (BSB).

Interestingly, if you skip ahead to John 20:22, you'll read that after Jesus was resurrected, right before His ascension, He breathed the Holy Spirit on His disciples, then told them to wait in Jerusalem until the Holy Spirit came on them.

The disciples received a lot of training from Jesus on waiting and observed Him as He waited. After His resurrection, they were being tested again in trusting God's timing. Jesus asked them to wait to receive power and to be His witnesses. On the day of Pentecost, after seven weeks of praying and waiting, Acts 2:1-4 records that Peter was filled with the Holy Spirit, with power from on high to become a bold witness. Because they waited faithfully, God gave the disciples this amazing gift of the Holy Spirit who would catapult the message of the gospel to the whole world.

The fact that Jesus waited for the right time to move inspired the disciples to become waiters on God's right time. What a powerful juxtaposition for His chosen who saw the contrast between those who had no regard for God's timing—who had their own agenda for how things should go—and Jesus, who wholeheartedly submitted to the timing of God. Jesus' perfect example would have prepared them to do what is humanly not natural—to WAIT.

Waiting on God's timing positioned them to become deeper followers—bolder witnesses—not just fans or silent approvers.

God is Lord over time. Sometimes we think something will never happen; but at the right time, what God wants to happen will happen. While we wait, we must accept what He's doing and allowing today and not just skip ahead to what we're anticipating.

Today you are where you need to be. Do you see that God has a time for everything in your life? Whatever season you're going through, whatever time of life you're in, you are there on purpose. God does not delay.

Maybe you have a dream in your heart and you're waiting. Keep your eyes on Him; stay faithful and obedient in your waiting. Even in loss, tragedy, and unmet expectations, God is always right on time.

Maybe you have a great financial need or a marriage or relational need. Trusting God's timing doesn't mean you're always going to get your provision exactly when you think you need it. We love those missionary stories where someone is praying for food and then the knock comes on the door at just the right moment, when their last morsel of food was gone. However, we've experienced at ATC that sometimes God allows for the money *not* to come when we think it should come. Later, we realize how He used the waiting to help us develop more trust, better strategies, and better planning. Even in our need, He comes through according to His sovereign plan that works for the greater good and is still on time.

GUARDING YOUR MENTAL HEALTH IN THE WAVES OF WAITING

The symptoms of depression include: sadness, emptiness, hopelessness, irritability, angry outbursts, loss of interest in things you used to enjoy, trouble sleeping, fatigue, feelings of worthlessness, fixating on past failures, and trouble concentrating.[28] One might have thoughts of death and somatic symptoms like aches and pains that are unexplained. The grief and loss you can experience while waiting for something can contribute to depression. You can easily lose hope when you feel so disappointed and let down by God.

It can be tempting to look to anything but God to satisfy and numb with food or sex or drugs or people or other diversions. But these methods don't help; they create more pain. Conversely, changing our thinking can bring healing. While you wait, believe that God is who He says He is. He is still good, He is still on your side, He is still for you, and He still loves you. Put faith in His agenda and timing.

He knows what He's doing, and He always moves toward our good, whether His answer is yes, no, or wait. *How* we wait can protect us from depression. Declaring the goodness of God's timing is a grounding truth that will provide an umbrella from the depression that can accompany unrealized dreams and unanswered prayers.

While you wait, try these practical suggestions to shield you from the storm clouds of depression. Invite people to pray for you and with you. Share your pain with a few individuals you trust; a support system makes the difference between sinking into a full-blown depression versus riding the waves of difficult thoughts. Surround yourself with positive influences and limit exposure to people and places that would trigger pain. It's okay to set a boundary when you need to; those limits don't have to be forever, just during the time that it's hardest to wait.

Ask the Lord to help you to wait well and wait with grace. Choose not to take your frustration out on others. It can be easy to complain, but keep a Christ-like attitude. Keep your faith in God by spending time in His Word, thanking Him for answers to prayer, developing a heart of contentment for what He has already given you, and trusting His sovereignty in your situation.

God is working your miracle out. He's also working *you* out. Remind your soul that Jesus will move right on time in a way that provides His best for you.

Recap and Engage

Truths to Calm Mental Storms: God wants to use my waiting to grow me into His image. He is always on time, and even when He delays, He is up to something good.

Lies to Refute: God's making me wait because I'm not loved or because He's not good. This time of waiting has no purpose.

Take It to Heart: Are you waiting for something right now? Do you see how it could lead to depression for you to keep dwelling on what you don't have yet? Try out one of the tips listed in this chapter. Share your struggles in the wait. If you don't have one already, begin a gratitude journal to protect your heart from discontentment and to remind you to be grateful for what you already have.

I would like to challenge you to consider slowing down in your devotional time. Sometimes we can be in a hurry with God, in a hurry with prayer and reading Scripture. Slow. Down. Let yourself wait on God. Practice waiting by taking 5-10 minutes (or longer) after reading Scripture and saying a prayer of just being quiet. Listen. You might be distracted at first. That's normal. Ignore the interruption. Focus on the fact that God is a good God who works in His own time. Think about what you just read about the Lord and meditate on that concept. Slowly, let Him speak to you. It might be a whisper or a simple thought. Write it down. This is one of the ways the Holy Spirit connects with our spirit—when we wait.

Prayer: *Lord, help me to trust in Your timing and endure with patience. Make us more like You and let not this waiting be wasted. Thank You, Lord! In Jesus' name, amen.*

Choose to Overcome Shame With Shalom

Read: John 8

Take a deep breath and imagine . . . A cool breeze tosses fluttering butterflies gently into the air. Peaceful stillness is delightfully interrupted by the harmony of the toucan, pelican, and peacock each calling to its own kind. Above, the birds soar majestically to get a breathtaking view of the rainbow of flowers and glimmering sea. A lioness pounces playfully with a zebra who fearlessly joins in on the fun. The forest echoes with its usual sounds, while the glow of the morning sunlight illuminates the grassy meadow.

Just a day in the life of the most magical place on earth. No, not Disney World. This is a place of true paradise and wonder. It's none other than the garden of God, the Garden of Eden. This idyllic world is not fantasy. It once existed, and Scripture teaches us that it has forever been banned from human entry. Yet, to appreciate the depth of Jesus' ministry to the woman whose story opens John 8, we must travel back to this place.

Caught in the act of adultery, the woman was a pawn for the religious leaders who tried to trap Jesus and find fault with Him. But they could not succeed. Jesus' ministry to this broken woman gives us hope and whole healing for a deep malady of the soul—shame. By revisiting the beginning of time, we find answers to the origin and healing of this mental storm that plagued her and still plagues all of humanity. A time when sin did not exist, and when relationships were perfect.

Shame-Free Days

In Genesis 2:13-25, we find that the Lord God took the man and put him in the Garden of Eden to work it and take care of it. He gave man a clear commandment:

> "You are free to eat from any tree in the garden; but you must not eat from the tree of the knowledge of good and evil, for when you eat of it you will surely die." . . . The Lord God said, "It is not good for the man to be alone. I will make a helper suitable for him."

God had Adam name all the animals, but in the meanwhile, no suitable helper was found for Adam.

> So the Lord God caused the man to fall into a deep sleep; and while he was sleeping, he took one of the man's ribs and then closed up the place with flesh. Then the Lord God made a woman from the rib he had taken out of the man, and he brought her to the man. The man said, "This is now bone of my bones and flesh of my flesh; she shall be called 'woman' for she was taken out of man." For this reason a man will leave his father and mother and be united to his wife, and they become one flesh. Adam and his wife were both naked, and they felt no shame.

What contrast to the lady pulled from the act of adultery in the New Testament—naked and full of shame. Shame-gorged is the state of many people today who, intimidated by others and afraid to speak, sabotage themselves. Shame is defined as the sense of feeling not good enough, flawed, and deficient. Distinct from its close cousins, humiliation or embarrassment, shame feels that deep down, there is something innately wrong with you. While guilt is feeling badly for something you did, shame is feeling badly for who you are.

It's hard to fathom that at one point in the history of humankind, there was no shame. No insecurity. No comparison. No expectations for performance. No one to tell people they didn't measure up. Only the voice of truth and affirmation that comes from our loving heavenly Father and Creator and the intimacy of His real, affirming love.

Before sin and shame entered the world, Adam and Eve had perfect communion with God, and therefore, with one another. They were free to be completely vulnerable. When there's no shame, we don't have to hide. There is no fear. Only perfect love. Perfect safety. Perfect trust, perfect peace. Quite literally, it's heaven on earth.

But then, dreaded Genesis chapter 3. Talk about a turn of events. The serpent tempted Eve to the point where she doubted God and saw herself as deficient. That she was missing out. That she couldn't trust God and that He was withholding from her.

Those thoughts led to the downfall of humanity. When she shared the fruit with Adam and he ate too, their eyes were actually opened to their own depravity, to their deficiencies . . . and they felt shame for the very first time.

The Aftermath of Shame

The first couple experienced a few reactions to this newfound shame. These reactions reflect three defenses those who research shame, like Dr. Brené Brown, tell us that we use today. These three ways in which we tend to respond to shame may seem self-protective but actually hurt our relationships.[29]

We move *away* and hide.
We move *toward* and perform.
We move *against* and fight.

Immediately after Adam and Eve ate of the fruit, their eyes were opened, and they realized they were naked. Aware of their shame, they decided to cover their vulnerability. No, they weren't inventing the first line of fashion, they were hiding their pain.

When we start feeling bad about ourselves, some of us react like the turtle that crawls back into its shell at the moment of fear. We begin to hide and withdraw. A hurtful word is spoken and we feel left out or like we're not as good as others, so we go quiet. Deep down, we feel rejected, but we'd rather just keep to ourselves. I'm not going to put myself out there, thank you very much; I will not risk getting hurt.

A second way people respond to shame is to look to people for approval and perform. I feel flawed, but if I can do this thing really well, then for at least a moment, I won't feel so bad. If I can get you to like me, or if I can please you by performing well or by doing more—then somehow, I can measure up.

The way the serpent deceived Eve to eat the fruit in the first place was to tempt her to find her own way to make herself good. God said she was enough, but the serpent tempted her to doubt God's Word, so she took the decision into her own hands and tried to earn or make a way for a better life.

Maybe you relate. As long as you are performing, achieving, or over achieving, you feel loved and loveable and good enough, but if someone does not approve of you or like you or include you, it's over. If someone criticizes you, you feel like you have failed. The performance treadmill is exhausting. You can never be perfect or constantly achieve the standards you may set for yourself. That mindset may seem laudable to others—look at how hard she works and how well she performs—but it's a trap because you always feel the tension and pressure to do more, bigger, and better.

A final reaction to shame is moving against and fighting. We see this in the way Adam blamed Eve, who blamed the serpent. Their shame led them to turn on each other. The way this shame reaction plays out in relationships is this: I feel shame, but if I can make you feel bad for a moment, it takes away from my own pain. Sometimes we are reacting in shame, and we don't even realize it. Exploring the three responses can help us become more aware of the shame underlying why we act and react the way we do.

I often tell our students at Adult & Teen Challenge, "You may think you have anger issues, but you really have shame issues. Your shame is being triggered, and you're not responding to it or dealing with it properly. That's why you're acting out."

One litmus test that indicates you are responding to shame is how you handle criticism. If you find yourself coming unglued by someone telling you that you need to improve or that you are wrong or that you fell short—then you might be someone who has layers of shame that need to be addressed.

Shame, Pride, and Lies: A Deadly Trio

The dynamics of shame play out in any relationship, especially in a conflict. Conflict can occur between coworkers, parent and child, siblings, and spouses or partners. Let me give you an example of something that happened recently in my life.

George and I were traveling with our children from the suburbs into the city of Houston. As we drove up to skyscrapers lining the horizon, I yelled, "Look, kids, it's the Houston skyline!"

I had always loved running alongside the NYC skyline when I lived in West New York. The kids and I started oohing over the buildings. George then told me, not loud enough for the kids to hear (but their little ears hear every decibel), "Uh, that's not the Houston skyline."

"It's not?"

He proceeded to tell me that the real Houston skyline was located in some other part of Houston. Now, he grew up in Houston, and as a New Jersey native, I figured he was right, so I had to retract my comment and carry on.

In no way was George trying to throw a jab at me, but I got quiet and realized that his comment triggered shame. It made me feel dumb, like I didn't know what I was talking about—which connects with this unhealthy expectation I have of myself to know everything. I'm not proud of it, but I realized in that moment, pride reared its ugly head. Pride is always at the root of every conflict. Shame's right up there with it.

It's ironic how shame and pride go hand in hand. In both scenarios, you look at yourself and how you lack or don't measure up in some way. Pride and shame are self-focused feelings.

Personally, my unhealthy expectation of myself to know everything came from childhood, where I was filled with shame, ridiculed, and subjected to discrimination. I had this false perception that I didn't have a lot going for me except for my academic ability and smarts, so that's where I rested my identity. When my intellect or knowledge got threatened, I felt like I was nothing.

I'm sharing this with you because there's a principle here. You may be placing your identity, confidence and self-worth in something—and when that something is stripped away or when someone challenges it—you feel shame. Deep down, you feel like you don't matter anymore. And that is a lie from the devil.

In John 8, Jesus shared a powerful nugget of wisdom with the Jews who believed in Him. In the midst of Pharisees accusing Him and challenging His authority, Jesus turned to His followers and said, "If you hold to my teaching, you are really my disciples. Then you will know the truth, and the truth will set you free" (John 8:32). He called the devil the murderous father of lies, in whom there is no truth. Every thought behind shame connects back to the deception in the Garden. These thoughts are lies, rooted in the pit of hell, to keep people captive and in mental duress.

Lies often take root in our childhood through different experiences with caregivers and circumstances. Not only can our hurts, horrors, and hungers damage us, our honors can as well. What we achieve that makes us feel "good enough" characterizes an "honor." It becomes a source of pride, a false god, so to speak. Our identity is meant to be in Christ, not in our performance.

When Christ came into my life, He gave me my worth and value. Any intelligence or ability I have are simply His gifts to accomplish what He's called me to do. I have been entrusted with those things to give Him glory, not to find glory for myself. These gifts were never intended for me to find worth or value. That's the world's mentality.

> For the world offers only a craving for physical pleasure, a craving for everything we see, and pride in our achievements and possessions. These are not from the Father, but are from this world. And this world is fading away, along with everything that people crave. But anyone who does what pleases God will live forever. (1 John 2:16-17 NLT)

This concept is so contrary to how we raise our children. We tend to reinforce our kids' accomplishments. We post them on social media. Pride wells in our hearts as parents for their successful performances. However, according to Jesus, to whom much is given, much is required. Our gifts were never meant to make us feel better, but to glorify God and magnify His kingdom. If we don't use them for that, we fall short. That's what it means to live life well—to use our gifts for His glory.

But from time to time, even when we know the truth and are walking it out, old shame can get triggered. Like that day in Houston.

There were three ways I could respond to that shame of feeling dumb. I could withdraw, go quiet, and just stop talking—effectively disengaging myself from communication. Or I could react by getting louder or aggressive, challenging George and getting competitive, "What do you mean that's not the skyline? That's crazy; you don't know what you're talking about!" I could try to make him feel bad rather than wallow in my own shame. Or, I could try to please: "George, you're right. Hey, do you want a snack?"

In any one of these scenarios, whether I retreat, get aggressive, or go into pleasing and performing, the relationship has been stunted because I impulsively reacted based on my feelings and thoughts rather than choosing to acknowledge my feelings and talk through them honestly with someone I loved and trusted.

What response would oppose shame? The truth. The truth sets us free! I could have told George, "This might sound silly, but I just had this moment of shame come over me, where I felt dumb, like I didn't know anything." That vulnerability would have allowed George to validate me, remind me that it's perfectly okay to be wrong, and point me to my worth in Christ. Even when we've been walking with the Lord for a long time, we can all use a reminder every now and then.

Jesus Ministers Truth to Shame

See, it's easy. Confess your shame and get rid of it. I *wish* it were so simple. Getting rid of shame is difficult, and we certainly can't do it in our own strength.

This is where Jesus comes to the rescue. In His encounter with the broken, sinful woman caught in the act of adultery, He rescued her from the accusers who would condemn her and stone her, just to make a point. Can you imagine the profundity of this woman's shame? How would she ever recover from such an embarrassing moment? It would be like your pastors discovering you in the moment of your dirtiest, most shameful sin and dragging you out through the church or posting pictures of you on social media for everyone to see.

This woman's predicament was horrifying. Yet Jesus redeemed her from her shame. She could not hide, but Jesus covered her. She could not perform, but Jesus had the right answers for her. She could not even fight back, but Jesus fought in her defense. Jesus did what she could not do, thereby freeing her from shame.

He assured her that He would not condemn her for her sin but also instructed her to leave her life of sin. No longer captive to her old habits and relationships, the woman was freed to live a life of wholeness, with her head held high.

Jesus later explains the foundation for freedom—the truth. You can only be free if you know the truth, if you hold to it, and if you let it be your source every day. He explains that the truth would help you become free and stay that way.

The Greek word for truth is *aletheia*, which refers to universal truth and undebatable fact.[30]

Four times in John 8, the Son of God emphasized that unlike the devil, He is the source of freedom-delivering truth.

So how does this apply to shame? Knowing who you are according to how Jesus sees you marks the truth about your worth. You won't need someone to acknowledge you, like you, or approve of you. God has already done all of these because you are His child. Believing the truth that despite people's rejection, you are accepted by God, allows you to boldly face the temptation to withdraw. Meditating on the truth of your worth in Christ protects you from angrily defending yourself and trying to make others small.

The Truth is Key

Which shame reaction characterizes you most of the time? Have you noticed that you hide, perform, or get angry in your relationships, or some combination or all of the above?

Here's the truth about shame—if it's not properly dealt with, it won't just go away. Shame gets stored and compounded.

Let's say you're an adult having a conversation with your boss. She tells you that somehow you didn't perform the way she expected, and you start to feel bad and deficient. But not just a little bad. I'm talking really bad, like it ruins your day.

It could be because your current failure has triggered a past inadequacy, a deeper sense of shame, thereby reinforcing an identity of defectiveness. So you're really not just upset about what happened with your boss, you're upset because it connects with previous shame, and the snowball has gotten bigger.

Shame that has been entrenched in our hearts and minds from childhood tends to stick. And when the negative feelings and thoughts around our childhood shame aren't challenged as we grow up, we start reacting to others from shame.

When shame surfaces, we must seek God and allow His truth to remind us of who we are and what we should think about ourselves and others.

Shame stays when we accept and focus on others' judgment of us; we combat the power of shame by accepting how Jesus sees us. The more we understand and believe what our Heavenly Father thinks about us, the less shame prevails.

From Shame to Shalom

Let's look back at the ministry of God to see how He provides a remedy to the shame of Adam and Eve, setting the pattern for Jesus, who lived to please His Father.

First, He went to them. Genesis 3 records that in the cool of day, God went and sought them and asked, "Where are you?"

We can't get over our shame without the pursuit of our loving Heavenly Father who sees us in our sin and beckons us into His presence. We have to let ourselves be found; then we seek Him back. God invites us, like He did for Adam and Eve, to come out of hiding, out of performing, and out of fighting.

Luke 15 tells the story of the prodigal son. Take a moment to read the story before you continue.

When the prodigal son found himself in the pig's pen after squandering his father's inheritance, making a disaster of his life, and wallowing in shame, he decided to pursue his father. But the father, symbolic of our heavenly Father, was already running toward his son, ready to receive the broken and repentant, shame-stained sinner.

After pursuing Adam and Eve in the garden, God covered their shame. He provided garments from animal skins, requiring animal blood to be shed. These garments symbolized the robe of righteousness we will all wear one day because of the blood Christ shed on the cross.

God took their weak, flawed, fig-leaf covering that would not last and covered it with His righteousness. 2 Corinthians 5:21 says that "God made him who had no sin to be sin for us, that in him we might become the righteousness of God."

Righteousness is defined as being in right standing with God. It's part of the armor of God—His breastplate—which covers our heart. So when we feel shame in our hearts or minds, when the enemy's wicked schemes come, we must remember that we are His and we are made right with God. We are loved. Because of Jesus, we have worth. We don't need to perform. We wear His righteousness, protection, and armor.

Our shame won't go away on its own. We don't measure up to the standards set by the world. We fall short of the glory of God, but His blood covers us, washes away our sins, and gives us hope for the future.

Finally, God gave Adam and Eve boundaries through His Word, His instruction. God told them what they could and could not do. His Word was to guide them and become a blueprint for their lives, and in the same way, the Word is our anchor against the waves of shame. When lies creep in, we must refute them with Truth!

Only the Word of Truth will defeat the lies of shame. Lies disrupted the shalom of Eden; truth—the Word of God—is the only thing that can restore shalom.

Shalom is a state of bliss, of harmony and perfect peace which characterized the garden of God and the hearts and minds of all present. The shalom of God was His presence; it still is. Satan shattered shalom in the garden by challenging the presence of God through sinful disobedience.

The enemy's tactics haven't changed much. Lies still disrupt shalom, God's presence in our lives, and bring shame. However, Jesus explained in John 8 that the truth sets us free. He did not condemn the woman caught in adultery or judge her and issue a death sentence. Instead, He invited her to a life of freedom by giving up sinful thoughts and habits.

"Go and sin no more" means to be free to live your life without the bondage of shame by walking in the blessing of following God's commands. Beware, our shame is often caused by our choice to sin and wallow in negative thoughts; freedom comes when we give these up and let God's Word permeate our minds so much that we obey Him, even in our thought life.

The I AM Conquers Your I AM NOT

At the end of John 8, Jesus made a profound statement to His bewildered accusers. They were confused about Jesus' statement that He existed before Abraham, but Jesus declared emphatically, "before Abraham was born, I am!"

The Jewish leaders were outraged at His audacity. Through this profound statement, He likened His identity and status with the Great I AM, Yahweh—the one and only God who revealed this name to Moses at the burning bush.

In Exodus 3:13-14, "Moses said to God, 'Suppose I go to the Israelites and say to them, "The God of your fathers has sent me to you," and they ask me, "What is his name?" Then what shall I tell them?' God said to Moses, 'I AM WHO I AM. This is what you are to say to the Israelites: "I AM has sent me to you."

Do you see the significance of that name, in light of shame? Everything we are not, that we cannot be, God *is*. And because He is, I can be whatever He needs me to be, I can do anything He wants me to do, and I have everything I need. I don't need to impress anyone else. I am free to be me because God says I am.

Shame taunts us to believe, "I am not _______ enough." We fill in the blank with our past deficiencies, with how people have accused us. But Jesus' declaration dares us to believe, "I do not care what shame says. My God is the great I Am! My God is what I don't have to be. My God is enough, and therefore, I am enough." When shame tries to steal shalom, the truth of God's Word fights back like a great defender and offensive lineman all at once.

The enemy uses shame as a weapon to keep us rooted in pride and separated from true communion with the Lord and true fellowship with one another. But when we stand on the promises of God by truly meditating on His Word and letting it fight against the darts of shame, here's something we can count on:

> No weapon that is formed against thee shall prosper, and every tongue that shall rise against thee in judgment thou shalt condemn. This is the heritage of the servants of the Lord, and their righteousness is of me, saith the Lord. (Isa. 54:17 KJB)

Isn't that awesome? God fights our shame, every voice and weapon turned against us. He gives us righteousness. He is our peace.

In case you've ever wondered how Jesus could see you in your mess and still love you, He proves that every life matters to Him in the account of John 8. Although some commentators suggest that the story of the woman caught in the act of adultery may not have been part of the original text, the account reveals the consistent heart of Jesus for every life. It also shows His power over shame—His ability to minister to the depths of people's pain.

Because of my childhood perceptions, I questioned: Was I truly loveable, even when I failed? If God made me beautiful, why did I feel flawed? Perhaps you can relate.

Shame stems from childhood wounds and snowballs as future hurts compound old insecurities. Shame interferes with our relationships in subtle ways causing loneliness, conflict, insecurity, and competition.

If these words describe the way you connect with others, confess to God that you are willing to make changes to experience His freedom. Start with your thoughts; your behaviors will soon follow to give you true peace. Satan tried to steal shalom in the garden of Eden, and the result was shame for humankind. But God's truth redeems life and restores shalom. You and I overcome shame by meditating on and living in obedience to the truth.

Recap and Engage

Truths to Calm Mental Storms: Jesus is enough for me. I am who He says I am.

Lies to Refute: My weakness disqualifies me, my sin defines me, and others' opinions dictate who I am.

Take It to Heart: A clue that you are responding in shame is understanding the three typical responses to shame: withdrawing, performing/ pleasing, or fighting. The next time you find yourself in a shame reaction, take a moment to evaluate your feelings. If you find that shame is the feeling underlying your behavior, take it to the Lord. Separate yourself for a moment and let His Word affirm you. Let Him remind you that when you feel not enough, He is enough. He is the great I Am! Free yourself by releasing yourself from the expectations you or others may have placed on you.

Prayer: *Lord, thank You that I don't have to live in the lie that I'm not enough. Thank You that You are enough, and because I identify with You, I am enough. Forgive me of my pride which gets in the way, and help me not to let shame rule the way I engage with others. Thank You for the freedom that comes by living out God's Word. In Jesus' name, amen.*

Choose to See How God Sees

Read: John 9

In graduate school, I found the Rorschach oddly fascinating. The controversial personality test consists of random inkblots. What patients saw in the pictures impacted their diagnosis and treatment plan and opened a window into thought processes that might otherwise have gone undetected.

Could it be that your outlook on life reveals a window into your innermost thought processes? What if you could learn to see the world differently? Could that impact your level of confidence and security and your ability to get along with others?

In John 9 we read about Jesus' ministry to a man born blind. Here was a man who was never able to see with his eyes, yet after his encounter with Jesus, God used him to help others see beyond their natural sight. Not only was his outward blindness healed, Jesus addressed the blindness of his soul and healed him wholly.

People assumed the man was born blind because of sin, a traditional Jewish thought that suffering emanated from weakness in personal devotion to the Lord. This man would have been judged.

The shame of sickness in a family is real. It is not unusual for people dealing with infertility or a sick child to silently struggle when others judge, ostracize, and blame them. The blind man and his family also experienced this shame.

When the disciples first saw the blind man, they asked Jesus who had sinned to cause the blindness.

Jesus taught them an important truth: "This happened so that the works of God might be displayed in [the man's] life" (John 9:3).

Contrary to what the world thought, God had chosen this family to walk through this blindness, with full knowledge that one day, this man's healing would be a testimony to the healing power of God through Jesus.

I Was Blind But Now I See

When Jesus encountered the blind man, He spit on the ground, made mud with His saliva, applied it like balm to the man's eyes, and instructed him to wash it off in the pool of Siloam. By faith, the blind man obeyed and came home seeing. As documented in many of Christ's miracles, Jesus asked the man to participate in his own miracle, and his part plus God's part equaled something spectacular.

Of course, the man's transformation did not go unnoticed.

"How were your eyes opened?" demanded the religious authorities. It was unthinkable that Jesus would defy the "rules" and heal a sinful, unlearned man—especially on their prescribed day of rest.

It's important to remember why Jesus did miracles.

God's goal was for all people, the religious leaders and all players involved, to have eternal life. Later in the Gospel of John, we read in John 20:30-31 that "Jesus performed many other signs in the presence of his disciples, which are not recorded in this book. But these are written that you may believe that Jesus is the Messiah, the Son of God, and that by believing you may have life in his name."

The Pharisees threw the healed man out of the synagogue and claimed once again that his or his parents' sin had caused his blindness in the first place.

After the Pharisees finished with the man, Jesus took the miracle to another level. He revealed Himself to the healed man and told him that He was the Messiah who came into the world to make distinctions clear. "I entered this world to render judgment—to give sight to the blind and to show those who think they see that they are blind" (John 9:39 NLT).

The religious leaders provoked Jesus, asking how He could have the audacity to imply that they were blind. "If you were blind, you wouldn't be guilty," Jesus replied. "But you remain guilty because you claim you can see (John 9:41 NLT). Since they claimed to see perfectly, they were now holding themselves accountable, and therefore, guilty for their faults and oversights.

HOW DO YOU SEE?

How's your eyesight? Do you think you have all the answers when in fact your vision is distorted? Are there beliefs in your life you assume to be true, that could actually be steering you in a wrong direction? Are they possibly impacting your relationships with others and yourself?

I'd like to divert our attention to another passage of Scripture in which people were assigned with the task of "seeing" and *how* they saw things changed everything. In Numbers 13 and 14, God told Moses to send twelve spies on a reconnaissance mission of the Promised Land. For forty days they were to "see what kind of land it was and what kind of people lived there," and to bring back fruit from the land.

God had promised to give the land to Israel, and of that fact, there should have been no doubt. However, ten of the spies disregarded God's promise and based their judgments on what they saw in the natural. Reporting nothing but problems, they spread fear in the camp.

Meanwhile, the other two spies, Joshua and Caleb, saw victory through eyes of faith and reminded the people of God's promise.

What does this say to us? When we leave God out of the picture, what lies before us can seem hopeless and impossible.

HOW WE SEE AFFECTS EVERYTHING

These twelve spies made their reports and decisions based on their perspective. Ten left God out of the picture. The other two saw through eyes of faith in God in four distinct ways.

Joshua and Caleb saw *God* rightly.

Over and over, God told His people He had given them the land of Canaan. In Leviticus, He gave them rules about how they were to live when they entered the land. Joshua and Caleb had these promises etched in their minds. With each obstacle Joshua and Caleb saw, they chose to trust in the promises of God. We can imagine Joshua and Caleb beginning to think, "Oh wow, those guys are big, but our God is bigger. Oh wow, there are a lot of people to fight, but our God can do anything. He's going to get us through this!"

On the other hand, each passing obstacle filled the other ten spies with fear, and they became discouraged. Discouragement is one of the number one tricks of the enemy. When we start to lose sight of who God is, we become easily discouraged.

Joshua and Caleb saw God's ability; the others failed to take God's power and protection into account. Joshua and Caleb reminded the people of the characteristics and promises of God. If God was pleased with them, He would lead them, be their shepherd, and guide them in the new land. Joshua and Caleb took God at His word.

Joshua and Caleb saw *themselves* rightly.

The other ten spies saw themselves like grasshoppers—incapable and completely disadvantaged compared to the giants opposing them. On the other hand, Joshua and Caleb saw themselves with the ability to fight the enemy. Joshua and Caleb had no doubt that they could go into the land and take possession of it, with God on their side.

Joshua and Caleb saw *others* rightly.

In Chapter 14, Caleb pled, "We should go up and take possession of this land, because we can certainly do it!" While the other ten spies saw the people as too big to attack, Joshua and Caleb had confidence. They held onto God's promise to deliver them; they saw the enemies as grasshoppers. "Don't be afraid of the people," they urged, "for we will devour them. Their protection is gone, but the Lord is with us."

Joshua and Caleb saw *their situation* with God's eyes.

Joshua and Caleb saw possibility and potential while the rest saw only problems and a hopeless situation

Joshua and Caleb's view of God, of themselves, of others, and of their situation was based on what God said; the vision of the others was totally God-less.

Do You See Others How God Sees?

What is your vision like? When you look at your life and what you're dealing with right now, do you see what God sees? Do you see your family, spouse, and children through the eyes of God? Do you see yourself as somehow flawed? Or are you really seeing yourself through God's eyes? Do you see your situation, the setbacks, the joys, and the bad report you've been given through the eyes of God? Do you see the opportunities He has placed ahead of you?

I was at a women's conference once when the speaker asked us to partner up with the stranger sitting next to us and stare into her eyes for an uncomfortable two minutes of silence. At the end of those two minutes, we were prompted to share what we had seen. After that time of sharing, we were instructed to repeat the exercise; this time we were to ask God what He saw when He looked at the person beside us. Whoa. What a profound difference. Most of us were in tears, struck by the wonder of God's heart, moved by what He saw in the soul of His beloved creation.

What would happen if we really saw people the way God saw them? Remember the story of Samuel evaluating Jesse's sons to pick the next king? God instructed Samuel not to look at the outward appearance, but to the heart.

Goliath, the giant, saw only the external side of David. "He disdained him: for he was but a youth, and ruddy, and of a fair countenance" (1 Sam. 17:42 KJB). Satan wants us to focus on the outside, the external, not on what is eternal and important. The enemy is a liar and accuser and wants us to judge and condemn others. Our human tendency is to judge ourselves by our good intentions and others by their worst actions.

Like the blind man in John 9, try putting on God's glasses. They are the same pair that Joshua and Caleb wore. If you find yourself thinking something inappropriate, ask God to open your eyes as He did for Samuel. If you find yourself frequently annoyed with the same person or having ill feelings about a certain group of people, confess that to the Lord, and He will open your eyes. God sees each person as one of His beloved. He not only has a purpose and unique plan for each of His creation, He also gave His Son's life to demonstrate His unending love for each of us. If God views people that way, then we should imitate, regardless of what we see with our natural eyes.

God told my friend Julie Johnston to buy rose-colored glasses one day when she felt prompted to visit a friend in the ICU. Julie knew this friend was self-conscious about visitors in the hospital due to the fact that she would not have makeup on. When Julie's friend saw her, she was at first uncomfortable, saying her hair and makeup were undone. Julie whipped out her glasses. Her friend looked puzzled, and Julie remarked, "You look great through these glasses." She reminded her that that's how God sees us, through rose-colored glasses, tinted by the blood of Jesus. Since His blood covers each believer, and the blood of His Son is precious to God, we are precious and beautiful in His sight.

Do You See Yourself As God Sees You?

Like those ten spies, do you see problems instead of possibilities? Do you focus on your failures, inadequacies, and setbacks? You find it hard to believe God's promises for you. Sadly, even though He says in His Word that you are forgiven, beautiful, healed, worthy, loved and loveable, provided for, and chosen, you don't see yourself that way.

Or do you see yourself more highly than you ought? Do you take pride in something that really doesn't make you better than others? Maybe you grew up feeling like you're only as good as you perform.

Let Jesus heal your blindness! You may know the story of Gideon in the book of Judges 6-8. God sends an angel to call him to the incredible task of delivering Israel from the Midianites. The angel calls him "mighty warrior," but Gideon saw himself this way: "Pardon me, my lord," Gideon replied, "but how can I save Israel? My clan is the weakest in Manasseh, and I am the least in my family" (Judg. 6:15).

Gideon had to be convinced that God saw him very differently than how he saw himself. The neat thing was that once he was convinced, he walked in his destiny. You and I cannot fulfill God's purposes for our own lives if we don't see ourselves as God sees us.

We must perceive our failures and imperfections rightly—we have all sinned and fallen short of the glory of God. We must see our strengths and gifts in light of the fact that He has entrusted us with those talents, and we must take care of and use them for His purpose and glory.

God can heal your self-image. I am living proof of that in myself and in those I counsel. In one of my darkest seasons of insecurity, I decided to type out twenty Scriptures that I believed would reprogram my thoughts. I posted them everywhere and read them constantly until they became rote. I was serious about changing, but it took discipline. Just like Jesus touched the blind man, the healing of our self-vision is only possible with God's touch. But we must line our thinking up with God's. Write down His truths about you, speak them over yourself in a mirror. Commit them to memory, and you will begin to see yourself the way God sees you: with potential and purpose.

Do You See Your World As God Sees It?

In order to see our situation the way God sees it, we must adjust our vision in three areas. First, we must focus on God's ability. He is able to meet whatever need we face, to give us peace, to fight our impossible battles, and to see us through. When we focus on God's ability, we begin to see potential, not probabilities.

Focus on how God is bigger than any problem. There is power in praise, especially when we pray. Praising God is saying that we love Him for all He is and all He's done. When we focus on God's ability, our inadequacy or lack of human strength seems less significant.

Next, we must meditate on His benefits. The psalmist wrote in chapter 103:1-2, "Praise the Lord, O my soul . . . and forget not all his benefits." Sometimes we forget what He's done for us. I'd like to think that every time Joshua and Caleb saw a giant in the promised land, they disciplined their minds to remember the faithfulness of God. Maybe they even talked about it with each other. "Remember how He provided quail? Remember going through that Red Sea? That was amazing! Somehow, He's going to give us this land."

That's what you and I need to do, no matter what we face. Remember how God has provided and declare He will do it again.

Finally, we must fix our eyes on God's promises. All twelve spies had heard God's promises; they were leaders. In Deuteronomy 1:30-

31, Moses tried to encourage the people by reminding them of God's provision. He said, "The Lord your God who is going before you, will fight for you, as he did for you in Egypt, before your very eyes, and in the wilderness. There you saw how the Lord your God carried you, as a father carries his son, all the way you went until you reached this place."

Just as the children of Israel had a choice, you and I have a choice to fix our eyes on God's promises, on what He said He would do, especially those promises based on His Word. He is our provider, need-meeter, helper, and ever-present friend.

Some time ago, I had to have oral surgery. The car accident which killed my dad caused severe injury to my teeth. For years, I had put off the surgery because it was too emotional for me, but I finally did it. At first, the swelling and the pain triggered a lot of the emotion and traumatic memories of that scary night, but I had a choice. I could either focus on my dad's death and the pain of that time in my life, or I could focus on God's provision. This scar is a memory of God's faithfulness! Choosing to see it His way has given me so much peace.

HEALED VISION

As we focus on God's ability, forget not His benefits, and fix our eyes on His promises, we begin to see our situations the way He does.

Ask God to open your eyes to see your situation with eyes of faith rather than eyes of fear. When the servant of Elisha once struggled to see his situation rightly, and started to fill with fear, Elisha prayed in 2 Kings 6:17, "O Lord, please open his eyes that he may see. So the Lord opened the eyes of the young man, and he saw, and behold, the mountain was full of horses and chariots of fire all around Elisha!" (ESV). That's awesome! If we trust the Lord and are walking with Him, we have the Commander of the armies of heaven fighting on our side.

The wrong view is costly. Could it be that the way we see ourselves, others, or our situation is getting in the way of a destiny God might have for us?

You and I are called to see with the eyes of God. I love the concept of fixer-upper shows. Gifted people can look at a dilapidated house or a space that was previously purposed for something else and see new life, possibilities, and usefulness. That's how God sees us: with purpose, potential, and promise.

How we see is vital. "The eye is the lamp of the body. If your eyes are healthy, your whole body will be full of light." Jesus taught in Matthew 6:22-23 that "if your eyes are unhealthy, your whole body will be full of darkness." The Messiah invited us in the beginning chapter of John to come and see. He knows when our sight needs adjustment. When we veer toward blindness, He heals us. We must focus on who He is and who we are because of Him. Focusing on God's Word with faith in His ability and promises will allow us to see ourselves, our situations, and others the way God does. Abundant life comes from healed vision and true sight.

Recap and Engage

Truths to Calm Mental Storms: The lens through which I view life affects the way I perceive and interpret what I experience. When necessary, that lens can be corrected. Studying God's Word, spending time in His presence, and remembering His faithfulness in my life can help me see God, myself, others, and my circumstances through a clearer lens.

Lies to Refute: My suffering is always a direct result of my sin or shame. All the bad things that have happened to me have been given by God as punishment or because I am a bad person.

Take It to Heart: Do you struggle with your vision? Will you ask Jesus to heal you? Which aspect is your biggest challenge—people, yourself, or your circumstances? Will you apply the principles of this chapter to those problem spots so that your vision can be corrected?

Prayer: *Lord, forgive me for my distorted view of self and others and help me to see my life and circumstances with Your right perspective. I realize the importance of proper sight. Be Thou my vision, Lord. Help me to have Your eyes today. In Jesus' name, amen.*

Choose to Follow God's Voice

Read: John 10

I did my training in clinical psychology in the Bronx, New York. There's nothing like the sights, sounds, and smells of New York City. One of my most memorable experiences was working at Bronx Lebanon Hospital's inpatient psychiatric unit. One of the patients I had was an elderly gentleman who had been homeless for years and carried a diagnosis of schizophrenia.

During my interview, he told me he had been in and out of the hospital for years. It had been months since he had taken any medication. He described hearing audible voices all the time. They were always with him. I asked him if he wanted to stop hearing voices. He looked at me, puzzled, and said, "No!" These voices were his friends; why would he ever want them to leave? The voices explained his existence, and they filled the aching void in his life.

Voices. We all respond to so-called voices in our head.

Think about your own internal dialogue. You think and rethink a difficult situation, ruminating about what you said. An internal voice of judgment makes you wish you would have been more patient or prepared. The voice of unforgiveness reminds you how you were treated unfairly. You secretly stress out when you compare yourself to others. You worry about how to make ends meet and get everything done—the voice of fear.

Pastor Steven Furtick, in his book *Crash the Chatterbox*, calls this between-the-ears dialogue the "chatterbox," the endless stream of thoughts that run through our minds. These condemning, worrisome thoughts are often pitted against God's thoughts of love and hope and forgiveness. It can feel like a war between your ears, and the barrage can be tormenting.

There are actually many voices we can listen to: God's voice, Satan's temptations, our own human voice, or other people's voices.

Our own voice and the voice of others can be shaped by the Holy Spirit, governed by the sinful nature, or hijacked by the enemy.

Jesus, Creator of humankind and sympathetic to our human condition, knows we need help with voices. He understands our tendency to be bombarded and confused with inner thoughts. In John 10, He explains that He is the Good Shepherd whose true sheep listen to His voice. This teaching frustrated the Jews, who mocked His authority and were miffed by His audacity. "How could He liken Himself to the One true Shepherd, God Almighty?" Yet, Jesus ministers to those who are willing to listen about the way to overcome the battle in our minds and defeat the negative voices.

Voices Go Way Back

The voices we battle have been entrenched in our hearts and minds from the time we were little children. When she was in elementary school, my daughter Caris and I were doing our nightly routine of "cuddle-time." She seemed quiet and finally confessed, "Mama, I'm bad."

"Huh? What happened?"

She explained that she felt like she didn't measure up (there's our old vice, shame) because she was short. As we talked, I realized how deeply insecure she felt because of this physical characteristic. Everyone in her second grade class was inches taller, and she felt significantly inferior. We were able to talk, challenge the lie, and help her see herself in light of God's truth. As always, God's Word had an answer, this time in 1 Samuel 16:7. "The Lord does not look at the things people look at. People look at the outward appearance, but the Lord looks at the heart." My daughter was comforted by the truth of God's Word, and although the physical characteristic persists, she realizes that it does not make her "not enough" or less than others.

I love this saying from the Ultimate Journey curriculum, "A lie unchallenged becomes the truth we live by."[31]

The lies we're told as children about who we are, who God is, and who others are get planted into the soil of our minds. What we think about ourselves as children directly correlates to what we believe about ourselves as teenagers and adults. That's why even when we *know* God loves us, we may not *feel* loved.

THE SCIENCE BEHIND VOICES

Research shows that both our negative and positive thought patterns actually impact the structure and biochemistry of our brains.

Neural pathways are forged in our brains with repetition. After much practice, the behavior becomes automatic, and the neural result is a pathway well-marked because the behavior has been repeated often.

It works the same with our thoughts. When we repeatedly think about failing and being worth nothing, we reinforce those neural pathways in our brains. Those thoughts take up cortical space in our brains and interfere with positive thought circuits. We are literally crowding out room for healthy thoughts.

Research also suggests that focusing on negative thoughts like fear, worry, and self-condemnation actually impacts our brains negatively. It slows the brain down and changes the brain's ability to think, remember, and form new neural connections. Over time, toxic, negative thoughts are being shown to lead to all kinds of illness—not just mental illness, but physical as well.

On the contrary, thinking positive, hopeful, joyful thoughts decreases cortisol and produces serotonin, which contributes to general well-being in our brain and helps our brain function at peak capacity. Positive thoughts, in general, support brain growth and strengthen our prefrontal cortex, which helps us plan and reason better.[32]

How we think affects everything. It's fascinating to me that science is catching up with God's Word and discovering what the Bible has said all along in Proverbs 23:7. "As he thinks in his heart, so is he" (NKJV).

We become what we think. The voice we choose to listen to impacts not just our thought life, but our relationships, our physical health, and our entire beings. God wants our thoughts to reflect His voice and truth about us because that will bring spiritual, emotional, and physical life to us in abundance.

Whose Voice Matters?

In John 10:1-5, Jesus referred to Himself as the Good Shepherd. He explained that sheep stay near the shepherd so they can hear and follow his trusted voice. Sheep run away from the voice of strangers. We can learn so much from these animals.

When we decide to follow Christ, we become His sheep and need to heed the simple animals' example—to stay close enough to hear, recognize, and follow His voice. Too often, instead of running from a negative voice, we allow it to linger in our minds and we become more familiar with it than the voice of the Shepherd. That needs to change.

The enemy knows that when we are trapped in this cycle of negativity, it paralyzes us, weakens our ability to withstand temptation, and renders us ineffective as Christians. As the Bible teaches, the devil uses our difficult situations as part of his wicked schemes. When we lose sight of God, Satan's fiery darts of doubt, insecurity, fear, and pride find their target.

Exposing the Enemy's Voice

John 8:44 describes Satan as the father of lies, so when we listen to lies about who we are, we are really listening to the enemy. "[The devil] was a murderer from the beginning, not holding to the truth, for there is no truth in him. When he lies, he speaks his native language, for he is a liar and the father of lies." When we are not walking closely with God or don't understand His Word, we are more prone to believe Satan's lies and accusations that make us feel guilty, ashamed, and condemned. These are not God's thoughts.

As alluded to earlier, the devil can attempt to get a foothold by using childhood lies. These can become absurd thoughts that distract us and diminish our witness.

When I was little, I grew up with parents who came to this country with eight dollars, literally, in hand. They had to learn the ropes—the language, the styles, the food, the music—and like many immigrants, both worlds existed in tension. When I went to school, I was one of the only brown kids in a sea of white children. I was called names and faced other types of discrimination. I felt rejected and inferior. Even in Indian culture, my skin color was less favorable and that was made known to me on several occasions. A lie took seed in my mind that I was undesirable and "not enough." Thankfully, over time, through His Word and Spirit and through friends, I learned to embrace how God made me, and I have developed confidence in the Lord.

Even when we experience victory in an area, from time to time, an old lie can creep back unknowingly into our minds. The issue resurfaced for me after a recent trip back home to New Jersey when an aunty reached for my underarm chub and stated, "I don't know why they think you're too skinny. Look, you're healthy." Several aunties told me my eyes were sunken and I looked tired. After a week of the comments, I couldn't help but feel that old feeling of ugly.

Without realizing it, I carried that thought home when I returned to Texas. It wasn't a conscious thought, but all of a sudden I was obsessed with eye makeup and undereye coverup. Don't you just hate the lying voice of the enemy? It's terrible when you start to give into it. And that's exactly what I was doing!

You know what finally broke the power of that lying voice? I brought it to the light. One of my favorite counseling verses is Ephesians 5:11, which says, "Have nothing to do with the fruitless deeds of darkness, but rather expose them." John 12:46 says, "I have come as a light to shine in this dark world, so that all who put their trust in me will no longer remain in the dark" (NLT).

I call it the flashlight effect. Telling a friend about my private inner struggle held a flashlight to it. When I told this friend, the power of this fruitless thought of darkness was exposed, brought to the light, and could not stay. God affirmed me and my worth during my time of prayer, and even in a funny way. That same day, a random stranger from the grocery store complimented me on, of all things, my eyes.

The devil would love for us to stay blinded in lies because it truly inhibits us and can become a foothold. When I was dealing with the feeling-ugly-thing, I simply thought of it as an old insecurity coming back. But God showed me it was more than that. It was a distraction used by the powers of darkness. My aunties never meant to hurt me, but the way I interpreted their words was a lie: I am *not* fearfully and wonderfully made. I am *not* a masterpiece. I chose to interpret their concern as criticism and their care as condemnation. I let an old voice dictate the way I heard them, which led to my becoming stuck in a lie.

Ironically, that lie threatened to derail me from the very mission God has uniquely entrusted to me, which is to help people see themselves through the eyes of God. Because I fed those thoughts, looking for additional examples to support the lie, and because I continued to dwell on it, the lie became a trap.

Do you relate? In what way has the enemy been trying to get a hold on you? Distract you? Lie to you? It's time to expose some of those fruitless deeds and thoughts of darkness. God wants you to combat them in the name of Jesus so the devil cannot keep you bound and stifled by them. God wants us to follow His voice.

The Incomparable Voice of God

So what does God's voice sound like? We recognize God's voice because it always gives life, heals, directs, and restores. God's voice is genuine, trustworthy, and always true. Jesus said, "I am the way and the truth and the life" (John 14:6). God's voice is always consistent with His Word, which is infallible, unchanging, and cannot lie.

The voice of God promises us perfect peace when our minds are stayed on Him (Isa. 26:3). The voice of God is filled with grace and unfailing love. He defends us, draws us close, and convicts us of sin so we can confess and be cleansed from all unrighteousness.

The voice of God is sovereign over all. He made Himself known to Job, asking, "Have you ever given orders to the morning, or shown the dawn its place? . . . Can you raise your voice to the clouds and cover yourself with a flood of water? Do you send the lightning bolts on their way? Do they report to you, 'Here we are?'" (Job 38:12, 34-35). God's voice directs all creation. How could His voice not also give perfect direction to our lives?

In the following chart, notice the contrast between the voice of God and the negative voice that wants to take root at times.

The lying voice says . . .	God's voice of truth says . . .
You can't.	In Christ, you can.
You aren't good enough.	I have equipped you with everything you need.
Have fear.	Don't be afraid; I am with you.
You're ugly and worthless. You're a mistake.	You are the work of my hands. I made you and I don't make mistakes!
You're alone.	I am always with you.
You need that drug or that person to be happy.	I completely satisfy ALL your needs.
Pornography doesn't hurt you.	Keeping your heart, eyes, and hands pure lets you have the most fulfilling relationships.
Just give up. What's the point of trying or doing the right thing?	Your labor in the Lord is not in vain. I see you. You will reap a harvest if you do not give up.
You can never be forgiven.	In Christ, you have been forgiven of all your sins.
You are not loved.	I have loved you with an everlasting love (Jer. 31:3).
You are forgotten.	I will not forget you! See I have engraved you in the palms of my hands (Isa. 49:15-16).
Just die. You are insignificant.	Choose life! I give you abundant life. I sent my Son in payment for your life. Your life matters!

Reading the Bible helps us understand this contrast between the voice of God and that of the enemy. Revelation 12 tells us that Satan stands before God accusing believers day and night. This might be true, but Jesus is there to defend us before our Judge, to stand between us and our accuser and declare that we are His. "Who then is the one who condemns? No one. Christ Jesus who died—more than that, who was raised to life—is at the right hand of God and is also interceding for us" (Rom. 8:34).

Belief in Christ is so important because it creates an allegiance between us and the Father through belief in the Son. This puts us on the right side of the battle. "Believe the works, that you may know and understand that the Father is in me, and I in the Father" (John 10:38). Our decision to listen to God's voice allies us with Him when faced with accusation.

Still, Small Voice

1 Kings 19 records the legendary story of Elijah, an incredible prophet of God. He had just had an undeniably victorious encounter with the prophets of Baal and proved God was the one true God. However, the news that wicked queen Jezebel sought his life, sent him running for his life and feeling defeated and depressed. He hid in a cave, feeling totally alone. But God met him there. He gave him food to strengthen him and reminded him of his purpose. The Lord said,

> "Go out, and stand on the mountain before the Lord." And behold, the Lord passed by, and a great and strong wind tore into the mountains and broke the rocks in pieces before the Lord, but the Lord was not in the wind; and after the wind an earthquake, but the Lord was not in the earthquake; and after the earthquake a fire, but the Lord was not in the fire; and after the fire a still small voice. (1 Kings 19:11-12 NKJV)

Don't you wish God's voice would just totally power out the other voices in our heads that tell us to be afraid, that we're not good enough, and that we somehow lack?

But God's voice is the still, small voice of truth.

We will miss it if we don't listen for it or if we are too far from Him to hear it. The enemy's voice will drown out God's voice if we let the cares of life ring louder.

Choosing the Right Voice

So how do we change? How do we listen to God's voice above the rest, stop the habit of negative thinking, and stop letting sinful thoughts reign in our lives?

Romans 12:2 instructs us to be transformed by the renewing of our minds. To do that, to overcome the fiery darts of the enemy and our own sinful desires, we must do what those smart sheep did—listen, recognize, and follow the voice of God, forsaking every other voice.

We can only do this with the help of the Holy Spirit. We must draw close to Him. We don't stand a chance against the constant noise unless we are armed with our Sword. We cannot get familiar with God's voice unless we spend time with Him. Podcasts and Christian music are great, but nothing compares to the alive and active Word of God. There is power in prioritizing. Plan to daily read the Word, pray, praise God, and then be still for a few minutes so you can hear His voice. He will talk to you and make Himself known. I hear His still, small voice whenever I finally get quiet—He speaks forgiveness, direction, caution, and love.

In the *Screwtape Letters*, C. S. Lewis records a series of letters between a veteran demon and a novice demon who is trying to secure the soul of a young man. In one of these letters, the elder demon writes, "It is funny how mortals always picture us putting things into their minds: in reality our best work is done by keeping things out."[33] The devil wants for all the truths Scripture records about God and who we are in Christ to be kept out of our mind. But the Holy Spirit, as described in John 14, is our Divine Reminder through the Word of God!

James 1:22 says that we can't merely listen to the Word and so deceive ourselves. We need to obey it—follow Him in our actions, our words, and our relationships with others. Forgive when God tells us to forgive, love others first, be humble, and serve. We need to agree with what God says about us and our situations and let only God's truth come from our mouths.

How often do you belittle yourself and mutter voices of doubt and fear? Start declaring God's truth about you and your situation. Obey His voice by actually doing what He says to do and by only declaring His truth (not any lies) about yourself.

If you feel like you're not hearing the voice of God, maybe there's an area of your thought life where sin reigns—pride, jealousy, worry, or unforgiveness. Sin separates us from God. Confess it and choose to do what's right. When we obey, we welcome the Holy Spirit to keep speaking to us. When we follow, we become attuned to His voice.

Finally, run from other voices. God implores us to take an inventory of the media—social media, music, television, and movies—we mindlessly feed our minds. We need to silence them in order to hear God. Refuse the enemy any prime time or space in your mind. Become aware of the negative voices. Our feelings are great indicators of our thought life. When we feel anxious or depressed, it's usually because we've allowed negative thoughts to overtake us. We need to take captive every thought and make it obedient to Christ like it says in 2 Corinthians 10:5. "We tear down arguments and every presumption set up against the knowledge of God; and we take captive every thought to make it obedient to Christ" (BSB).

God gave me a picture of what it means to take captive every thought—oddly, while attending a rodeo in Houston. I marveled at the calf-wranglers strategically chasing the calf, tying its legs, and rendering it powerless. They were focused, relentless, and persistent. Like a calf wrangler, we need to wrangle thoughts skillfully, taking hold of them by the root, to prevent them from snowballing into a stronghold.

Run from bad thoughts using the Word of God like Jesus did when Satan tempted Him. Combat lies with the God's Word. James 4:7 says "Submit to God. Resist the devil and he will flee from you" (NKJV).

God's Word really is a guide for how we should think. Try a thought check based on Philippians 4:8. "Finally, brothers and sisters, whatever is true, whatever is noble, whatever is right, whatever is pure, whatever is lovely, whatever is admirable—if anything is excellent or praiseworthy—think about such things."

Do your thoughts line up? Or do you dwell on lies, half-truths, all things dishonorable, impure, shameful, or mediocre? If so, run.

What You Sow Grows

God's Word says we get to choose which voice we listen to. We get to select what grows in the garden of our minds. If I plant bluebonnet seeds, what's going to grow? If I sow godly seeds of love and hope and truth in my mind, that's the kind of life I will enjoy. If I sow seeds of hurt and bitterness and impure thoughts, that's what I will reap in my life. You and I get to garden our own minds. We get to determine what grows by choosing which seeds we plant, by truly checking our thoughts and determining whose voice we heed.

God beckons us to listen to His voice. Stop listening to the voice of the enemy. Stop entertaining evil thoughts that will destroy you. Open the door to a life totally yielded to God and His voice. Choose to meditate on God's promises, keep your focus on Him, and think only on the truth. Obey God and let His voice drown out everyone else's.

If you feel like a slave to negative voices, the first step to victory is to become one of God's sheep and commit to making Jesus the Lord of your thought life. Then pull out the lie-weeds and plant truth.

RECAP AND ENGAGE

Truths to Calm Mental Storms: In Christ, I am a new creation, and I become new by thinking what He wants me to think and listening to His voice.

Lies to Refute: It's not a big deal for me to keep thinking negatively about myself. I can never change how I think and become someone new.

Take It to Heart: Which thoughts do you need to uproot? I love feelings because they are indicators of what we are thinking. Have you felt down recently? What thoughts underlie those feelings? Spend time evaluating and doing a thought check. Review the chart provided in this chapter, contrasting the lying voice to God's voice of truth. Identify which lies you need to replace, confess any wrongful thoughts and purposely bring your thoughts into alignment with the truth of God's Word. Daily declare the truth—God's voice—this week over your life.

Prayer: *Lord, would You help us to listen to Your voice and choose Your truth over every lying, negative, defeating thought? Help us by Your Holy Spirit to think Your way, and heal our minds. In Jesus' name, amen.*

Choose to View Loss Rightly

Read: John 11

For all the differences of opinion that exist today about everything under the sun, I believe we can all agree on one thing. Losing someone you love stinks.

The death of a loved one is one of the most difficult events a person can experience, especially when unexpected. Grief can turn into depression and can lead to an unfulfilled life if not properly processed.

Years ago, George and I suffered a miscarriage. Although we prayed earnestly for God to spare the baby's life, God chose to bring baby Selah's soul to heaven. Even still, we clung to and continue to believe the principle of John 11—Jesus is greater than the storm of death, grief, and bereavement. Jesus gives hope to all who grieve and shows His power over death, foreshadowing the ultimate resurrection of believers.

When Jesus heard that His close friend Lazarus was sick, He purposely waited to go to him, knowing that Father God would get more glory from what He had planned than from what man expected.

Jesus revealed part of His mission on earth: to conquer death.

That's super comforting to me, especially with news of war, natural disasters, epidemics, and untimely deaths. In John 16:33, Jesus made a tough promise: "In this world you will have trouble. But take heart! I have overcome the world." Suffering is part of our pilgrimage, but Jesus overcame our troubles—even death.

Stages of Grief

In college I studied theories by experts like Elizabeth Kubler-Ross, who posited that we go through five stages when we face death: denial/isolation, anger, bargaining, depression, and acceptance. We all grieve in our own way, but understanding the stages can help.

During grief, people go through feelings of denial. We may isolate to avoid reminders of the truth, and well-meaning words of comfort can sting in this stage if we are not ready to handle the reality of the loss.

When denial is no longer possible, people can feel deep anger, like life is unfair. I remember that after we spent a few minutes at my dad's funeral and returned to our hospital room, someone suggested we watch a movie. Everyone meant well, but I erupted with anger. "My dad just died! How can we think about watching a movie?"

Grief unfolds uniquely for every individual in mourning, but anger is a common feeling. Asking yourself what it stems from can be helpful. Often, there is anger at the circumstances, the individual who died, God or another spiritual figure who may have promised hope. Quite often, people feel angry at the new life they have to face without their loved one. For some people, it might seem safer to express anger than it is to process the pain, sadness and fear that truly underlies it.

Bargaining involves negotiating, often trying to make a deal with God like, "God, if you heal him, I will do this or that." Bargaining can help someone feel in control in the face of a helpless situation. In this stage, people often make "if only" statements to combat how vulnerable and helpless they feel. "If only I had driven that night, he would still be here." Or, "If only we had tried that procedure."

Feelings of depression set in when we let ourselves feel the full weight of our sadness. Our loved one is gone. It's normal to have waves of sadness. This sadness can turn into a clinical depression if the symptoms become more pervasive, lasting all day and every day for weeks and months. Isolation can contribute to sadness. Spending time with others to process emotions is critical. Maintaining habits of worship and the Word, taking care of our bodies, and making choices that lead to healthy mindsets can help prevent clinical depression.

Following healthy practices and keeping Biblical mindsets can allow a person to come to acceptance. The fact that one has accepted a loss does not mean they are "over it," but rather, that they have come to terms with what has happened and continue to move forward.

Acceptance can take years and isn't always achieved. When people focus only on their loved one's death, it can lead to bitterness, loss of purpose and trust, and worsening symptoms of grief.

THE TRUTH ABOUT DEATH

How do we protect ourselves from becoming susceptible to clinical depression or other types of mental illness? We must guard our thoughts so an *unchallenged lie* does not become our personal truth. In order to enjoy Jesus' abundant life, we must actively combat these lies. Let's consider several examples of how Jesus countered the false assumptions about loss in John 11 and shows us the right way to think.

Mary and Martha, siblings of Lazarus, sent word to Jesus that their brother was sick. Sickness, suffering, and death happen to everyone, even to those who fully follow Jesus. No one could question the depth of relationship this family enjoyed with Jesus. The sisters described Lazarus as *the one Jesus loved.* Yet for reasons not made clear yet, Jesus waited to go to Lazarus.

When God delays, we sometimes believe that He has not answered our prayer in time. But remember, God is always on time. He has a bigger plan, a higher purpose.

The fact that our omniscient God sees the big picture and the greater good is a healing truth. We may entertain the idea that death and sickness surely cannot be God's will and occur because of sin, lack of faith, or prayerlessness. The truth is that God allows sickness at times so that the Son may be glorified through it. Similarly, we may assume that untimely death cannot be part of God's plan.

If I were writing my own life story, I would not have taken my dad away when I was so young. But God is always up to something, even when we can't see it. This is a Scriptural principle. Jesus described Himself and the death He would face on the cross in John 12:24, "Very truly I tell you, unless a kernel of wheat falls to the ground and dies, it remains only a single seed. But if it dies, it produces many seeds."

God's math is so different from our two-plus-two. When we think of death, we might think subtraction; but God sees multiplication and exponential growth. Death or loss may look like a puzzle piece that doesn't fit because it's dark and sad, but God works that piece into the whole story that He's weaving together to create a glorious masterpiece.

Loss Clears the Stage for New Purpose

God has master-minded your loss to fulfill His purposes for your life. Maybe, like me, you didn't expect your loss. You prayed for healing or some other outcome, but it didn't happen the way you expected. You may feel anxious because you are not in control. Why? Couldn't it have been some other way?

The better question to ask is *what.* "Lord, what do you see that I don't see? What are you birthing through my loss? What is the purpose of this pain?" Often, these answers don't come right away, and even when we think we may have figured them out, we've only touched on a fraction of the mysterious plan God has for our lives.

Time is a great eye-opener. With time, God shows us how He can use the saddest, the hardest, and the most painful things to fulfill His purposes for our lives.

I longed for my dad to come back to life. When I was growing up, we watched soap operas—*Days of Our Lives*—don't judge. Sometimes a character would die and somehow come back to life a few years later. Because I didn't spend time at the funeral or see my dad get buried, in my innocent mind, I fantasized that maybe there was some mistake. I so badly wanted my dad to be written back into my story.

Despite my fantasies, I recognize that I have become who I am today because of my loss and the pain I suffered. Even when I served at Mukti Mission in India, I connected with the orphaned kids because I, too, had lost a parent. We can be aversive to pain, but as Dr. Samuel Chand writes in his excellent book, *Leadership Pain*, "Pain is the classroom for growth and can be our greatest teacher."[34]

Sometimes the lessons God has for us through someone's death or suffering are more powerful than if He had sent healing.

The Truth About God in Loss

Have you ever wondered where God is when something terrible happens? Like Mary and Martha reasoned, "Lord, if You had been here, my brother would not have died," we assume that if God was there, bad things would not happen. We think God should prevent bad things from occurring, but that is not reality. His hand of mercy *does* shield the believer from many things, as stated in Psalm 91:1. "He who dwells in the shelter of the Most High shall rest in the shadow of the Almighty." However, we live in a fallen world where evil happens. When Adam sinned in the garden and gave over his God-entrusted authority over the earth to the prince of darkness, the enemy's ways of sin began to prevail.

However, even in our lowest moments, God is there. The Spirit of God knew when Lazarus was dying, when he had died, and what would happen after his death. God was there.

God is ever-present. He does not change. But there is nothing like death, loss, and suffering to make you question the goodness of God. Is God who He says He is? Does He care? How could a good God allow such a horrible thing to happen? And ultimately, can I really trust Him? In those moments, we need to grasp the truth that His nature does not change, even when our circumstances do.

The shortest verse in the Bible, John 11:35, states, "Jesus wept." In those simple words, we see the heart of God and His humanity, tenderness, and compassion. Why the tears? Jesus was troubled at the pervasive enemy of humankind: death. More than sad, He was indignant. He knew that one day, He would defeat death once and for all. Even though Jesus foresees the outcome and knows the greater good that will come out of *all* we experience, He still understands our sorrow, sympathizes with us in our weakness, and mourns with us in our pain. Because He cares, He invites us to cast our cares on Him.

In the same way, the Lord uses our losses to reveal more of Himself to us. Sometimes it's during our darkest seasons that we experience the true goodness and nature of God because we recognize how much we need Him. We sense we are being carried; we feel Him pulling us through.

God's resurrection power allows us to see the glory of God despite our loss. Jesus' ultimate purpose for all we experience in life is for us to believe that God sent Jesus to save us. Our God is able to do the impossible on many levels—not just resurrecting us to eternal life, but also giving us peace in the midst of our brokenness. Jesus knows the outcome, both for this life and for the one eternal.

Joshua Learns to Overcome Grief and Sorrow

Two days before my dad died, on the day we left India for the airport to come back to New York, my extended family gathered at my dad's family home in Kerala to send us off. As was our custom before a trip, my Christian family spent a while in prayer and reading from the Word. All of my cousins, aunts, and uncles were gathered together, about thirty people. Interestingly, my dad's dad picked my mom to read the Bible before this large group of people. He told her to read from Joshua 1. My mom thought it strange that she was asked to read, and of all passages, this passage; but she recognized much later that the Lord was actually speaking to her and preparing her for what would come, giving her instruction for how she should live her life and handle the loss she was about to experience. Read this Scripture my mom was asked to read, Joshua 1:1-9.

> After the death of Moses the servant of the Lord, the Lord said to Joshua son of Nun, Moses' aide: "Moses my servant is dead. Now then, you and all these people, get ready to cross the Jordan River into the land I am about to give to them—to the Israelites. I will give you every place where you set your foot, as I promised Moses. Your territory will extend from the desert to Lebanon, and from the great river, the Euphrates—all the Hittite country—to the Mediterranean Sea in the west. No one will be able to stand against you all the days of your life. As I was with Moses, so I will be with you; I will never leave you nor forsake you. Be strong and

> courageous, because you will lead these people to inherit the land I swore to their ancestors to give them.
>
> "Be strong and very courageous. Be careful to obey all the law my servant Moses gave you; do not turn from it to the right or to the left, that you may be successful wherever you go. Keep this Book of the Law always on your lips; meditate on it day and night, so that you may be careful to do everything written in it. Then you will be prosperous and successful. Have I not commanded you? Be strong and courageous. Do not be afraid; do not be discouraged, for the Lord your God will be with you wherever you go."

What anchoring words! I am so encouraged by how God revealed Himself to Joshua when his beloved mentor Moses died and he was assigned to lead the Israelites. In his loss and grieving, God told Joshua that He would be with him and stay right by his side; the Word of God would be his key. God actually used the loss to reveal more of Himself to Joshua, just as He would for Martha and Mary.

Death has a way of rocking our security; it's why insurance agents are so successful at convincing us to seek bigger life insurance plans, to help offset that feeling. The Lord saw the fear written all over Joshua's face as he faced his new assignment. Who could blame him? Immediately, Joshua would face a trial—crossing the Jordan during its flood stage. With no boat, Joshua would have to rely on God. Forced to walk through the trials of leading these people on his own, without his earthly mentor, Joshua grew in ways that he would never have experienced. His faith muscles were exercised in ways that stretched him, and probably even hurt.

But notice how God answered the unspoken question of how Joshua would get through the pain. He challenged Joshua to base his courage on the Word. "Be careful to obey the law . . . Do not turn from it to the right or to the left, that you [will] be successful wherever you go. Keep this Book of the Law always on your lips; meditate on it day and night, so that you may be careful to do everything written in it. Then you will be prosperous and successful" (Josh. 1:7-8).

What got Joshua through was his dependence on the counsel of the Word of God. In the same way, when we survive a loss, we must never let this Book depart from our mouths. We must meditate on it; it must be on our minds and in our thoughts. We must follow it and carefully obey it.

Let the Scriptures anchor you through your storm; keep praying them even in the midst the pain; defy every lying voice of the enemy. Remember Psalm 1, "Blessed is the one . . . whose delight is in the law of the Lord . . . that person is like a tree planted by streams of water, which yield its fruit in season and whose leaf does not wither—whatever they do prospers."

Joshua found himself in a very painful season, but as he relied on the Word of the Lord, he prospered and was victorious. God fought the battles, Joshua obeyed, and they had great success.

My mom depended on God and prayed about everything, from parking spaces to our future spouses. She became a widow at the age of thirty-eight and never remarried, but she prayed each of her three children into a relationship with God and a successful future—education, careers, happy marriages with beautiful children, and hearts to serve the Lord. In an age where statistics against single parent homes and kids are pretty slim, this is miraculous. This is the work of God, a testimony to His power and His faithfulness. He never once left our side as He guided us through His Word.

It's humbling to think that the Lord would give my family a specific Scripture to anchor us, even before our storm occurred. He is no respecter of persons; He longs to speak personally to you, through Scripture, in the darkest circumstances of *your* life.

Where, O Death Is Your Sting?

To me, nothing offers more hope and allows us to come to the stage of true acceptance like the truth that God overcame death once and for all.

"But Christ has indeed been raised from the dead, the firstfruits of those who have fallen asleep. For since death came through a man, the resurrection of the death comes also through a man. For as in Adam all die, so in Christ all will be made alive" (1 Cor. 15:20-22).

The last evil force Jesus will defeat is death.

"Then the end will come, when he hands over the kingdom to God the Father after he has destroyed all dominion, authority and power. For he must reign until he has put all his enemies under his feet. The last enemy to be destroyed is death" (1 Cor. 15:24-26).

Jesus removed the sting of death, along with every other source of trial and tribulation.

Whole Healing After Loss

After loss, abundant mental wellness happens when we maintain the right perspective, aligning our thoughts with the Word of God. In Mary and Martha's case, their brother came back to life. Most of us will never see a deceased loved one resurrected. However, as Christians, we have a future hope of being reunited in heaven; this truth serves as an anchor.

If you're facing loss today, remember that God will use the loss to reveal Himself in a fresh way, to confirm His identity, and to grow your character.

Don't forget who He is. He hasn't changed.

Don't forget who you are. You are more than a conqueror because of the Conqueror who lives inside you; you have victory over every loss.

Don't forget that abiding in God's Word every day is your most effective tool when striving to keep His perspective.

And finally, press on. "Therefore, my dear brothers and sisters, stand firm. Let nothing move you. Always give yourselves fully to the work of the Lord, because you know that your labor in the Lord is not in vain" (1 Cor. 15:58).

Recap and Engage

Truths to Calm Mental Storms: God has purposed my loss for the glory of God. Jesus is greater than death and provides hope for all in the grave and all surviving the loss of a loved one.

Lies to Refute: I am alone in my loss. God's character must have changed somehow because I am facing pain.

Take It to Heart: Consider the losses you've suffered. Maybe the death of a loved one. Maybe a time when you lost your innocence, or it was taken from you. Your brain's record of those losses can be triggered by someone looking at you the wrong way, not acknowledging you, or not including you. All of a sudden, you can feel down, or like a helpless little child. You might mentally return to that original place of deep loss where you felt hard feelings: rejection, isolation, loneliness, fear, and insecurity.

Do you relate to the assumptions that God wasn't there, God didn't care, or God couldn't use your pain as part of His plan? Confess your doubts, anger, and concerns to the Lord.

Affirm that He is the Resurrection and the Life. He conquered death. He understands our pain and He will see us through. Comfort yourself with the fact that this life is temporary, and one day He will erase your sorrows and wipe your tears. Pick a few truths to meditate on as you walk through this season.

Prayer: *Lord, help me keep Your perspective in my life and losses. Thank You that You don't waste my pain. I trust You to see me through. I trust You to weave my darkest moments into a glorious piece of art. I trust You to shape me into Your image as I meditate on Your Word day and night. In Jesus' name, amen.*

Choose to Surrender

Read: John 12

"Today's the day!" She twirled excitedly as she prepared for the guests who were coming. The aroma of delicious lamb roasting and bread baking filled the festive air as friends gathered together to finalize the meal preparations.

"Every hand to the plow!" her sister commanded cheerfully from the other room. The sisters had great reason to celebrate their guest of honor. After all, He had just miraculously raised their brother Lazarus from the dead. Not your everyday occurrence in Bethany.

Some time ago, Jesus had commended Mary for sitting at His feet and hanging on to His words, but this time, she made sure to be helpful, at least before the Master arrived. She took her place along with Martha and the other women of the town stirring, dicing, arranging, tidying, and her favorite—taste-tasting.

"Ooh, Martha! You did it again! This soup is . . . mmm . . . so good!" As she bustled about, her mind drifted. Today was the day. Their friend was coming over, but there was even more. Mary had a gift for Jesus. Excitement bubbled within—the feeling you get when you know you've gotten the right present for someone you love dearly, someone who is hard to shop for. She couldn't wait to present her gift.

His words echoed in her mind, "The reason my Father loves me is that I lay down my life—only to take it up again" (John 10:17). "I am the resurrection and the life" (John 11:25).

When Jesus arrived, Mary slipped away. What she felt compelled to do would probably be met with criticism. She didn't want to draw attention to herself, but she knew this could be her last chance.

As Martha served dinner, Mary made her way to her Master. Quietly, dutifully, she took her treasure of a pound of costly spikenard and poured it on Jesus. Letting down her hair, she wiped His feet with it. Gasps went up, eyes glared at her, but she didn't care. Her singular purpose was to worship Him and give Him the best of what she had.

The fragrance of the ointment consumed the house, even overpowering the aroma of the savory food on the table. She hoped the scent would linger on Jesus until the day of His arrest and crucifixion. It would serve as a precious memory of her devotion.

While onlookers, including the disciple who would betray Jesus, insulted her for what they perceived to be wasteful, Jesus defended her.

"Hush!" Jesus took command of the brewing storm of criticism. "'Leave her alone,' Jesus replied. 'It was intended that she should save this perfume for the day of my burial. You will always have the poor among you, but you will not always have me'" (John 12:7-8).

Contrary to the opinion of the bystanders, the humble disciple Mary, known for sitting at Jesus' feet, was prodigal in love. Prodigal: reckless in abandon, profuse in generosity, and extravagant in obedience. Mary had actually listened and perceived a truth everyone else seemed to miss. Her Savior was about to give His life for them. Mary's magnanimous gift to Jesus foreshadowed the Savior's gift and ultimate sacrifice.

Surrendered Despite the Storm

After Lazarus' resurrection, the religious leaders grew increasingly intent on murdering the Messiah. Yet, the masses seemed to be enamored with the Son of Man.

The next day a great crowd greeted Jesus as He entered Jerusalem on a small, unimpressive animal, so unlike kings of that day. Exuberant with hope, they spread their cloaks on the ground and waved their palm branches. They believed their political Savior was going to free them from the oppression of Rome. "Hosanna! Save us now!"

Of course, this crowd changed their tune less than a week later. The opinion of the people, whether positive or negative, didn't faze Jesus. He was unwaveringly committed to the Father's agenda, plowing ahead to the cross, despite what people wanted or expected.

During this tentative time many came to believe, even a few of the chief rulers, but they hid their faith, "for they loved the praise of men more than the praise of God" (John 12:43 KJV). Tucked in this verse is a precious truth. It's impossible to be wholly surrendered, recklessly abandoned to God, if your desire is to please people. You'll miss out, inhibited from the freedom of an abundant, full life in Christ.

Scripture speaks to the fear of repercussion and encourages us to be unabashedly unashamed. "Yet if anyone suffers as a Christian, let him not be ashamed, but let him glorify God in that name" (1 Pet. 4:16 ESV). "For whoever is ashamed of me and of my words, of him will the Son of Man be ashamed when he comes in his glory and the glory of the Father and of the holy angels" (Luke 9:26 ESV).

Unlike the shallow loyalty of certain leaders and the deceptive, two-faced adherence of the betraying disciple Judas, Mary's reckless devotion was unhindered. She served as a portrayal of Jesus' reckless love that is deep, lavish, and inexplicable. He went to the cross because of you and me. He's unashamed of us; He identifies with us and all of humanity and faced the darkest night anyone could ever imagine by taking the weight of our sin.

Jesus lived with total surrender. We, as His followers, must follow Him in surrender. Does reckless devotion benefit our mental well-being? In a way, the answer doesn't even matter. We are called to die to self. No questions asked. But the truth is that as we follow Jesus without abandon, He always provides, blesses, and guides.

Saying Yes to Self-Surrender

I enjoy watching George play with our kids. When our son was younger, George liked to toss Luke around and put him into martial arts holds. He taught Luke ways to get out of the holds, and Luke would try with all his might. But he was usually forced to surrender.

Of course, with your loving dad, it's fun. But surrendering to someone you don't like is the last thing you want to do. It's giving up your pride and saying, "You win, I lose. I give up."

Centuries ago, a few young men found themselves in a very difficult situation—Daniel, Shadrach, Meshach, and Abednego. Their country was besieged by another nation and forced to surrender. The king of the ruling nation ordered that several men from the royal court of the surrendering country be forced into royal servitude. Ripped from their families, their traditions, and their *normal,* they were forced to surrender to the service of the king, his country, and its ways.

To surrender is to yield to the power, control, or possession of another upon compulsion or demand. It means to cease resistance to an opponent and submit to their authority. Most of us resist surrender because we resist the notion of being controlled. Let's be real—we like being in control. It's one reason people are so afraid to fly; they lack control. However, surrender is critical for a Christian's walk, and we must be willing to say, "Lord, I totally yield to whatever situation You put before me."

The Savior's Sermonette on Surrender

In John 12, when the Greeks requested an audience with the Jews, He responded with a homily on surrender.

> Very truly I tell you, unless a kernel of wheat falls to the ground and dies, it remains only a single seed. But if it dies, it produces many seeds. Anyone who loves their life will lose it, while anyone who hates their life in this world will keep it for eternal life. Whoever serves me must follow me; and where I am, my servant also will be. My Father will honor the one who serves me." (John 12:24-26)

In essence, Jesus explained that He must surrender His life for the greater good of all people. We might be tempted to think it was easy for Jesus to surrender because He was God, but He was also fully human. He experienced pain and sympathized with our weaknesses. He dreaded the cross. In fact, Scripture records that He prayed at the Garden of Gethsemane, at the foot of the Mount of Olives, just before going to the cross: "Father take this cup from Me! I really don't want to do this! But if this is the only way, and if this is Your way, I will" (Luke 22:42, author's paraphrase). Although Christ was in anguish, He resolved to do it God's way. He fully surrendered to the will of the Father.

We might also think that it was easy for Jesus to surrender because He knew He would rise again. Yet the reality of the resurrection did not negate the agony of the crucifixion. Despite how difficult it would be, Jesus believed the benefit far outweighed the cost. He was willing to yield to His Father's plan because He trusted Him.

Jesus is our perfect model for surrender. He does not ask us to do anything He has not already done. He commands us to do what He did.

Flesh Opposes Surrender

In Matthew 16:21-23, we get a more detailed account of Jesus anticipating the cross. When Jesus predicted His death, Peter was not so thrilled about the prospect of his friend and Savior dying.

> From that time on Jesus began to explain to his disciples that he must go to Jerusalem and suffer many things at the hands of the elders, the chief priests and the teachers of the law, and that he must be killed and on the third day be raised to life. Peter took him aside and began to rebuke him. "Never, Lord!" he said. "This shall never happen to you!" Jesus turned and said to Peter, "Get behind me, Satan! You are a stumbling block to me; you do not have in mind the concerns of God, but merely human concerns."

There are two truths to glean from this passage: self-life opposes surrender, and Satan opposes surrender.

Peter reasoned that Jesus should not suffer. This resistance to Jesus' surrendered life exemplifies how the self-life resists surrender. The self-life is self-protective and takes the easy route. It's ambitious and designed to make self look and feel good. The self-life does not want to give up control.

The danger of the self-life is that we can confess Jesus is Lord and still remain on the throne of our lives. We don't really make Jesus the Lord and we risk denying Jesus. This is the very thing Peter did three times. He denied Jesus. He acted like he did not know Him.

If we do not live a life surrendered to the plan of God, when we are tested or tempted or in a situation in which we feel overwhelmed or afraid, we will fall into the trap of denying Jesus. As if we don't even know Him, we will return to our old self-life ways of coping and numbing from our problems, including drugs, alcohol, poor relationships, and unhealthy habits.

Satan also resists surrender. When Peter rebuked Jesus, he used the same Greek word, *epitimao*, Jesus used when He rebuked the wind and waves. It means to "charge sharply, tax with fault, admonish."[35]

In his rebuke, Peter accused and found fault with Jesus, thereby taking on the voice of the devil. He found fault with the voice of truth, totally clashing with the plan of God and trying to take authority.

Jesus' surrendered life is completely offensive to the enemy. It's contrary to his wicked schemes. Just as Peter tried to get Jesus to spare Himself, Satan says to you and me, "Never! This should not happen to you. Don't give up your life. Don't surrender all." Satan comes against you and me with the same temptation because he is threatened by our completely yielded, submitted lives to the Lord.

Jesus Is Pleased With Surrender

Jesus' affirmation of Mary's extravagant gift, symbolic of her surrendered life, shows that surrender pleases Him. Not only does it please Him, but knowing that we are living for the right reasons gives us purpose and fills us with a sense of joy and accomplishment. Peter's opposition to Jesus' surrender was prompted by a spirit of selfishness and foolishness. In rebuking this spirit, Jesus was communicating His displeasure with the self-life. A life centered on one's own needs and agenda does not please God. A life that is not pleasing to God will not be blessed and cannot experience everlasting joy and peace.

Imagine a strong, able-bodied horse that has the genes, muscular build, and potential to become a prizewinning racehorse. Now, picture this horse being untameable and not surrendered to its master. It doesn't matter how much potential the horse has; it is useless without surrender. On the other hand, a horse with potential that is willing to be taught and trained can be used to do great things.

We are like these horses! We may feel like we don't have a lot of potential, but that doesn't matter when our hearts are totally surrendered to God, and we say, "Lord, have Your way in my life! I surrender my deceit, my desire to look good, and all my pretense!" When this is our prayer, God can use us!

"God chose the foolish things of the world to shame the wise; God chose the weak things of the world to shame the strong" (1 Cor. 1:27). He can use the fully yielded person whom the world would disqualify to bring Him glory and do awesome things. He can take our one talent and multiply it if we are totally surrendered. In fact, that's the way that God will use us most powerfully.

THE COST OF SURRENDER

Jesus expects us to deny ourselves, take up our cross, and follow Jesus. This is a choice on our part, an act of our own free will. Jesus showed us the way to practice the following three aspects of surrender.

Deny self.

To deny self, we must empty ourselves and put the desire of Christ and His will above our own. Deny our appetites, desires, and ambitions and totally surrender to God's way. Christ modeled this for us. Think of a cup. What if I wanted to fill it with tea? I'd need a clean, empty cup. If it had juice or water or worse, dirt, in it, I would need to empty it in order to be able to use it. In the same way, you and I need to be empty cups.

Does this mean that we become a blank slate? No personality, no interests? Forget our education or background? No!

God uniquely created us to do different things in the Kingdom of God. We have different functions in the body of Christ, and when we surrender our appetites, desires, and ambitions, He shapes them into something He can use.

When God called George into the ministry, He spoke to him about surrendering his corporate career. George was used to his comfortable way of life; the financial cushion meant peace of mind. But God took George to a place of surrender. He said, "Lord, I will do anything for you. Any job, anything to serve you."

Finally, the Lord opened a door at Teen Challenge in the field of bookkeeping, the area of George's education. God used George's specific bend and background, and George surrendered to the plan of God. He wasn't deterred by not being paid and began to volunteer forty to fifty hours weekly. God stretched our faith that first year of marriage and showed Himself powerful. George had to become empty in order to be used.

The same with me. I had to empty myself of all my training and background in order to be used. I had to die to the world's answers for solutions in people's lives, die to reliance on my education, and become a surrendered student to the Word of God. Not coincidentally, that's when God opened the door for me to start a counseling ministry.

Take Up Your Cross

The cross is a symbol of cruel punishment by death—a horrible death instrument. Practically, it means to die to ourselves. We must crucify the flesh and constantly battle against our own tendency to sin, against the enemy, and against the hatred of the world. Just like Galatians 2:20 states, "I have been crucified with Christ and I no longer live, but Christ lives in me," we must be willing to suffer and experience whatever God would have us experience. This is the surrendered life.

Follow Christ

To follow Jesus and join Him is to get on the same side as Christ, to take His side and not the enemy's side, and to cleave and conform wholly to His example (Rom. 12:1-2).

If you're reading this and thinking you can't deny yourself and just join yourself with Christ, it's okay. The Lord will work it out *in* you. He is not asking you to give Him your perfect surrender in your own strength; in fact, we can't do so by our own might, but only by His will and the power of the Holy Spirit. What we must do is ask God to help us and then trust that He will.

Andrew Murray was a great preacher who studied in Scotland and preached revival in South Africa back in the 1800s. He wrote the following in his timeless sermon "Absolute Surrender:"

> When God has begun the work of absolute surrender in you, and when God has accepted your surrender, then God holds Himself

> bound to care for it and to keep it! Will you believe that? If God allows the sun to shine upon you moment by moment, without intermission, will not God let His life shine upon you every moment? And why have you not experienced it?
>
> Give yourself absolutely to the will of God . . . Say absolutely to the Lord God: By Thy grace I desire to do Thy will in everything, every moment of every day. Say: Lord God, not a word upon my tongue but for Thy glory, not a movement of my temper but for Thy Glory, not an affection of love or hate in my heart but for Thy glory, and according to Thy blessed will'" (pp. 14-15).[36]

I encourage you to make this prayer of submission your own. "Lord, help me to have in mind the things of God, not the things of men. Help me to come to You, deny myself, die to myself, and follow You." Ask yourself in what areas of your life you feed the flesh and struggle to surrender.

The Why Behind Surrender

Our decision to surrender affects our whole health. Without it, we may feel like we are in a fight, which is true, because we are resisting God's perfect plan for our lives. However, when we surrender, we find eternal life, joy, peace, and purpose. We will wake up with a sense of duty, and even if our service ends in death, we find life for eternity in Christ.

Our surrender also has eternal rewards. In Matthew 16:27, Jesus shares the promise of surrender. "For the Son of Man is going to come in his Father's glory with his angels, and then he will reward each person according to what they have done."

We don't know what our reward will look like, but Scripture teaches us that our reward will be commensurate with our sacrifice.

"So we make it our goal to please him, whether we are at home in the body or away from it. For we must all appear before the judgment seat of Christ, that each of us may receive what is due us for the things done while in the body, whether good or bad" (2 Cor. 5:9-10).

Even though the Bible is quite clear that surrendering all to Jesus comes with great benefits, I'll admit, when I studied this at first, I felt twinges of fear when I considered saying, "Lord, do *whatever* you want with my life." (I mean, can't I have a tiny say in it? Like, God can You please spare us from pain and sorrow and suffering?)

"God, am I really good with You doing whatever You want with my kids and marriage . . . with my career and future? But, Lord, I've been through so much. I'm afraid, Lord. I don't want to experience pain again, like I did with the loss of my dad."

As I reflected, I recognized that my immediate reaction was based on a distorted view of God. As though He's cruel and heartless, as though He is just waiting for me to surrender so that He can hurt me.

Friends, that's just wrong. The wrong view of God is a hindrance to the idea of surrender because it leads to fear. And fear leads to a desire to control. We need to get our view of God right before we will be willing to choose to surrender. We may go through the motions, feeling like we have no choice but to surrender. But it won't last. We'll go back to our same old controlling selves.

But when we see God for who He really is—loving, kind, caring, and there for us—then we give ourselves cheerfully because we know that our God is a *good Father* and that we can trust Him.

I invite each of you to make this your prayer: "Lord, more than anything else I want to be at a place where I fully surrender all." There is no greater joy and freedom than to be able to honestly say, "I, and all I have, are Yours. Do with me whatever seems good to You."

Surrendered People

Earlier I referenced Daniel and his three friends who were forced to surrender to King Nebuchadnezzar of Persia. The king erected a statue of himself and expected everyone to bow to it, including these Jewish men who served as his officials.

Their example of unwavering surrender to God inspires and challenges me. "Shadrach, Meshach, and Abednego replied to him, 'King Nebuchadnezzar, we do not need to defend ourselves before you in this matter. If we are thrown into the blazing furnace, the God we serve is able to deliver us from it, and he will deliver us from Your Majesty's hand. But even if he does not, we want you to know, Your Majesty, that we will not serve your gods or worship the image of gold you have set up'" (Dan. 3:16-18). Willing to face whatever God had for them, they declared in essence the following:

Even if He does not save us, we will not serve any other god!

Even if He does not, we pledge total allegiance to God.

Even if He does not answer the way we may hope He answers, we trust Him to defend us.

Even if things don't go the way we plan, we choose to worship God!

Even if He puts us to suffering, we will serve God and Him alone!

Friend, I invite you to respond to the call of God to surrender. I urge you to strip yourself of yourself. To take up your cross and deny yourself. "God, not my way. Have Your way."

I rebuke every attempt of the enemy to resist this moment in your life. This is a time to renew your commitment to surrender. Your surrender brings freedom and peace. When you give up control, you are no longer anxious. You don't have to figure it all out. You just trust God to work it out.

Every Adult & Teen Challenge student I have seen who has been successful in his or her healing journey and future life has totally surrendered, given up any life agenda, and trusted God.

I think of my friends Austin and Sarah Baughman, married for over ten years with three precious children. Both Austin and Sarah came into the program full of themselves but broken down by their own futile attempts to live life. At different points in their journey, not knowing each other, in different ATC programs, they chose to say yes to Jesus. Their yes led them to each other as they recognized the same passion for the Lord and the same desire to serve Him with everything they had. Now they have purpose, freedom, joy, and a beautifully blessed life. All because of their willingness to surrender.

The Lord invites us to surrender not only our lives, but our responses, how we treat others, our time, future, pride, and gifts to the Lord. The blessing is eternal, and it's a life worthy of God's praise.

Recap and Engage

Truths to Calm Mental Storms: A surrendered life is the most blessed life, for when you give your life away, God has a way of giving it back with more.

Lies to Refute: It's my life, and I can do whatever I want to please me when I feel like it. It's my world; I need to defend my rights.

Take It to Heart: Consider which areas of your life you still hold on to. Is it your finances? Do you have a hard time letting go of your children? What are you afraid of? Bring these areas of concern and these fears to the Lord; share them with a friend. God understands your hesitation but will always move us into a place of greater faith. We grow when we're not comfortable. Remember that Mary's secret to surrender was her devotion, time spent at Jesus' feet listening and meditating, letting His words sink in deeply. We must do the same daily!

Prayer: *Lord, forgive me for the ways I have tried to live my life in my own strength, securing and defending my own rights, following my own agenda, and serving my selfish purposes. I realize that by holding on, I am not letting go and trusting You to provide and see me through. Father, help me to be at Your feet. Please help me to choose surrender, and thank You that You work everything in my life out and that I am Yours. What freedom, joy, and peace to know that You are taking care of me. In Jesus' name, amen.*

Choose to Love Like Jesus

Read: John 13

Have you ever felt compelled to do something that required sacrifice or letting go of your plans?

During the 2020 pandemic, God prompted us to leave the city we had settled our family in for over ten years to move back to George's hometown and move his precious parents in with us. This was no easy move. Our kids were content in their schools, and we loved our jobs and church. However, because the Holy Spirit urged us, we felt compelled. So we packed up our four kids, our dog and belongings in San Antonio, and two U-Hauls later, we were settled in Houston and starting over. Although it took great effort and sacrifice, tremendous blessing has come from being obedient.

Sometimes God asks us to do hard things which don't make sense on paper. At Adult & Teen Challenge, whether student or staff, not a day goes by that we are not stretched, challenged, or tested.

In John 13, Jesus practiced and taught one of the most important commandments God gave. With over 1600 commands in the Bible, Jesus summed them all up into two foundational ones. First, love God with every fiber of your being—soul, body and spirit (Mark 12:30). And second, love your neighbor as yourself (Mark 12:31). If we get these two right, we have obeyed the essence of all the other commandments.

Jesus explained that loving others is essential to our spiritual walk and to the fullness of our life on earth. Peace of mind goes hand in hand with loving like Jesus.

An Uncommon Love

University President John Roberson McQuilkin resigned from his job at the height of his career to care for his wife Muriel, diagnosed with early dementia. The pair had built a life serving the Lord, even as missionaries to Japan. Robertson tried to continue his regular responsibilities when they got the distressing news that Muriel had early Alzheimer's disease, but his wife became full of fear when he left the house and attempted to follow him on foot. He took the road less traveled and followed Jesus' footsteps in giving up his life for his bride.

It's rare to find such examples of unconditional love. A love that is lavish, giving, and selfless. A love that does not need to be returned. We live in a world where we're so easily offended. If someone doesn't make mention of us, if someone gets the better seat or the bigger piece of the pie, if someone looks at us the wrong way, or God forbid, drives too slow, we get offended—often even outraged.

In common culture, love is temporal, as fleeting as the seasons. Our world is sadly in short supply of true, unending love.

Responding to an Unprecedented Act of Love

In John 13, Jesus washed the disciples' feet. This was no spur-of-the-moment act of love. Jesus planned and prepared. He sought the Father. Knowing His time on earth was coming to an imminent end, it was time to show His disciples just how much He loved them.

Uncharacteristic of a rabbi, Jesus took off His outer robe and proceeded to perform the menial task of foot washing. Usually reserved for servants of the home, His act was an act of extreme devotion. Never did anyone with "higher" status wash the feet of their subordinates. Truly, by this unusual action, Jesus assumed the status of a slave.

Can you imagine how the disciples felt? They were becoming increasingly aware that this teacher they hung around with was no ordinary rabbi. He was the Messiah, the actual Son of God. The Savior of the world. He was greater than the emperor, than Caesar himself, greater than any Jewish priest. This was God incarnate. You and I can't even imagine the president of our country touching our feet, and our feet are relatively clean. The Messiah touched the dirtiest, filthiest part of the disciples' bodies. Their calloused, scaly feet touched everything dirty outside. Now Jesus was going to wash those feet.

Notice there are different reactions to Jesus' display of love. Characteristically, outspoken Peter couldn't bear the thought of the Savior of the world doing such a menial task for him.

We tend to judge Peter for his impetuous nature, but some of us respond to God's love in the same way. "God, I don't deserve Your kindness, forgiveness, and mercy. I can't let You love me in parts where what I've done is disgusting. I am unworthy of Your love."

When Peter finally realized Jesus was serious and that he needed to have his feet washed in order to be cleansed, Peter thought he would go for the whole package deal. "Then wash everything, Lord."

Jesus assured Peter that he only needed his feet cleaned. This symbolized the cleansing work of the cross, complete in and of itself to cleanse our souls from sin.

Then there's the reaction of Judas, whose feet were also washed. Just like the other twelve, this chosen disciple had every opportunity to grow and give his life to the Lord. Jesus loved him to the end and didn't exclude him from the chance to be cleansed from his sin. Jesus gave him the opportunity to turn from his wicked ways. Yet, this man would not ignore the prompting of the devil. The devil tempts all of us to walk away, to seek self, and to look out for number one. Judas, unlike the other disciples, chose to let those lies sink into his heart and mind. His sinful act of stealing from the treasury opened the door for the devil to taunt him, lie to him, and entice him. When Jesus predicted that Judas would betray Him and dismissed Judas from the room, the Bible says that Satan entered Judas.

There are only three times we read in John's gospel that Jesus is deeply troubled. The Greek word *tarasso* means vexed in spirit.[37] In John 11:33, at the tomb of Lazarus, Jesus was troubled at death. In John 12:27, Jesus was troubled at the prospect of the cross. In John 13:21, Jesus was deeply troubled at the thought that someone would betray Him. Why was the Master so troubled? Because one of His own chose a path apart from Him. Because this soul was going to the hands of the enemy. His sinful choices secured his fate.

Jesus' purpose was to save every soul, including Judas. But Judas was created with the gift of choice, like all of us.

You want to know what distresses Jesus, what distresses God? Losing a soul. Every life matters deeply to our Creator. No matter what you've done, no matter what you're going to do. Every soul is worth His coming to earth and His agonizing death on the cross. Every soul.

Judas could have reacted to Jesus' act of love with humble gratitude. Instead, filled with selfish ambition, his heart remained hard. Maybe thoughts of the Jewish leaders rewarding him and giving him a place of honor filled his mind. Whatever, Judas chose to betray his friend, setting the stage for Jesus' capture—a dreadful choice leading to the eternal damnation of his own soul.

Two totally different reactions to Jesus' love. *Jesus, I'm not good enough for you, so I won't let You love me.* And *Jesus, You're not good enough for me, so I won't love You.* To which do you relate?

Receiving Unconditional Love

What about the other disciples who received Jesus' act of love? They let themselves be washed. No questions asked. They received the love Jesus was giving them. Therein lies an important principle. God's love is something we must receive. It's there for the taking, but if we don't receive it, if we don't believe His Word and accept His sacrifices, His love won't penetrate our hearts and change our lives.

Too many Christians walk around handicapped, disabled by thoughts that they are alone and unloved. Life dealt them many hard blows. The reality is that no matter who neglected you, abused you, tortured you, hated you, betrayed you, and abandoned you, you are loved. You are wanted. You belong. You are loved by the One who made you, who believes in you, and who has a purpose for your life.

Fully receiving God's love is to become like a cool glass brimming over with refreshing cold water. There's something about the love of God; it can't help but spill over and be poured out onto others.

By contrast, with every other kind of love we have a tendency to become selfish, protective, and jealous. We don't want others to experience the intimacy we might have with our spouse, for example, or even with our child. But God's love is different. The love of God was never meant to fill us so we just sit fat and full of His goodness.

His agape was entrusted to us so that we would pour it out. In fact, Jesus gave His disciples a new command, a new purpose and call. The disciples were to love others with the love they just received. They were to first love the other followers of Christ so all people would know they were His followers.

The command to love isn't a suggestion; Jesus used the strongest possible word to indicate that He was not playing. He called His followers to the same radical love He had not only shown them in the act of foot washing, but which He showed them through His years with them, and which He was about to show them at the cross.

An Out-of-This-World Love

What does *agape*, unconditional love look like? It's a love that puts others' needs before self, like the university president I mentioned earlier. You put your ambitions, preferences, and dreams aside so that someone else can have preferential treatment. This love is not based on tit for tat. It is based on sacrifice, surrender, laying down of pride, and laying down of self. It's a love that embodies the principle Paul describes in Galatians, "I have been crucified with Christ and I no longer live, but Christ lives in me" (Gal. 2:20).

And the crazy thing is that God expects us to show this kind of love, not just to people who deserve it, our family and friends, but even to strangers and to our enemies. "Love your enemies," Jesus challenged, "and pray for those who persecute you" (Matt. 5:44 BSB). This kind of love, as Paul taught in 1 Corinthians 13, is patient, kind, not jealous, not demanding of its own way, not conceited or proud. It always rejoices in truth, always hopes, and always perseveres.

This is not an easy love we can offer in our own strength. This love is challenged when we encounter those who are different, betray us, or get on our nerves. Luke 6:32-36 emphasizes this.

> If you love those who love you, what credit is that to you? Even sinners love those who love them. And if you do good to those who are good to you, what credit is that to you? Even sinners do that. And if you lend to those from whom you expect repayment,

> what credit is that to you? Even sinners lend to sinners, expecting to be repaid in full. But love your enemies, do good to them, and lend to them without expecting to get anything back. Then your reward will be great, and you will be children of the Most High, because he is kind to the ungrateful and wicked. Be merciful, just as your Father is merciful.

The only way to live out this uncommon love is through Jesus. We need the Holy Spirit. He must fill us and fuel us with this love.

How to Agape: Know Who You Are

Jesus, knowing who He was and where He was going, washed His disciples' feet. He was supremely aware that His time on earth was coming to an end. He knew He was the King of the Universe, who stepped away from heaven to bring God's love to earth, so the world's definition of honor and prestige didn't bother him. He was unscathed by people's accusations and accolades.

How did He live that way? He was solely concerned with the heart of God.

What a way to live! Imagine what it would be like to truly not care what people thought and go solely about the Father's business. How freeing to every aspect of life.

To love unconditionally, we must remember who we are and be confident in our identity as children of God.

It can be humiliating not to fight back when others offend us—like we're not looking out for ourselves. But when we trust God, we can respond to others with His love because we are confident in Him. It's not about whether we think a person deserves love or not. We can die to self because we are secure in our identity in Christ.

Jesus, knowing His purpose, was also aware His time was short. Similarly, we must love when we have the opportunity today.

Have you ever felt nudged to say something kind to someone, but you didn't do so? I can recall several missed opportunities because of my own busyness, agenda, and self-focus. God has also given me the joy of loving selflessly and seizing the moment. I remember feeling a tug to go visit my mom in New Jersey, especially to go see one of her best friends who was like an aunt to me. Alice Aunty had been diagnosed with pancreatic cancer, which was progressing rapidly. Covid still raged, and I had many obligations at home and work in Houston. But I could not ignore the nudge I felt to go see them. God is so good, and I am so grateful that I had one more visit with my sweet aunt. I got to love on her and laugh with her and let her know what a difference she made to my life. She passed away just a short while afterward. Sometimes those moments never come again. We must love while it is still day. Agape love calls us to put feelings, inconveniences, bad moods, and distractions aside and let God use us to bring His love to others.

How to Agape: Love When It's Hard

Have you experienced giving a gift to someone who did not seem to appreciate it? When my children were young, they would spend what seemed like hours making a birthday card for a friend. I couldn't help but feel sad for them if their friend paid little attention to their labor of love. However, in the shuffle of gift opening and tossing wrapping paper, with cake and ice cream on the horizon, no hard feelings were kept. They would carry on their friendship with no love lost.

Children are forgiving and so willing to love. I have heard countless stories of the daughter waiting for her father to pick her up every time he promised, and even though most of the time he never showed up, she would wait with hopeful expectation. As she got older, that wishful thinking would produce a calloused heart, skeptical of love, untrusting of promises.

Jesus exemplified that in agape love we must love despite the reactions, criticisms, objections, and the responses of people. Love anyway. Despite the fact that Judas would not reciprocate, and that Peter would have momentary lapses of love, and that all of the disciples would fall short in their love at different times, Jesus loved anyway. "While we were yet sinners, Christ died for us" (Rom. 5:8 KJB).

Have you ever tried loving someone who was difficult to love? They don't know the sacrifice it takes for you to be there and help them. This is the kind of love many mothers show their children, as my mom showed me. They give and give, knowing the child will probably never understand until much later. But they do it anyway.

Christ's love was not motivated by the disciples' responses—it was motivated by the Father's "well done." When we love others, we do it for the Lord, not for ourselves or the person receiving the love.

In John 13:11, Jesus illustrates the principle that we must love even those who seem unworthy of love, who aren't kind to us, who will hurt us, and who even act like an enemy toward us. Why? Because despite their actions and choices, they are still people of value.

Jesus demonstrated this type of love to Judas. He knew who was going to hand Him over to His enemies. He knew the intent of Judas' heart but loved him anyway. We must love even those unworthy of love because Jesus values every life. He gives every soul a chance. Despite what one has done or will do, He sees each life as valuable.

We must pay attention and look deeply. Jesus knew Judas would betray Him, but He loved him anyway and showed him the same grace and mercy that He showed others. Every single person around you, at the grocery store, at your school, even online—is worth loving . . . because God says so.

The Results of Reckless Love

Jesus closed out His instruction by emphasizing how powerful love is, how it sends a message loud and clear to the onlooking world. In John 13:35, He explained that the disciples' love for one another would prove to the world that they were His disciples. In the same way, our love for each other is proof to the unsaved world that we are true followers of Christ. "By this all men will know that you are my disciples, if you have love for one another." Love is a statement.

Unconditional love between believers brings blessings as well. The principle of Proverbs 11:25 is true every time: "Those who refresh others will themselves be refreshed" (NLT).

In fact, Jesus exemplified that true joy comes from loving others deeply and unconditionally. Loving one another, giving ourselves away as the Lord leads, contributes to an abundant mental life. Even research has found that nursing home residents who care for plants and animals fare better than those who are not responsible for anything or anyone else. Science has popularized the idea that altruistic love has incredible impact on one's emotional well-being and relationships.[38]

But the Lord asks us to do it, not for what we will get in return.

The love of God doesn't make sense, and the way He calls us to love others might seem a little crazy. The Father's love is reckless, selfless, and unconditional. And He calls us to love that way. Love takes risks, love values, love dies to self, love puts the other first, and love trusts God.

As you embrace the reckless love of God, be challenged to be reckless with your love for others. Chase others down. Fight for them and pray until they're found. Tell them about the God who loves them. Speak truth and love them with your words no matter what they say.

Love comes with a cost and requires you to let go and be vulnerable. It would be easier to not love. C. S. Lewis, in *The Four Loves*, captures this: "To love is to be vulnerable. Love anything, and your heart will certainly be wrung and possibly broken. If you want to make sure of keeping it intact, you must give your heart to no one, not even to an animal. Wrap it carefully round with hobbies and little luxuries. Avoid all entanglements. Lock it up safe in the casket or coffin of your selfishness. But in that casket—safe, dark, motionless, airless—it will change. It will not be broken. Instead, it will become unbreakable, impenetrable, irredeemable."[39]

Love is costly and dirty, but it is worth it. A life spent in love is a life well spent.

Recap and Engage

Truths to Calm Mental Storms: Jesus' unconditional love for me allows me to love others His way, but I must receive His love daily and walk in it.

Lies to Refute: I am not good enough for Jesus' love. Jesus' love is not good enough for me.

Take It To Heart: We are not measured by our *intentions* to love but by our actual actions. It's really not just the thought that counts. Is there anyone you struggle to love? I dare you to love. You heard me. I double dog dare you. It's a love dare. For one week, I challenge you to love a person in your life you have struggled to agape love. Ask God who this person should be. Pray for them. Forgive. Pray for them like they're your best friend or your family. Get a little crazy and wash their feet.

Prayer: *Father, thank You for the perfect example of Jesus' unconditional love. Forgive me for falling short of that kind of love. Help me to follow You in love and fill me with Your Spirit that I may love selflessly and recklessly. Thank You for challenging me and for giving me the help I need to love others. In Jesus' name, amen.*

Choose to Trust God When Anxious

Read: John 14

Mom didn't even know what a bucket list was, but we encouraged her to write one. She had lived her whole life for others, raising her children sacrificially and always giving to those in need. Since Mom was approaching seventy years of age, my sister Julie asked if there was anything she wanted to still experience. Without hesitation, Mom exclaimed, "The Grand Canyon." So into the bucket it went, and it became our new family mission to get her there.

My sister, brother, and I made plans for our families to converge at the Grand Canyon for a week-long vacation the following summer. George, the kids, and I would drive from Texas, while the rest flew from the Northeast. We had stopped in Albuquerque for a few hours when I noticed five missed calls from our neighbor who was feeding our dog back at home. We had nicknamed Paws, our sweet black mouth cur, "Houdini," and I figured my neighbor was calling me about yet another incident of Paws escaping. Notorious on our block, he doesn't usually go far and comes back right away, but it was an ongoing (and amusing) battle between George and Paws to keep him contained in our fenced-in property with everything from cinder blocks to cacti.

To our surprise, this wasn't about the escape artist. "There's water everywhere," my neighbor said frantically when we finally connected. The water heater in the upstairs attic had burst, causing water to flood through the ceiling of the master bathroom and spill through the house. "It's bad. Everything is drenched."

We were crushed. Just a year before, we had saved up to rip out the old carpet in our home and replace it with a beautiful wood laminate. The floor was already belting and buckling. After turning off the water, our neighbors, John and Diane, quickly began the process of moving furniture to try to salvage what they could. As soon as we found out, we called the insurance to start a claim, and we began to pray.

"Lord, You know what's best. Show us if we should continue on to Arizona. Thank You for Your timely provision through our neighbors and friends." As soon as we prayed, we felt God's peace about moving forward and spending the next week with our family. Our insurance company assured us they would handle the process of drying things out and starting the claim on our home, reminding us that we wouldn't be able to stay in our home anyway. We decided to let God's peace fill our hearts and not let this trouble dampen the time we were going to spend with the family we loved and hardly saw.

Peace was only possible because God provided for us through other people. Our amazing neighbors served as gatekeepers and would let in whoever needed to come in. We reached out to our pastors Joel and Sabrina Garza, who had just gone through a flood in their own home. They gave us wisdom about how to proceed, offering to do an inventory of our soaked mess while we weren't there. I remember Sabrina telling me with such confidence, "You will see how God will work this out for good."

She was so right. God gave us favor with our insurance company, who acted quickly and were extremely generous. Although we had to live out of a hotel for a while, we thanked God that it happened during the summer while the kids were out of school. By the time it was all said and done, God gave us a repainted home with new floors and furniture. It was all so humbling how God gave people, provision, and peace during a time of trouble.

The Trouble with Trouble

When Judas the traitor had gone, Jesus addressed the remaining disciples' fears, in an effort to prepare them for a huge shift—God the Son would leave them, but God the Holy Spirit would come and fill them.

This was a hard pill to swallow. They had given up everything to follow Him, and now Jesus was going to leave them? He was preparing an eternal home for them in the future? By believing in Him, they would be able to do greater things than they had seen Jesus do? It was a lot to take in.

On top of that, Jesus was going to send someone they didn't know. "The Helper (Comforter, Advocate, Intercessor—Counselor, Strengthener, Standby), the Holy Spirit, whom the Father will send in My name [in My place, to represent Me and act on My behalf], He will teach you all things. And He will help you remember everything that I have told you" (John 14:26 AMP).

Perceiving their distress, Jesus taught them an important principle for storm whispering, for hushing the waves of fear and anxiety that plague our minds today. A statement that echoes throughout John 14 is "Let not your hearts be troubled." How easy it is to let trouble overwhelm us and let it steal our peace.

When's the last time trouble took peace from you? Trouble can come through anything that triggers stress—a bad medical report, a job difficulty, a strained relationship, or underperforming in school. Trouble can come through financial struggles, moving, a child's bad attitude, regaining the twenty pounds you just lost, or the death of a loved one. Every day we are pummeled with things that try to steal our peace.

As used in John 14:1, trouble is defined as something that causes "inward commotion, takes away calmness of mind, disquiets, makes restless and stirs up, renders one anxious or distressed, perplexes the mind by suggesting doubts, or strikes one's spirit with fear and dread."[40] Think about each of these definitions. Basically, what Jesus is saying to His beloved is: "I have the answer to heal your mind, as well as your body and spirit. You want your oppression to be taken care of on earth; I have a bigger plan for peace on earth. And, I am going to give you peace as well, eternal peace."

In John 16:33, Jesus made a promise none of us necessarily delight in: "In this world you will have trouble." But then He assures us, "Take heart! I have overcome the world." He prefaced this statement with the fact that although He would leave His disciples, He would leave with them His peace. His peace would supersede every trouble. Yet, trouble would be real.

Our Lord understands what it feels like to be troubled—distressed to the point of dread. Ponder that. Even though Jesus knew the outcome, His soul was troubled because He was human. However, He didn't linger there, and in this passage, Jesus offered a wholistic approach to healing the anxiety of the mind. He encouraged the disciples to believe in Him, to think eternally, and to receive the Holy Spirit.

Belief—the Antidote for Anxiety

When we're anxious, we're choosing to believe what we can see, but Jesus says, "Believe what you can't see." When we're stressed out, we've let the "I" in anxiety become our focus. I can't do this, I won't be able to finish that, I don't have what it takes, I'm a failure. When we're stressed out, we play out every negative thing that could possibly happen. Our minds become incredibly imaginative as we play the "What If?" game. What if that happens and someone gets hurt? What if they get hurt and they die? And on and on. Jesus says that in order to overcome trouble, we must look not to what we can see or the things we imagine or fear most, but to the invisible One to handle things.

"You believe in the Father; believe also in Me." We cannot overcome our mental storms, our feelings of distress, or our emotional struggles without belief in Jesus. Many might wish there was another way. Give me a pill to fix it; give me ten statements to repeat; give me nineteen exercises to do every day to make pain go away.

Yet Jesus told His devoted followers that nothing was going to help their troubled souls but believing in who He said He was. They already worshiped the Father; now He was challenging them to open their minds to understand that there was no other way to the One True God except through Him. "I am the Way, the Truth, and the Life" is the central tenet to the Gospel of John, to remind us that there is no other way to abundant life except through Jesus and through the truth He taught and encouraged us to live by.

A recurring motif in the Gospel of John, the Greek word for believe is *pisteuo.* It means to be persuaded of something, or to place confidence and conviction in God's rescuing ability.[41] Jesus told them to put their confidence in the fact that God had it all under control. He's so sovereign that He already had a future place for His followers, and Jesus was the way to get there. In fact, Jesus explained that there is no other way to the Father and all that God offers except through Him.

Belief. What if, in the middle of your greatest anxiety, you simply believed God? You believed that He was going to take care of everything and work it all out? You trusted Him to work things out beyond your ability to comprehend? What if you believed that He had a plan for your future, despite what you can see or understand in the present?

Jesus simply stated we could believe Him to be who He says He is in the middle of our trouble. He is God, He is good, He is loving, He is present, He is our healer. And like the old chorus goes, "Because He lives, I can face tomorrow."[42] I can have hope amid tragedy and triumph.

Have you ever had a bout of insomnia? Usually it's a sign of anxiety. No, it's not your pillow or your spouse or roommate snoring. You're having trouble sleeping because you're worried and stressed, and you're carrying that pain with you as you hit the sack. Recently, I woke up with my jaw hurting, and I realized I was clenching my teeth again, another anxious behavior. It served as a signal to me that I hadn't been truly giving my concerns and responsibilities to the Lord. Somewhere deep down, I didn't believe He could handle it. Somewhere, subconsciously, I thought I needed to pick it back up and strive to figure it out on my own.

Instead of trying to resolve our own issues, we get rest when we say, "Lord, I trust You to take care of what I can't and what I don't see. I believe You."

John 14 records Jesus teaching His disciples about their future home. In essence, He tells them to fix their gaze on eternity. No matter what is confusing about life on earth or what seems controversial or hard, we have an eternal life that awaits us. No matter how bad it gets right now, there is heaven to look forward to, and we have a Savior who is coming back.

MARANATHA

I was a teenager during the 90s in New Jersey, and during that time, Christian radio stations featured Maranatha Music, an upbeat, folk-rock style of hymns and worship songs.

The word maranatha intrigued me. Used only once in the KJV, in 1 Corinthians 16:22, it is a word of Aramaic origin meaning "Our Lord is coming, and He will judge those who treat him with contempt" (author's paraphrase).[43] The verse states, "If any man love not the Lord Jesus Christ, let him be Anathema Maranatha." Paul warned of the curse and judgment.[44]

However, it was also an expression of encouragement to the believer. The Romans ruled when Paul wrote his letters to the Corinthians and the other early churches; this was a dangerous time for believers. People were expected to declare that Caesar was lord, and if they did not, they would be persecuted, tortured, and killed. Christians would greet and comfort each other with the word maranatha, much like the Jews embraced each other with the word shalom.

The word maranatha served as a constant reminder that the Lord is coming. Imagine how powerful that one word would have been to encourage the persecuted Christians. In His teaching in John, Jesus instructed them to maranatha—keep your gaze ahead. Be careful not to focus on material or temporal things because Jesus is coming. Strive to keep your eyes on what pleases the Lord because Jesus is coming. It was a word of hope, a directive to look up.

Let's apply this principle to our anxiety or stress. Jesus says, "Maranatha!" If you're overwhelmed by a circumstance and the unknown, "Maranatha!" If you are stressed or burdened over the troubles you face today, "Maranatha!" Jesus told His disciples to shift their attention to the fact that Jesus was sovereign, more powerful, and greater than their biggest fears.

Lest you think I'm trying to encourage you to live in denial or dismiss any present concerns, remember that Jesus came to give us perspective. Maranatha is a word of perspective. Whatever we might be facing is bad, but think about it in light of eternity. He will take care of us. Jesus knows we will have trouble on earth, but He has overcome and He sent us His Comforter to give us peace.

An Uneven Trade

Knowing how crushing His departure would be to the apostles, Jesus promised that the Holy Spirit, the Comforter or Advocate, would come in His place. Through the presence of the Holy Spirit, the disciples would not need to fear or worry. God Himself would come down and dwell within their hearts to fight every storm. The Holy Spirit would serve as His peace for their problems. Truth in their trouble. Support in their stress.

Maybe you're wondering, how? How do we walk in the peace of the Holy Spirit when trouble comes?

I love the picture of the Israelites in the First Passover. In faith, the Israeli people had applied blood to their doorposts. When the Lord passed by, they were spared the deaths of their firstborns. The trouble did not sweep over them. They believed and God used their act of faith and obedience to save them. In exchange, He gave them joy and peace. Peace was theirs because they acted in faith. They didn't sit there passively but began to do something about what they believed.

What does that look like for you and me? Actively apply your faith to your storm. Declare God is bigger. Bring others to agree with you in prayer. Know that the Holy Spirit is there to help you. Receive His help through the Word of God, enlightening your mind with Truth and through worship. Worshiping God is one of your greatest weapons in life's battles and storms. Declare He is with you!

You may know the Scripture, "Do not be anxious about anything, but in every situation, by prayer and petition, present your requests to God. And the peace of God, which transcends all understanding, will guard your hearts and your minds in Christ Jesus" (Phil. 4:6-7). Don't give into your feelings, which tend to overwhelm. Instead, admit the following: "Lord, I don't have the strength in myself to handle this problem. I need You to take over. You have every ability to fight my battles and handle this storm. I declare my confidence in You. In my weakness, You are strong!"

Jesus taught His disciples that the way they could show their love for Him was to keep His commands. This included their response to stress. It includes our response to stress. We must remember that worry is not of God; it's masterminded by the enemy to make something bigger than it seems. Isn't that what the devil did when he fell from heaven? As an angel of God, created by God to worship Him, Satan fell like lightning (Luke 10:18) because he thought in his heart that he could be bigger and better than God.

Think about what we stress over. We make it bigger and more important than God. Bigger and better than God? Yikes! My problems are not bigger than God. Camping out in worry and anxiety is not of God, and to love Jesus is to receive His Holy Spirit. Let Him be your advocate the next time the enemy tempts you to camp out in fear of what you can't see all the way.

Waves of Worry Swept Over Me

I don't think I was ever as tempted to be anxious as when I was pregnant. After losing Selah, our first baby, twelve weeks into pregnancy, being pregnant afterwards four more times was a complicated bundle of wonder, beauty, joy and stress because nothing was guaranteed. Is it ever? I had believed God with my first baby and He allowed the baby to die for reasons I could not understand.

My second time around, I started gaining weight at a rapid pace at around thirty-two weeks. Doctors ran tests and found that our daughter had a stomach obstruction that caused an excessive amount of amniotic fluid. On top of that, she had intrauterine growth restriction (meaning that she was incredibly small due to poor nourishment in utero), and I had pre-eclampsia.

Jadyn would need surgery right after birth. We would need to give birth at a hospital three hours from our home because no pediatric surgeons practiced in our city. Five weeks before my due date, we visited the doctor in St. Louis where I would give birth. My blood pressure was so high they admitted me.

Stress and anxiety filled my mind. "Lord, is the baby going to be okay? Lord, You promised!"

I had recently changed employment, and my insurance was just switching over to my new job. We were unsure if it would cover the hospital stay and impending surgery. "Father, can You miraculously heal this baby? How are we going to afford this?"

George and I were two years into marriage, barely thirty years old. "Lord, what about our home—who will take care of it while I am here?" My mom was supposed to come for the delivery; George's mom, too. What about the natural birth I had prayed for? Nothing was going as planned. My mind swirled with dismay.

As I stated in the chapter on choosing to worship God, I had a choice to make. While George traveled the three hours back home to get some things for me, I looked at all the things that were not going according to plan. Would I trust God? Would I trust in what He was doing and allowing? Would I let my mind stay troubled or would I embrace God's peace?

Not long after, I was admitted. Although I had initially shown no signs of being in labor, I started to have genuine labor contractions. While George was gone, the doctors confirmed that I was going into labor, five weeks early. In that moment, God in His mercy opened my eyes. Had I not been admitted on that day, who knows what would have happened to me or the baby. God knew she would be born the next day. Just as Jesus knew the future for His disciples, God knew the future for me.

My faith grew as I started to open my eyes to the ways He was providing in the middle of such a stressful situation. We were sent to a hospital where my cousin Sajeena had become chief resident of the Ob-Gyn unit; needless to say, we immediately received special treatment. Not only that, it turned out that the most renowned surgeon in the world for the complication Jadyn had—duodenal atresia—worked at that hospital. If she was to have the surgery, she would be in the best human hands possible. By His grace, I had a super supportive faculty team at Evangel who was ready and eager to take the load of classes I was responsible to teach. Despite the fact that I had to be on intense medication during delivery, God answered my prayer and allowed me to go through the pain of childbirth without any numbing or epidural, with George by my side. To top it all off, both moms found flights on the same day and were able to witness their first granddaughter being born. God worked it out! He did it!

I could have been overwhelmed with stress in the days to follow as our four-pound miracle underwent surgery and spent weeks in the NICU, but God gave us supernatural peace. He even bonded our moms, who banded in prayer for our daughter's life. It's odd to say that I have fond memories of St. Louis Children's Hospital, even all the NICU sounds, but I do because it was a time when God stretched my faith and held my family close in the storm.

A couple years later, when Liana was born, she sustained a high fever of unknown origin and had to be hospitalized at two weeks old for a week. We were a week away from my sister's wedding in California where I was to be her maid of honor. George was to officiate the service and our babies were to be flower girls. Fear of losing this baby taunted me, but God sustained me with His peace. I decided to spend the hours in the hospital sewing her little flower girl dress and trusting God was going to use this for good. Believe me, I struggled to keep peace, but He helped me. And God gets the glory; He got us out of the hospital and onto a flight just in the nick of time for George to proclaim the couple husband and wife. Not every storm ends with a happy ending, but every storm can end with His peace.

What I learned and have continued to experience is that through every troubling season, God wants to stretch our faith, remind us about the future, and strengthen us with His Spirit.

Don't Worry; Be Happy

What's so scary about a stressful situation is the unknown. We don't know how it's all going to work out; we don't know if there will be the answered prayers and perfect timing. We think the fairytale is our version of the happy ending, but I'm reminded of a statement Gary

Thomas made about marriage—"What if God intended marriage for our holiness, not for our happiness? What if life isn't just about being happy, but being holy?"[45]

Sometimes in the middle of stress, we feel gypped. Aren't most of us pursuing happiness? Doesn't God want us to be happy? Maybe not.

God doesn't give to us as the world gives. The world's definition is anything goes; there is no one or best way. Jesus' teaching is absolutely contrary. He is the only way. The point of this life is not to be happy but to look like Jesus, to reflect Him and glorify Him; that's the only way we will ever experience true joy.

My brother Tobin went through a Bob Marley phase in high school. It was Bob Marley all day, and one song I didn't mind was his version of "Don't worry. Be happy." Jesus' prescription for happiness—freedom from the weight of the world's trouble—comes solely as a result of our relationship with the Father, through Jesus, that allows the Holy Spirit to dwell in our hearts.

If this is true that Jesus is the answer, why do so many Christians struggle with anxiety? Is it lack of faith? What are we doing wrong?

I think the reality is that we can be so easily swayed. We are all prone to wander, and sometimes the billows of this life can be so overwhelming that we lose sight of the greatness of God in our storms. Even Peter, the only one to walk on water besides Jesus, sank when his view of the waves became bigger than the God he followed.

As a leader in a Christian ministry, I have been tempted to be stressed out by the constant pressures of financial demands and people's severe problems. However, when I sit before God and peel back the layers of my desire to perform and my tendency to overdo, I realize I just need to relax and let God handle it. I need to believe He is who He is, receive His comfort, and keep my eyes on what is eternal. I try to fix what I can—any unhealthy perspectives—and correct any lies in my own mind that persist, then trust Him to do the rest. Circumstances might not seem to change right away, but *everything in me* changes because I have shifted from burdened to belief.

Everything's Gonna Be Alright in the End

The disciples so took this to heart, that later, Peter, in his epistle, encouraged believers to not be troubled. He said in 1 Peter 3:12-15, "For the eyes of the Lord are over the righteous, and his ears are open unto their prayers . . . be not afraid of their terror, neither be troubled; but sanctify the Lord in your hearts" (KJV). In plain English, Peter said, "Don't stress!" If you're doing the right thing, don't sweat what's happening around you; just stay humble before God. Stay holy, and He will take care of you.

"Let us also lay aside every weight, and sin which clings so closely, and let us run with endurance the race that is set before us, looking to Jesus, the founder and perfecter of our faith" (ESV). Just as Jesus showed His disciples in John 14 that humility was the key to staying anxiety-free, we're reminded in Hebrews 12:1-2 that we can resist the enemy by trusting God to take care of us.

In my personal time of trouble with the water heater flood, we were amazed how God used the challenges to set things up. Just a year after the flood, God would call us to move to Houston. Because of the flood, we got new paint, new floors, and new fixtures throughout the entire house; it was practically brand new and in ideal condition to sell quickly. God had worked it all out or our good.

Not only that, God showed His lovingkindness as well. A few months before our Grand Canyon trip, I was rearranging furniture and placed a box with our family and baby albums underneath our bed. They stayed there for quite a while. In fact, I noticed the box and moved it just before we left for the trip. Had the Lord not shown me, all our family albums would have been ruined in the flood. God spared them and showed His care for my heart as a mom.

Our visit to the Grand Canyon gave us a powerful metaphor. Through a guided tour with a group called Answers in Genesis, we learned scientific evidence has been discovered that indicates the breathtaking canyon is a result of the cataclysmic flood of Noah's day.

Just as the canyon resulted from a monumental storm, God made something beautiful from the flood in our home. The enemy tempted us to focus on the immediate difficulty and problems. But we trusted God. His peace is available during any storm when we believe His Word, keep an eternal focus, and let the Spirit of God reign within. I pray that you will embrace His peace today.

Recap and Engage

Truths to Calm Mental Storms: Jesus is my answer to peace amid all of life's storms.

Lies to Refute: My troubles are too big for God; I cannot overcome anxiety. There is no hope for me. I can find peace any way I like.

Take It To Heart: What causes you the most anxiety today? Take a few moments to write down your five most typical stressors.

Evaluate patterns in your life. Do you tend to get stressed out during particular times of the day, or particular times of the month? Are there certain circumstances that are consistent? For example, is your stress usually about financial issues, health problems, people and your dealings with them, performance issues, or something else?

Be honest with yourself to determine whether pride might contribute to your anxiety. Ask yourself: "Do I want others to think of me a certain way, and does this make my stress level increase? Am I afraid to disappoint people? Do I expect myself to handle this or figure this out?"

Confess to God any pride or unbelief and ask Him to help you by His Spirit to replace that worry with belief. Declare His greatness in the unknowns of your situation.

Prayer: *Lord, thank You for the perfect peace You came to earth to give me through the presence of the Holy Spirit. I depend on Your help for overcoming the troubles in my life today and thank You that the results are up to You. I face no storm alone. I trust You! In Jesus' name, amen.*

Choose to Abide

Read: John 15

I have a word for you. The buck does NOT stop with you. It's not all on you.

It's okay if you don't have this. You won't make it or break it. You don't need to be perfect. Your wrinkles can show. Your kids don't need to be like their kids. You don't need to be thin or muscular. You don't always need to have the right thing to say. Your church doesn't need to be as big as their church. Your house doesn't need to be perfectly put together. You are not responsible for others' emotions and choices. You don't need to make it all happen!

Do you ever get tired of all the pressure the world puts on you and you put on yourself? I do. I have expected high performance of myself, and I've beaten myself up when I didn't get it right. The proverbial inner critic never seems to tire. We let the world dictate our self-expectations, and we come unglued when we don't measure up.

Jesus ministered to His chosen in John 15 to help them break free from the pressuring, enslaving mindsets of the world. To prevent them from plastering a worldly philosophy onto their faith in Christ, Jesus cleared a few things up. Judaism, steeped in rule-following and excessive tradition, had become overwhelmingly burdensome for people to follow. Left and right, they were breaking rules and falling short. The people rebelled. They couldn't keep *all* of the Law, so they decided to let it all go. The Pharisees prided themselves in their rule-following and outward perfection, but their hearts did not reflect the true love of God the Father. So God sent His Son to seek and to save the lost and free them from their self-expectations.

God Gardening 101

I am certainly not a gardening pro, but I love playing in the dirt—preferably without gloves. Unless I'm dealing with sharp thorns or prickly weeds, I like to feel the dirt on my hands and under my nails. Recently, we planted some zinnias from seed. They grew to be stunning, waving hello in the wind with their spectacular hues. George's pride was his kumquat tree which he faithfully tended in San Antonio; we gave out those citrus gems like candy. There's nothing like eating your homegrown herbs and vegetables.

I feel like the Lord talks to me while I'm tending to the plants. Be consistent with pulling out those weeds of sin and pride, Dolly, before they take deep root. Remove what's dead to make room for new life. Cut back on areas of low growth to make room for more Kingdom depth and fullness. So many spiritual lessons from playing in the dirt.

The Jews were agriculturalists and very familiar with plant imagery, which explains why Jesus—always real and relevant—used it often. John 15 opens with a reference to viticulture, a fun word that defines the science of vine dressing. Using this imagery, Jesus taught the disciples about true discipleship—that following Him was a way of thinking, a way of living, and a supernatural experience out of this world, and often contrary to it.

Jesus' opening statement in John 15:1 was more than a nice lesson on planting. He called Himself the true Vine, and God the Father, master gardener. Vines and vineyards were sacred images in Judaism. Israel was pictured as a vine, as we read in Psalm 80:7-9: "Restore us, God Almighty; make your face shine on us, that we may be saved. You transplanted a vine from Egypt; you drove out the nations and planted it. You cleared the ground for it, and it took root and filled the land." In the Old Testament, the nation was chastened for not bearing fruit. Hosea 10:1-2 described Israel as "a spreading vine; he brought forth fruit for himself. As his fruit increased, he built more altars; as his land prospered, he adorned his sacred stones. Their heart is deceitful, and now they must bear their guilt. The Lord will demolish their altars and destroy their sacred stones." Later in Hosea 14:4 and 7, God promises to "heal their waywardness and love them freely, for my anger has turned from them . . . People will dwell again in his shade; they will flourish like the grain, they will blossom like the vine—Israel's fame will be like the wine of Lebanon."

This imagery of Jesus being the Vine would have spoken to those who knew Scripture. Jesus saying, "I am the Vine" was an image of hope, but also of judgment. Israel had been chosen by God to be the vine, but they did not follow after God and did not bear fruit. So God the Father sent His Son to fulfill what they could not. How merciful that God had a plan for healing waywardness. In this final "I AM" declaration in the Gospel of John, Jesus was essentially saying that God's vineyard has one vine and people are branches growing from one stock. Israel was no longer guaranteed to be attached to Him. Every branch that didn't bear fruit would be cut off.

Let's make sure we have all our key players correct. God the Father is the master gardener. Jesus the Son is the *true* Vine—unlike every other vine that tried to be the true vine. He is the source of life by which everything else lives and breathes and has its being (Acts 17:28). No fruit is possible without Christ. There is no other source of life like Jesus; we can seek it in medicine and relationships and food and achievements or money, but nothing else breathes life like Jesus. Finally, we have the branches who shoot off from the vine. These represent the disciples, any of us who choose to follow Christ.

The Abiding Branch Bears Bananas

Let's explore branch life for a moment. At first glance, a branch may seem so unimportant, so just there. But a branch is really an offspring, an offshoot of the vine. You and I have the opportunity to be an offshoot of Christ, an extension of His heart and life on earth, His hands and feet. A branch becomes a conduit of the lifegiving flow of Jesus, perfectly positioned by the Father to do good works and impact the world around it.

What responsibilities does a branch have? To bear fruit. We can't do that on our own, so how do we do it? Simply by remaining or abiding in Him. Our main job is to remain in Him. Abiding equals fruit-bearing. A guaranteed winning formula.

So what does it mean to *meno*—the Greek word for abide? To abide means to tarry, to continue to be present, to be continually held, to endure, to survive, to not change to a different state, and to wait for.[46] The word is used in over one hundred verses in the New Testament in reference to a place where the disciples were to hang out somewhere a little longer. Jesus also used the word when He asked His disciples to stay awake as they were praying before His crucifixion—"Would you stay with me? Would you stay connected with me?"

Just as the Spirit of God descended onto Jesus at His baptism, He also remained in Him (John 1:33). Similarly, Jesus promised that the Spirit of God would remain on His disciples if they received Him (John 14:15-17).

Picture Jesus ministering to His disciples as He taught them. They were taking it in, but John was particularly moved by Jesus' teaching on *abide*. We know this because he used the word over and over in his writings. "Whoever claims to live in him must live [abide] as Jesus did" (1 John 2:6). "Anyone who loves their brother and sister lives [abides] in the light" (1 John 2:10). "The one who keeps God's commands lives [abides] in him, and he in them. And this is how we know that he lives [abides] in us: We know it by the Spirit he gave us" (1 John 3:24).

Remain, remain, remain, he said over and again to the early Christians. Their main role was to trust God and stay connected to Him in love. They didn't have what it took to produce fruit; all they needed to do was to worship and love Him by loving others.

Jesus answered the disciples' innermost questions about what it meant to be a branch.

What will happen if we don't fulfill branch duties of bearing fruit? To not bear fruit means jeopardizing our status in the vineyard—you could be cut off. A branch is to remain in Jesus' love, just as He abides in the Father's love. A dead branch is a useless branch because it cannot be fruitful on its own.

What can I expect will happen to me as a branch? I will be pruned so I can be more fruitful. To prune is to cleanse of filth or impurity and to cut off useless parts.[47]

When Jesus told His few that they would be pruned or cleansed to be positioned for more fruit-bearing, He reminded them that they were already clean because of the Word. The Word of God is enough to cleanse us. God's Word prunes our minds of unnecessary thoughts that distract us or derail us from the divine mission God has for us. God, in His mercy, prunes people out of our lives who distract us from fulfilling His purposes. Sometimes He removes a good activity to make room for something better. Pruning is the subtle version of what Jesus did to the temple in John 2, cleansing it from the things that didn't belong there and making room for what He intended.

Jesus also gives fair warning that as a branch the world will hate us because it hates Jesus. The world hates the message of the gospel. We will be persecuted and misunderstood because the world hates Jesus. However, as a branch connected to the Vine, there are great benefits. The wonder of wonders is that we can ask whatever we wish and it will be given us, to the Father's glory.

Whatever we wish? That's what Jesus said. That if we are connected to Christ, that's one of the perks. We ask according to His will because He is our sustenance. We are not asking for our personal gain or glory. Rather, we are in tune with His will and desires. Therefore what we wish will be what He wishes, and it will be done.

Finally, Jesus addresses why we should bear fruit. Fruit-bearing glorifies God the Father. We make God's name great when our lives bear the fruit of being connected with Jesus through the Holy Spirit.

What is this fruit? Totally contrary to the desires of the sinful nature, these characteristics are listed in Galatians 5:22-23—love, joy, peace, patience, kindness, goodness, faithfulness, gentleness and self-control. If we want any of those traits in our lives, we have to stay connected to the Vine, and that fruit will grow like mangoes or bananas in South India. God fertilizes the soil, provides the opportunities for us to grow, and waters the seed. He's the Gardener, after all. Our only job is to stay connected. And the benefit is that we will have the complete, full, abundant joy that comes from a life flowing out of connection with Him.

What's more is that we are promised a friend in high places; we get to be Jesus' friends if we do what He commands. As fruit-bearing branches, we've been chosen to do this, appointed to bear eternal fruit. Thus, our prayers will be answered.

The Pressure to Perform

How often do we spend time trying to make things happen? I'm a planner. I'm reminded of the ridiculous all-nighter that I pulled to get my daughter's two-year-old Sesame Street-themed birthday party right. Seriously? What if I just let some of those things go and decided to pray instead that my daughter would feel really loved, that the guests would feel welcomed, and that God would be blessed through the gathering? I wonder what would have changed if I hadn't made it about whether I had the perfect decor, or even deeper, whether I was doing a good enough job as a mom? Or the times that I've spent hours trying to "lecture" my kids, when praying for them and just staying connected to the Vine might have been more impactful.

I may or may not have confessed to you yet that I'm a recovering performance-addict. I'm not sure if that's a thing, but there it is, I'm coining the term. Wait, I just googled it and 239,000,000 results about performance addiction popped up in less than a second! So it is a thing. Not technically a professional diagnosis, but a true phenomenon in which we are tempted to find our worth in our achievement, our work, and relationships. Performance addiction has been defined as the belief that you will find love and respect by perfecting your appearance and achieving status.[48] Its close cousin is approval addiction, where others' admiration feeds your sense of worth.

We can love the fanfare and the applause and grow up feeling valuable when people notice us for what we do. But Jesus ministers to the heart and soul and teaches that without Him, it's all meaningless. Without Him, we can do nothing.

We can aim for love and joy and peace and grittiness and goodness in our own strength, and we can try to get others to admire us and award us for having these traits. But without abiding in Christ and allowing Him to do the work, the fruit is unsustainable. We may be able to perform in spurts, but at the end of the day, we will feel fake, the fruit will wither, and our efforts will all come tumbling down.

That's why preachers sometimes fail. I've had the opportunity to counsel many pastors and leaders in ministry over the years. I've seen great desires gone awry because of the lack of abiding. At some point, they knew they needed to spend time with the Lord, but the demands of ministry may have caused them to drift. They were so busy ministering to people that they didn't minister to the Lord.

Dr. Jim Bradford, pastor of Central Assembly in Springfield, Missouri, once said at a National ATC conference, "Ministry is toxic to my personal relationship with Jesus, and I've prayed to survive ministry." He understood that the demands of shepherding the sheep can cause the caretaker to feel weary and falsely draw life from things and people outside the Vine. He was careful to guard his personal devotion to the Lord to prevent this from happening.

Ironically, the rewards of ministry can contribute to a shift as well. Some can still deliver a good sermon without much prayer or a life of obedience because they are gifted communicators. They can still sing those songs and hit those keys and make things sound good even without a habit of personal worship. I'm still functioning, they rationalize subconsciously. Or they justify that a reward for their sacrifices in ministry is some personal pleasure. It doesn't hurt anybody.

Is there an antidote to the possibility of falling in ministry or in the Christian walk? Yes . . . abiding in the Vine.

What if we freed ourselves from the pressure to perform and trusted in Jesus to make anything good happen in our lives? What if we totally left the results up to Him? What would happen if we spent more time abiding in Him and loving others rather than trying to seek self-recognition or achieve personal goals?

Christ in us can accomplish wonders and miracles. He can do even more things than are recorded in the pages of Scripture; He is unlimited, and if we abide in the Vine, we have the source within us to make it happen.

This doesn't mean that we stop trying, like He's going to do it all and we're just marionettes He will move to action. We have been given a choice to exercise our free will to abide in Him. We get to act in obedience and allow our lives to be an overflow of His love to others.

The only way to get there is to get off the performance treadmill and replace performance with a life of prayer and devotion.

The Symbiotic Life

Staying connected with the Vine is essential to life. It's more than symbiosis, where two creatures might thrive off of each other.

Take sea animals for example, where two unlikely creatures link up to create a fearless duo that sustains life. Sea urchins are known to pair with carrier crabs, which have modified back legs to Uber these poisonous creatures on their backs as a defense mechanism. Both sides benefit because the sea urchin gets a ride to new places to feed, while the carrier crab is shielded from its prey. A win-win.

However, an urchin can get off the Lyft when he's ready and move to another host. Sometimes, we view our relationship with God like these animals feed off each other—we attach ourselves to Him for a while when we have a great need in our lives, but we ditch Him when things get better, when we have enjoyable relationships, when the bank account is steady, and when the weather is fair.

This won't work. We must remain attached like a baby's umbilical cord is attached to the placenta. Not to gross you out, but George and I had the privilege of viewing Luke's placenta after he was born. It was actually really profound. The midwife showed us the amazing "tree of life," the veins shaped like a tree, representing the life-giving source to the baby. What a great picture!

To have everlasting life, we must remain as connected to the Lord as a baby in the womb must remain connected to his mother for survival. We can't have an abundant mental life without staying connected to the Vine. We are like parasites that feed off Jesus, but we can't hurt Him; we can only be sustained with His power and truth. He is all in all. We don't have to perform in our own strength.

Remember that our job is not to produce fruit. The word is to bear, which means to bring forth or to carry. God does the producing. He waters, conditions the environment, and prepares the fruit. Fruit-bearing is a natural byproduct of abiding. God will even orchestrate the conditions, the people and places of our lives, so that we can be more fruitful.

Our only job is to cling.

Next time your friend asks you why you're reading your Bible and why you pray, say, "I'm practicing my cling." I am holding tight to Jesus. I glorify God by my clinging. I can love others by clinging. I bear fruit by clinging."

The world may not understand, but when you duck out of the rat race and rest in the fact that your duty as a disciple is to abide, you are most pleasing to God. We get to be called His friends if we do what He commands. True love for others comes from how strongly we cling to Him. I have been chosen, even ordained by God, to bear eternal fruit by getting my cling on.

RECAP AND ENGAGE

Truth to Live By: We don't have to perform to earn God's love. Our job is to stay tethered and attached to our life-giving source, Jesus. God prunes our lives to make room for His best.

Lies to Refute: The buck stops with me. If I don't make it happen, then no one can.

Take It to Heart: Do you have a go-to place to practice abiding? The Lord makes His home in our heart, but it helps when we have a physical place in our home set apart to be the venue for connection and clinging. I loved the Kendrick brothers' movie, *The War Room*, which inspired me to design my space to spend time with Jesus. Having this designated area can strengthen our walk with the Lord. In addition, a journal can allow us to document our prayer requests and His answers to praying *whatsoever we wish.*

Do you relate to living on the performance treadmill? Often this begins in childhood. We are validated by others when we do well in school or sports. We feel more powerful when others notice and inferior when they do not; thus, the need for approval becomes addictive. We strive to go bigger and do better. Treadmills can be dangerous. Let me tell you from personal experience—never pray on a treadmill with your eyes closed; long story, but it's a sure way to scrape up some knees. Treadmills take us nowhere. Confess to God where you have tried to earn approval from others rather than trying to please Him, our Creator.

Prayer: *Lord, thank You for being my Source of Life, for being the one true Vine. Thank You that joy and bearing fruit is the byproduct of seeking You with all I have. In Jesus' name, amen.*

CHOOSE TO CONFESS SIN AND BE FREE

Read: John 16

If you happen to walk by my house on a Saturday evening, don't be freaked out if the lights are out and you hear screaming voices inside.

Nothing crazy is happening. We're just playing one of our children's favorite games, Hide-and-Go-Seek-Tag, in the dark.

It was a weekend classic when the kids were younger, but even as they're older, we'll rerun it, especially when their close friends are visiting. We turn off all house lights but the porch light, and do the standard counting to twenty, while everyone darts around looking for a good hiding spot. Problem is, after a few rounds, there are only so many places you can lay low. And now that they're older, it's harder to hide in the cabinets. But it's still fun because we usually stay hidden for a minute and wait till the Seeker is somewhere else so we can make a mad dash for base, usually a couch in the living room.

When I played Hide-and-Go-Seek as a child, the whole house was fair play, including my mom's basement. That place was love-hate for me. Mom always had treasures in the basement, hidden jewels she forgot existed that I could use for an art project or decor. The only bad thing was that the basement sounds terrified me. The stairs squeaked eerily. The furnace breathed murderous threats. I was sure I could hear bugs crawling. One day during a game, I decided to brave it and find a hiding spot in the basement. I crawled up into one of the built-in shelves and listened intently for the seeker's footsteps. My heart pounded as loud as the guy in Edgar Allen Poe's "Tell-Tale Heart." (Why did they make us read horror stories in standardized high school education?) I waited in anticipation as the seeker creaked down the stairs. It was probably too spooky for her to rummage through the creepy room, so she took one big look around and started back up.

I was torn. Did I keep playing the dumb game and lose my sanity while I was at it? Or did I just give up and let myself be exposed?

Funny how that's the way sin works in our lives. It likes to stay hidden, in the dark, and it might not seem like a big deal, but while it's there, it takes a toll on your mental health. Sin takes a lot of energy to hide and cover up. This energy distracts you from the things you need to do and steals joy from your life.

Speak to Me in Plain English Por Favor

I had a calculus teacher in college who, the more he talked, the more confused I got. Has that ever happened to you? I think the disciples felt that way somewhat. John 16 records Jesus' ministry to His increasingly bewildered disciples. Jesus was saying goodbye; His disciples were in shock. He promised to send the Holy Spirit in His stead, but because they were overcome with sorrow at the thought of His departure, they held sidebar conversations.

"What is He talking about? We're not going to see Him, and then we'll see Him in a little while?" The timing of it all perplexed them.

Sensing their inner squall, the Storm Whisperer did it again. He told them about the ministry of the Holy Spirit, who would take Jesus' place on earth and dwell within them forever. He would convince the world of sin, righteousness, and judgment. He would guide them into all truth. He would speak only what God gave Him to say; He was not on His own, so He would be totally yielded to the Father. The Holy Spirit would also open people's minds to the future. All the while, He would bring glory to Jesus by taking what Jesus had and giving it to the disciples.

In comforting them, Jesus promised their grief would turn to joy. I can imagine the disciples flashing back to when Jesus read from Isaiah's scroll in the temple in Nazareth on the Sabbath.

"The Spirit of the Sovereign Lord is on me, because the Lord has anointed me to proclaim good news to the poor . . . to comfort all who mourn, and provide for those who grieve in Zion—to bestow on them a crown of beauty instead of ashes, the oil of joy instead of mourning, and a garment of praise instead of a spirit of despair" (Isa. 61:1-3).

Here it was. The promised Holy Spirit would turn their grief to joy. Their joy would be complete as they asked in Jesus' name anything of the Father. After all, the Father loved them.

Finally, when it seemed like they couldn't take it anymore, Jesus opened their minds and spoke with crystal clarity. Jesus declared that He came from the Father into the world and was now leaving the world and going back to the Father. Suddenly, it clicked! The disciples had been in the dark, but now Jesus revealed in plain English (okay, Aramaic) what was going on. Jesus came from God. And to clinch that, He told them in advance what was about to happen. They would all scatter, but Jesus would never be alone because He would be with the Father. And peace would thrive over trouble because Jesus had overcome the world.

We don't always understand the things of God right away, but we learn from these chosen few that joy comes when we stick with it, keep asking God, and keep hanging around Him. He will make things known to us. He will show us truth in increments and give us what we can handle.

The Work of the Holy Spirit to Heal Your Mind

What words do you think of when you think of the Holy Spirit? People think ethereal, holy, and out of this world, but also strange and weird. There are many misunderstandings of the Holy Spirit, and abuses in the way He is portrayed and said to work. Robert Morris, in his great book, *The God I Never Knew*, shares an excellent teaching on the way the Holy Spirit works in a believer's life today.[49] It can be summed up to say that the Holy Spirit is a helper, advocate, companion, and friend. His role is to direct, teach, correct, rebuke, and train in righteous and holy living.

Because *The Storm Whisperer* focuses on whole health, I'd like to emphasize the way the Holy Spirit heals our minds through conviction and guiding us into truth.

Have you ever been convicted and found guilty? Many of my friends at ATC have pretty hefty rap sheets. They'll attest to the fact that conviction is not a happy time because it usually means consequences. Conviction means time. Conviction means loss. Conviction means separation. However, conviction also means protection. It means provision. Conviction can also lead to transformation.

The Greek word for convict is *elegcho*, which means to find fault with and correct, to chide and admonish, to convince, and to convict.[50] The work of the Holy Spirit is to convince people that they are in sin and that they need to live righteously, or they will be judged. You and I might try, but we can't convince people. Conviction is the job of the Holy Spirit. *Elegcho* also means to bring to the light and expose.

Wow. I love that part of the definition. The job of the Holy Spirit in my life as a believer in Christ is to bring to the light, show me my faults, and call me to account. It doesn't sound great, but when I get convicted by the Holy Spirit, I have been given the gift of a chance. A choice—to change, to turn from my wicked ways and move into the path that He would have for me. My exposure leads me to freedom. When I'm found by the Holy Spirit, I can walk into the light and the darkness will no longer overtake me.

In my counseling office, I had the privilege of serving a young man I'll call Liam. After getting saved, Liam felt a calling to serve the Lord in full-time ministry one day. Slowly, he began stepping into that calling and volunteering his time in leadership roles. He loved his new life, his new friendships, and the new direction his life was taking. People trusted him, and he was growing more and more passionate about serving the Lord.

But there was one issue. He started to feel increasingly anxious and depressed. Finally a friend recommended counseling. Liam came to my office presenting with classic symptoms—he constantly worried and lived with a sense of dread and doom. He also felt worthless, irritable, sad, distracted, and even suicidal at times. I probed him about his childhood and incidents of trauma. I asked him about habits and addictions, which he denied. Then, I felt the Holy Spirit nudge me to read him one of my favorite Scriptures for counseling, "Have nothing to do with the fruitless deeds of darkness, but rather expose *(elegcho)* them . . . But everything exposed (*elegcho*) by the light becomes visible—and everything that is illuminated becomes a light." (Eph. 5:11, 13).

"In other words, Liam, if there is anything hidden in your life, any sin you're entertaining in the basement of your mind, it's time to let it come out of hiding. Once it comes out and is exposed to the light of Jesus and the truth of His Gospel, then the darkness can't stay, and everything will light up again."

I probed gently, "Liam, do you have anything you need to confess? Is there anything in your life you haven't told anybody?"

The young man paled and began to tear up as he revealed a secret occasional habit of pornography. He was too ashamed to tell his leadership that this was his continual battle; he tried to perform and act the Christian part to keep everyone off his scent. Liam wasn't intentionally hiding, he was too afraid of the consequences of being exposed.

The Power of Confession

Sin has a way of eating us up alive. And God knows that unconfessed sin will destroy us. Have you ever kept a gnawing secret? A neighbor confessed to me once that she had lied to her daughter's school and told them the girl lived at her grandmother's address. In the attempt to get her into a better school, every day after school both my neighbor and her mom would be present to pick up the high schooler. But the situation caused massive stress. They had to make up elaborate stories and keep up the appearances that she lived somewhere else. My friend admitted it was all exhausting. We talked about the freedom that would come from confessing, and how God has a way of blessing us when we do.

I don't know if my neighbor ever made any changes, but I saw, firsthand, the way unconfessed sin and hiding ate at a person's mind. She didn't sleep well, put on stress weight, and became overwhelmed with keeping up the story. Having to remember what she told whom and when contributed to distraction, confusion, and exhaustion. Unconfessed sin does that. It grows like a weed. In our backyard, poison ivy wraps around a few of our trees and will take over if left untouched. Eventually, it will choke out a tree. Hidden sin has this effect on our minds. You will feel like a fake, and no amount of worshiping can compensate for the way you sinned in private the night before. You will feel empty because you sense that your sin has created distance from God, and your prayers will feel ineffective.

Sin can change the way you think and can lead to future compromise. Left untended, it will destroy the good fruit God wants to produce in your life. Hidden sin will completely disconnect you from the Vine.

So, why don't we confess? We are afraid of experiencing the consequences, we think we deserve better, or we think we're not hurting anyone. We already know the third part is not true; we are deceiving ourselves if we live in sin and think it's okay. But we think if we confess, we will stop having fun. The sinful way seems more convenient. We think that when God rebukes us, it's going to suck the joy out of life. However, it's quite the opposite.

The Holy Spirit leads us into truth so that our joy may be full. His boundaries are for our good. When He corrects us, He is addressing us as a father addresses his son. "My son, do not make light of the Lord's discipline, and do not lose heart when he rebukes (elegcho) you" (Heb. 12:5). Again in Revelations, Jesus says, "Those whom I love I rebuke (elegcho) and discipline" (Rev. 3:19). Conviction from the Holy Spirit comes as an act of love from a Father who addresses a wayward son and says, "Get back in line! I love you and I have a plan for you. I want to bless you, and unconfessed sin hinders you from My blessing."

It's amazing how God led King David to a place of confession after the birth of his son with Bathsheba. God used the prophet Nathan to confront David. We see such a changed man when he confesses to the Lord. Psalm 51 is the record of his painful confession and his earnest cry to be reinstated with God. David knew there would be great consequences for the heinous sin he had committed, but He also trusted God to show mercy and do what seemed best to Him.

Is there any sin you need to confess in your life today?

THE POWER OF VULNERABILITY

I listened to a speaker at a women's conference who dared us to be fully transparent and vulnerable. I don't even remember her name, but I was touched by her transparency. It was strikingly refreshing and beautiful. She disclosed that in preparation for the event, she wanted to be seen as a powerful speaker and wanted to deliver an inspiring message, but the Lord kept redirecting her to share about confession and vulnerability.

The woman of God explained how she and her husband had struggled through a distant season of being on autopilot and going through the motions of ministry. It all came to a head when her husband confessed a sin. His vulnerability sparked her to be completely open with him. The conversation catapulted them into a week-long confessional. For a week, the two didn't spare each other any details. They laid out all of their innermost thoughts and dirty secrets. But while they did that, they listened; they didn't judge, they chose to forgive, they were real, and they loved. Experiencing the power of shame, brokenness, true openness, and freedom was life-changing.

So be honest with yourself. Does the thought of being so real with someone else sound revitalizing or frighteningly deadly? I think the reason people seek counseling is because they know they can be totally transparent with a counselor whose job is to listen without judging, to encourage, and to help. While there's benefit to talking with a counselor, without true confession and transparency with the people who are part of our everyday lives, we stunt our freedom.

One of the things I love about ATC is that people tend to be real. Unlike church where Sunday smiles are plastered on people's faces, when you hang around an ATC campus long enough, you'll notice people are not masking their issues. "I struggle with my mouth and with lust," someone will quickly admit, as soon as you get to know their name. That's some vulnerability. If a student is having a bad day, everyone knows it. Now, I'm not advocating for being ungracious when you struggle; there's a time and place to be vulnerable and confess. However, I do commend that many are learning to confess their sins and not hide it from people or from God.

The apostle John, probably moved by Jesus' teaching in this discourse, takes it to heart, and later admonishes the early Christians. 1 John 1:8-9 advises, "If we say we have no sin, we deceive ourselves, and the truth is not in us. If we confess our sins, He is faithful and just to forgive us our sins and to cleanse us from all unrighteousness" (BSB). The benefit of confession is freedom and cleansing. Wholeness. Not just spiritual healing, but emotional healing as well.

Liam became a new person as he dared to confess his struggle and receive accountability from others. We worked through his triggers and shame, and gradually the Lord set him free of a sin that had enslaved him. The cool byproduct was that all those symptoms dissipated as well.

Symptoms are like bad fruit growing because the branch has been disconnected from the Vine. Too often psychology and counseling focus on the bad fruit when we really should delve into the root issues that are causing separation between the Vine and the branch.

Repent and Repeat

Confession is one step, but there's another step to freedom. Jesus taught in John 16:20, "Very truly I tell you, you will weep and mourn while the world rejoices. You will grieve, but your grief will turn to joy." Jesus was talking about His death, and the joy that would follow at His reappearance. However, this verse foreshadows a principle of how grief over our sin (confession) can turn to joy when we are able to make an about-face.

Have you ever lost a key to something important? Stashed in a hidden place in our home is a portable fire safe in which we keep our important documents and valuable items, including our children's fallen baby teeth in labeled Ziploc baggies. (Don't ask—we didn't know where else to keep them.) Normally, we have the key to the safe stored in the same place, but after that Grand Canyon flood, all of our belongings were moved around and now I had no idea where to find the key. I was obsessed until I found it. Losing that key would mean losing access to our marriage license, family birth certificates, titles, and other objects of great treasure.

What if I told you that there was a key to entering into the presence of the Almighty, to experiencing the fullness of God, to being mentally whole, and to having our prayers answered? We have power to use this key through the Holy Spirit. This would be a crucial key that we would never want to misplace.

The key is repentance. Repentance? Sounds so meek and powerless, but ironically, it unlocks a great power in the spiritual realm and in our lives.

The step beyond confession is repentance. In the Hebrew, the word for repent used in the Bible is *nacham*, "to be sorry, to be moved to pity, to suffer grief, to rue, to regret, and to console oneself."[51]

Although I did not comprehend this principle in my early 20s, I found myself in a season of repentance that allowed a complete change of course for my life. When I graduated college, I was serving God on the outside, but deep down, I was thinking and living sinfully.

Mercifully, God stopped me in my tracks and convicted me. I felt so guilty about some of my choices, for acting like I had not known the Lord, when in fact, He had revealed Himself to me so lovingly and clearly. For three months, during a summer in graduate school, I could not stop crying. I played on-repeat songs like "Break my heart, oh God, for the things in my life, that break Yours." I grieved my sin, and I was deeply sorrowful for breaking the Lord's heart. He was my first Love, and I wanted to return to Him. I asked God to forgive me and restore me to Him; that's all I wanted. I wanted to be made new and to be used by Him again.

Looking back now, after that season of repentance, I realize that something lifted during that time. I was heard, forgiven, and healed! It was like I was free to be who God created me to be. God gave me the drive to pursue running a marathon and other dreams that had laid dormant in my life due to my sinful choices. Sin does that to you—buries your innate desires and gifts, masks your potential, and kills your dreams.

In college the Lord impressed on my heart a desire to serve Him as a missionary, but my sin stunted me. Now I was free to pursue His calling. After the summer of brokenness, I made plans to go on a mission trip to India the next summer. What a time that was! Total restoration and joy to be doing the will of God. I felt so grateful to be used by the Lord and serve abandoned children in an orphanage called Ramabai Mukti Mission.

While I was in India, free from the weight of sin, the Lord began to speak tenderly to me. One day I was reading Matthew 9, and He whispered to me through the words of verse 37, "The harvest is plentiful but the workers are few. Ask the Lord of the harvest, therefore, to send workers into his harvest field." I started to feel like God was asking me to be one of those laborers in the harvest. Could He be calling me? After I had disappointed Him so much?

I was not convinced, but the idea lingered deeply in my soul. Sweetly, as if to persuade me that it was His voice and His beckoning, I began to see Matthew 9:37 in the most random places, even on bumper stickers in the Hindu territory of India. I even saw it on billboards. I wondered if I was imagining it like the parched traveler seeing the mirage of water, but I could not shake the reality that the Lord was calling me to His service.

Repentance for me brought about three things. Repentance gave me freedom and joy. Repentance freed me from what had been holding me back. Repentance allowed me to step into God's calling.

Unconfessed sin had been a stumbling block, a barrier. But confession of my sin and my repentance allowed me to approach His throne of grace, and I prayed with confidence, knowing that my God and Maker was hearing me. He was giving me new direction for the future. I felt free and joyful.

All of the above are the work of the Holy Spirit, and I'm so glad Jesus gave Him to you and me. I love how He gently brings things to the light and gives us the courage to turn away so we can be healed.

Is there anything you are contemplating or flirting with that perhaps no one else can see? Will you let it come out of hiding? When sin is exposed, darkness cannot prevail and you can be brought back into the light.

Your light is worth shining!

Your life, untethered to sin and the weight of sin's oppression, is worth freeing. Perhaps some of your anxious and depressed thoughts are due to non-confession. Shine a search light into the deep crevices of your mind. Don't be afraid of what you're going to find; God sees it all, and it's His Holy Spirit drawing you to expose those things and make them right before God.

RECAP AND ENGAGE

Truths to Calm Mental Storms: My life is better off when I am open to God and to others about my struggles. God loves me so much that He came to guide me into truth.

Lies to Refute: My sin can stay hidden, and I will be okay.

Take it to Heart: Take time to confess your sin first to God. Write down what you have been struggling with, let His Holy Spirit lead you to Scriptures to read, and make yourself right with God. Experience His forgiveness.

Confess your sin to a friend you trust. Let this person keep you accountable and encourage you to be honest. Practice vulnerability with others and don't pick up the mask the next time you're tempted to cover up.

Prayer: *Lord, I need You. I come to You in humility, knowing that I'm a sinner. I thank You for the Holy Spirit guiding me into all truth and exposing my innermost desires and fears. Cleanse me and create in me a clean heart. Thank You for the joy that comes as I turn to You. In Jesus' name, amen.*

Choose to Pray Like Jesus Did

Read: John 17

In February 1958, a twenty-six-year-old pastor in rural Pennsylvania, Rev. David Wilkerson, sensed God telling him to sell his television. He was to set aside those late night TV-watching hours to pray instead.

Two weeks later, he felt drawn to a copy of Life magazine on his desk. He opened to the story of the Michael Farmer homicide in New York City. Seven teenage boys were on trial for his murder. As he looked at those faces, David Wilkerson started to cry, and he had this sudden, crazy but unshakeable thought, "Go to New York City and help those boys."

The amazing story of how Teen Challenge (TC) programs were born in New York and then spread all over the United States is chronicled in the *Cross and the Switchblade.* Prayer got TC started, and only prayer will carry out its mission.

In 2016, George and his leadership team experienced a similar compassion and call to reach out to adolescent boys in the state of Texas.

For a few decades, the ministry was called Teen Challenge because of its history but didn't actually serve teens anymore. It's sad to think that twelve to seventeen-year-olds have severe addiction and behavioral issues, but the need is great.

Today in Texas, we have programs that serve adolescent boys and girls, as well as adults. Each restored life and family is a bona fide miracle through the power of Jesus Christ and His presence. I've seen the power of prayer melt through the hardness of belligerent former addicts and turn them into soft-hearted vessels for Christ.

Many skeptics attribute the "answers" to prayer as coincidences or self-fulfilling prophecies, results that would occur because an individual is so committed to seeing these things happen.

Scientists have studied the effect of prayer on the brain, and science now concludes that prayer can change your brain and impact you positively in many ways.[52]

An article published by NBC news reported that prayer triggers the release of feel-good chemicals like oxytocin. Prayer was found to be effective in lowering a person's response to traumatic and negative events. MRI scans of individuals in Alcoholics Anonymous showed a significant difference in cravings after prayer and suggested that prayer actually helped to reduce their desire to use![53]

A Very Special Moment

John 17 is Jesus' longest recorded prayer in the Bible and expresses His ministry to the Father, His disciples, and all believers. Jesus was a man of prayer. Many times in Scripture, we read that He went off to be alone to spend time with His Father. This prayer was the end of His farewell discourse—His last private words with them.

In this passage, Jesus was teaching His disciples how to pray, by example. They had observed Jesus praying often and requested: "Lord, teach us to pray."

With the mental turmoil we experience in the climate of our world, we, too, can benefit from asking, "Lord, teach us to pray."

John 17 is a tender passage that records the heart of our Savior as He engages with His Father about twelve hours before His death on the cross.

The fact that we are privy to these words is something special. Some commentators refer to it as the holy of holies—"sanctum sanctorum." We must approach this text as worshippers, with a posture of humility.

John was so distinctly moved that he recorded every detail as a blueprint for believers to commune with God and to face life's storms. Prayer radically prepares us for anything we might encounter in life and leads to mental wellness and abundant life. After prayer, Jesus was ready to face the greatest trials of His life. No storm is too difficult to endure when we pray. Communing with the Father is the antidote to any mental distress.

Jesus Models How to Pray for Ourselves

In John 17:1-5, Jesus said again that His time was near. What Jesus anticipated was not easy. He prayed, "Now my [heart] is troubled, and what shall I say? 'Father, save me from this hour'? No, it was for this very reason I came to this hour. Father, glorify your name!" (John 12:27-28).

Despite the dread, Jesus was intent on glorifying God, for that was the reason He came to earth.

No matter what we go through, we must pray for God's glory. If we have a big exam or responsibility ahead, our prayer shouldn't just be, "Father, help me to do a good job in this." Rather, we should say, "Lord, help me to do this so Your name will be lifted high!"

At times we seek glory for ourselves. We want to be recognized and get upset when we are not. That's why entertainment through Facebook and social media causes depression. We observe what others are doing and how perfect their lives seem. If we don't think we compete, we get down.

That is not the heart of our Savior. His prayer teaches us to focus on the Father's glory, not our own.

Another word for glorify is to magnify; that's a good picture for us. Make His name big; make ours small. Just like John the Baptist explained, "He must increase; I must decrease" (John 3:30).

Pray for God's glory in your storm. Maybe you're dealing with a sickness, a difficult marriage, a problem with one of your children, loss, unemployment, or you just find yourself in a hard season of life. Pray for God to be glorified somehow.

You may not understand why you're going through the situation, but trust that God sees. Determine to walk through the trial making His name great. Pray Matthew 5:16—"Let your light so shine before men, that they may see your good works, and glorify your Father who is in heaven" (KJV).

Do you realize you have been given a holy assignment? At church, I recently met a couple with a cancer diagnosis, starting aggressive treatment. Although their worlds have been turned upside down, they see the finger of God, and have been led to pray for others in the midst of their greatest storm. "For we are God's handiwork, created in Christ Jesus to do good works, which God prepared in advance for us to do" (Eph. 2:10). No matter your calling in life, regardless of your career, your mission is to glorify God. You are on assignment where you have been placed.

Christ was able to pray, "I have brought you glory on earth by finishing the work you gave me to do" (John 17:4). What a wonderful example of how we can pray over ourselves: "Father, help me to bring You glory on earth by completing the work You gave me to do!"

It will never benefit you to compare yourself to others or worry about how your work does not look like theirs. That's when problems come. When we start to compare ourselves with each other, we are not wise (2 Cor. 10:12) and we get jealous!

Instead of looking at each other, our perspective should be vertical. "Lord, am I bringing You glory in my work? Am I accomplishing the task You have for me? You put me here at this job. You placed me in this family. You situated me in my current neighborhood. Thank You! Help me to make the most of every opportunity!" Turning your pity-party into prayer protects your thought life.

I love the verse about David in Acts 13:36. "Now when David had served God's purpose in his own generation, he fell asleep." David rested for eternity, having fulfilled his God-given destiny; what joy and peace!

You were born to do whatever it is God puts in front of your hands to do. He will make it happen as you trust and cooperate with Him. Jesus exemplifies the wave-whispering peace of a life that is mission-minded and utterly focused on God's glory. We can experience the same.

In addition to praying for God's glory, Jesus encouraged the right thoughts about God when we pray. Without the right perspective, we are vulnerable to mental attacks. Jesus showed us we must have the right view of God when we pray, just as He did.

In John 17:5, He mentioned the glory He had with God before the world began. Scripture gives us a glimpse into our glorious God, like this vision recorded in Daniel 7:9-10.

> As I looked, thrones were set in place and the Ancient of Days took his seat. His clothing was as white as snow; the hair of his head was white like wool. His throne was flaming with fire, and its wheels were all ablaze. A river of fire was flowing, coming out from before him. Thousands upon thousands attended him; ten thousand times ten thousand stood before him.

This is God! The God we talk to, the God you and I get to approach in prayer because of what our Lord and Savior has done. In Daniel 7:13-14, Daniel continues to describe what he saw.

> In my vision at night I looked, and there before me was one like a son of man, coming with the clouds of heaven. He approached the Ancient of Days and was led into his presence. He was given authority, glory and sovereign power; all nations and peoples of every language worshiped him.

When we pray, we must never lose sight of the awesome God we approach. Yes, He is our friend and the lover of our souls, but He is holy, terrifying, and to be feared. He is God!

Four Words to Pray for Others

Pray for protection.

"Holy Father, protect them by the power of your name"
John 17:11

Similar to His prayer in Matthew 6, "Deliver us from the evil one," Jesus prayed for our spiritual safety. He warned that the world would hate us because of Him, but that He would be our defender and guardian. Pray for protection of the mind against lies, accusations, and evil worldly philosophies for you and your loved ones.

Pray for deliverance from temptation and that you and your loved ones will stay committed and true to Jesus, no matter what. Pray you won't be deceived by false teachers. "Lord, protect us from the fiery darts of the enemy intended to derail our lives and trick us into settling for less than best."

Pray for joy.

I say these things while I am still in the world, so that they may have the full measure of my joy within them.
John 17:13

In John 17:13, Jesus prayed for our joy to be complete. Joy is the byproduct of living for Him and staying connected to the Vine. Joy is integral and actually a hallmark of the believer. You can be joyful when you have the right perspective and when you trust God to take your burdens.

"The joy of the Lord is your strength" (Neh. 8:10). He's a place of safety, refuge, stronghold, and protection. Joy keeps us strong despite external circumstances.

One of the enemy's greatest temptations is to attack joy through discouragement, using joy killers such as complaining, comparison, gossip, remaining in sin, living in the past, and fearing the future. Praying for joy means putting aside everything that hinders our joy. An attitude of joy leads to a victorious, mentally healthy life.

Consider how the apostles reacted when persecuted. "The apostles left the Sanhedrin, rejoicing because they had been counted worthy of suffering disgrace for the Name" (Acts 5:41).

Pray for joy in your life and in the lives of the believers in your sphere of influence. Pray against those killjoys, and pray that you might rejoice always because of Jesus.

Pray for sanctification.

Sanctify them by the truth; your word is truth.
John 17:17

Since 2011, George and I have been coaches for a church ministry called Junior Bible Quiz (JBQ), a program that teaches children the basics of the Bible. Ask any JBQ quizzer, and they will tell you that the word "sanctification means being separated from sin and set apart to serve God."[54]

Jesus prayed for His disciples to stand out from the world, and to be holy by His blood (Heb. 13:12). Holiness sets us apart. We should be set apart in the way we dress, talk, act, entertain ourselves, and keep company.

At first glance, a holy life might seem restrictive and oppressive, but it actually leads to freedom, joy, and peace. When we live sanctified and pure, we are not covered by a cloud of shame or guilt, and we can be whole.

Jesus teaches us to pray that our loved ones will remain pure and stay single-focused in their devotion to Him. Pray they would not sell out to the world's ideas or to the influence of social media or divisive politics, but that they would have courage to live pure and blameless lives.

I'm so glad my mom prayed for my sanctification; she prayed me out of many bad situations. George's parents are prayerful people, as well. George used to be an accountant for Enron, and he was on a fast track to management. All was well at first. I love how George's mom tells the story of how Enron went down. She saw that George was being influenced by the worldliness around him, and she and George's dad prayed earnestly for a way for George to get out of that environment so he could use his gifts for the Lord's work. She firmly believes that Enron shutting down was one way her prayers for George's holiness were answered.

Pray for unity.

I in them and you in me—so that they may be brought to complete unity.
John 17:23

Jesus prayed for His disciples, that they would be one. Unity is not the same as all being the same; that's uniformity. God's not offended by our variety, even in our worship. Just because we have different denominations who believe God's Word and worship Him differently does not mean we are not unified.

Unity, instead, is solidarity in the mission to let the lost world know about the love of our Father. Unity is singleness of heart and action (Jer. 32:39). Our unity is pleasing to God and is His desire. As a key to peace in our relationships, unity is the bedrock for relational wellness, which directly correlates with mental fortitude. In other words, the more peaceful our relationships, the stronger and more secure we are set up to feel in our thought life.

The late Rev. Dr. Martin Luther King, one of my heroes, took this prayer of our Lord to heart. He made unity his prayer, passion, and life mission. You can read his book of prayers and see that unity of the brothers and of the church and of all mankind was one of the major themes. As he prayed, God gave him a vision of that unity which inspired his most famous "I Have a Dream" speech.

His prayer and his efforts as a civil rights activist changed our nation, resulting in the voting rights of African-Americans, desegregation, labor rights, and other basic civil rights.

Dr. King exemplified what happens when we begin to pray to God for unity—things change! We begin to dream about unity, work toward it, and help bring it to life.

Paul urged us in Ephesians 4:3 to "make every effort to keep the unity of the Spirit through the bond of peace." We, too, can pray for unity in our church, that all of us, of different colors and backgrounds, will stand hand in hand, believing in the same triune God and the same Word. As Christian believers, we can let the whole world know about the unity God wants to have with all of His creation.

Friends, let's pray for unity in our marriages, families, and extended families. We are not the same, but God blesses our efforts to live together in unity. This is one of my favorite principles to teach at ATC. It comes from Psalm 133:1-3. "How good and pleasant it is when God's people live together in unity . . . For there the Lord bestows his blessing, even life forevermore."

The Amazing Reach of Prayer

I think it's amazing that we, as believers, were on Jesus' mind and heart when He prayed the night before His crucifixion. He prayed for each one of us, and we are answers to His prayer. Some prayers take a long time to be answered. Take heart and keep asking. God hears us!

In John 17:20-26, Jesus showed us how to pray for those we don't yet know who will be connected to God by our influence, like future grandchildren or future people we will serve.

Jesus prayed for us to be with Him and to see His glory. Likewise, we can pray that those we influence will know God's love and stay true to the straight and narrow path.

The fact that Jesus prayed for future generations of believers leads to a significant truth. When we pray for someone in our sphere of influence today, we touch their future generations. One of the best gifts we can give someone is to sincerely pray for them to the Father, in the name of Jesus, guided by the Holy Spirit. Our prayers today have a ripple effect and impact more than the here and now.

Our prayer life gives us significance as it truly impacts the Kingdom of God. Why does the enemy come against our prayer life so strongly? Why does it seem that every time we set a time to pray, some obstacle stands in the way? The enemy hates a praying Christian and knows that a prayerless Christian is powerless.

I told you about our house flood in 2019. The ceiling of our master bathroom caved in. Prior to leaving on that vacation, I had packed up my "War Room" supplies, my notecards, markers, prayer board, and missionary prayer cards into a neat pile onto my bathroom counter. Would you believe the ceiling caved in with water right on top of all of my prayer room stuff?

I was furious when I noticed this—then the idea fueled me to keep praying. God was my protector, and no devil would deter me from praying. "Lord, help me to be a woman of prayer, and help everyone reading this to become serious about prayer!"

I can't tell you how many times when I have been upset about something, worried, depressed, frustrated, or jealous, I took the feelings to the Lord, and He healed me. I am living proof that prayer to the one true God heals your mind and sets you free!

Be Inspired to Pray

I love the story of Corrie Ten Boom. She was a Dutch Christian who helped many Jews escape the Holocaust by hiding them. Corrie, her sister, and her father were sent to prison (where her father died). She and her sister were sent to the worst concentration camp, where her sister died. Corrie survived to share the story of God's love, provision, and forgiveness to millions. But do you know her backstory?

In 1844, Willem Ten Boom began a prayer gathering to pray for the return of the Jewish people to their promised land and for the peace of Jerusalem. The Jews were scattered, without a country or national identity. For one hundred years, through three generations, the Ten Booms met in his house in Holland to pray for the peace of Jerusalem.

You know what is amazing? Almost a century later, God used the Ten Boom family to save many Jews right from that very same house. In 1940, when Germans invaded Holland, Corrie and her sister used their home as a hiding place for many Jews.[55] The power of prayer to impact generations is amazing!

Lord, teach us to pray. Instead of complaining, getting angry, giving into temptation, wasting our time, worrying and being anxious, dwelling on the enemy's lies, and relying on our strength and wisdom, nudge us to pray.

As we look into Jesus' side of this intimate conversation with His Father, we get a glimpse into the purpose of prayer. So often we connect prayer with just the petition part of it—asking for the specific things we want or need. But the purpose of prayer is to connect with our Creator, to submit to Him, and to acknowledge that we depend on Him. It is to align our desires and will with His will.

Throughout John 17, Jesus acknowledged all the many things His Father had given Him: authority, words for believers, His name, and glory. In verse 10, He summed it up, praying, "All I have is yours and all you have is mine."

Jesus' intimate heart cry showed His utter humility, dependence, gratitude, and praise for His Father.

Prayer shows our dependence on God. Prayerlessness is a sign of pride and implies we don't need God. Whatever you are going through today, you can get through it only with Jesus.

Get into a church that prays together regularly. Connect with other believers who pray. It may significantly strengthen your faith to become part of a prayer group like Moms in Prayer. Find a group near you and pray the Scriptures over your children and schools. Praying together encourages us and helps us carry each other's burdens. We can agree with one another and ignite each other's faith as we pray. We can pray together for unity, joy, protection, and sanctification.

Begin a routine of family prayer. When counseling families, I have seen that implementing this one step of regularly gathering together to pray, read the Bible, and sing to God makes a huge difference. It's hard to stay in a fight with someone you pray with and for every night.

No matter our emotional storm or difficult season, when we pray according to Jesus' example, our minds are renewed and our relationships are strengthened. Our faith can be ignited as we see God perform miracles. Prayer is our greatest defense against mental storms and a powerful offensive weapon when they strike.

Recap and Engage

Truths to Calm Mental Storms: Prayer prepares me for the greatest of life's trials and gives me strength, unity, joy, and protection. I grow more like my Lord as I pray.

Lies to Refute: Prayer doesn't make a difference. It is a waste of time.

Take it to Heart: I want to encourage you to take your prayer life to the next level. Maybe you only pray for five minutes. Extend that to ten. Maybe your prayer time is solidly petition, meaning all you do is ask. Spend time thanking Him and praising Him. Confess your sins daily in prayer.

The next time you recognize negative thoughts, *choose* to replace them by writing down what is bothering you and praying Jesus' words over the matter. Pray for your protection against the evil one. Turn your complaint into a declaration that God is going to work it out.

What are you praying for that is bigger than what you can handle on your own? I am the product of prayer: godly parents, praying family, and praying friends. This book exists because many prayed *for you* as I wrote and as you are reading it today. God stretches our faith as we pray for the impossible.

Prayer: *Lord, thank You for the power of prayer, for the far reach of prayer. Prayer changes things and prayer changes me. Help me follow Your example and become a person of fervent prayer. Thank You for Your patience with me as I grow, and thank You for healing my mind. In Jesus' name, amen.*

Choose to Be Refined Through Trials

Read: John 18

I love words. Blessed and bloom are two of my favorites. These words and other hope-filled phrases embellish the walls of my home, our throw pillows, and decorative art. They convey promises and hope and serve as encouraging reminders to my soul.

I have to admit that I don't often think of the flipside of each of these words, but to get to the blessing, there is testing. We are blessed once we're pressed, squeezed, stressed, and pushed to our limits. We bloom when we are pruned, when we go through that paring down process. We bloom after we've gone through a winter season.

We tend not to remind ourselves of the other side of these coins, but as people of faith walking in mental wholeness, God's favor and blessing often results from a process of trials and testing. If I want to be used by God for His glory, I must be prepared for trials—many of them! Paul said, "Through many tribulations we must enter the kingdom of God" (Acts 14:22 ESV).

John 18 captures the story of Jesus on trial. In a harrowing turn of events, He was betrayed by Judas in a private place He frequented to pray, abandoned by His disciples and companions, and even disowned by one of His closest friends. The Savior was bound like a criminal and taken to first Annas, then Caiphas the Jewish high priest, and then Pilate the Roman governor to be tried. Jesus did not attempt to defend Himself. Instead, in His conversation with Pilate, He focused on the redemption of Pilate's soul, and gave Pilate the chance to state whether he believed Jesus was the King of the Jews (John 18:34). Jesus did not lose His composure or His peace on trial. Instead, He remained unwavering in His mission and steadfast in His devotion to the Father. He even told the pagan ruler that the reason He came into the world was to bear witness to the truth. Grace under pressure!

We all experience trials that can leave a scar and mar us if we do not maintain the right perspective. How we go through God's refining fire sets us apart and allows us to walk in greater strength and mental fortitude.

Jesus did not need to be refined; He was already perfect. Yet, He gave us an incredible example of how to walk through fire. His life was also the perfect example of living in favor; He did not lord it over others or use His platform to put others down. He kept the tension of favor and fire in perfect harmony.

Let's study the life of a young man in the Bible who struggled with this tension, like most of us do, and use his story, juxtaposed with favor and fire, for lessons on how to handle both.

Favor and Fire in Joseph's Life

I love a good story, and Genesis 37-39 captures the epic account of the life of Joseph. At the time we meet him in Scripture, he was a 17 year-old shepherd boy with a very interesting family. His dad was married to two sisters (can you get more complicated than that?) and later married a few more wives. They all lived together with all the kids, all boys but one girl! Talk about the makings of a family feud.

Joseph was the second youngest of all the brothers, the older son of Jacob's clearly favorite wife, Rachel. Because he was Rachel's, he was probably given a double portion and special treatment. Most likely, he was protected, sheltered, and not allowed or expected to do what his brothers had to do. And he was a tattle tale. Joseph might have been favored by Dad, but his brothers deeply resented him.

Twice, Joseph shared dreams with his brothers. In the first, his brothers' sheaves bowed to Joseph's sheaf. In the second, the sun, moon and eleven stars bowed to Joseph. Now, it's one thing to have crazy dreams, but when the dream borders on offensive, it's probably wise to keep it to yourself.

Joseph was favored. But he was foolish.

He bragged about his dreams. Maybe he was just excited with the first dream. He had probably heard stories of his father Jacob's and his grandfather Abraham's dreams. He must have been curious and amazed and eager to talk about it. But his constant talk rubbed his brothers the wrong way. We see Joseph lacked emotional intelligence and probably took some pride in his favored position and in the fact that he was so blessed.

Joseph's character had flaws—pride, boasting, and self-reliance. Some of this was probably due to his dysfunctional surroundings. Clearly, Joseph didn't know how to handle his favor, his platform, his dreams, or his promises.

This may be true for us, too. We may have the call of God on our lives. We may sense His favor and blessing, but we might not be ready to handle the platform He plans to give us. If we rise too quickly, we must be careful lest we take pride in position or find our worth and identity in how we perform rather than the fact that as His children, we are simply walking out what He gives us to do.

Joseph was in for a rude awakening. Just like that, he lost his favored status when his brothers sold him into slavery for just twenty pieces of silver. That's quite symbolic. Centuries later, Jesus would also be sold for the price of a slave, thirty pieces of silver.

Think about that silver. Just as it had to go through a refining process to become useful and something of worth, Joseph would have to undergo fire to fulfill God's purposes for his life.

THE REFINER'S FIRE

Let me define the concept of the refiner's fire, a phrase used at the end of the Old Testament. Zechariah, a young prophet, delivered a message from the Lord to the remnant—the third of Jews returning to Jerusalem after years of captivity in Babylon. "This third I will put into the fire; I will refine them like silver and test them like gold. They will call on my name and I will answer them; I will say, 'They are my people,' and they will say, 'The Lord is our God'" (Zech. 13:9).

The refining fire of God is often a testing, a purifying process that cleanses that which is impure and not useful from an item to make it useful and able to fulfill its purpose.

Just like fire tests silver and refines gold, the tests of our Christian faith examine what we are really made of. The fire can require us to wait for something we want, maybe an answer to our prayers. The fire can be an unexpected illness or physical ailment. The refining fire can be a person in our life who has this way of bringing out our dark side. The fire can be a difficulty we are facing at work.

Proverbs 17:3 says "The crucible is for silver, and the furnace is for gold, and the Lord tests hearts" (ESV).

Joseph was put to the test in an unfair situation that seemed unbearable. But with each trial of fire, his faulty character traits that were not useful to the Lord were burned away—his pride, boastfulness, and sense of worth that came from people's approval. Joseph may not have even realized he had those tendencies, but God saw them.

When we go through the refining fire, it might feel like we're going to die, but what is really dying is the stuff that hinders us from fulfilling God's purpose for our lives.

When gold and silver are purified, the precious metal is sifted out and then put to the fire to strip out its impurity. Who knew silver had so much impurity? Extracting the real gold and the real silver from these precious metals involves a laborious, intense process, with a lot of repetition of several key steps to make sure the metal is truly pure.

There is a principle here for calming our storms—the testing we endure today may serve its purpose for now. But likely, we will have to go through the crucible again as more impurities rise to the surface that need to be skimmed off through prayer and confession. Because of the mind-numbing pace of life, sometimes we move too fast to even realize these vices have taken us off course and prevented us from being effective for the Lord.

Further examination of Joseph's life shows this tug of war between favor and fire. He was favored by his dad but sold into slavery by jealous brothers.

God used the crucible of rejection and slavery to prune out what didn't belong. Then He turned that fire into a position of favor. Genesis 39:2 states, "And the Lord was with Joseph, and he was a prosperous man; and he was in the house of his master the Egyptian. And his master saw that the Lord was with him, and that the Lord made all that he did to prosper in his hand" (KJV).

God's presence in the fire turned it into a place of favor. What a turnaround! When His presence accompanies us in the fire, we are highly favored and blessed. No matter what comes, we will be okay.

God's Presence in the Fire Turns It Into Favor

What was once devastating turned into a place of favor. Potiphar singled Joseph out and entrusted him with the care of everything in his house. Sadly, Joseph was then falsely accused of seducing Potiphar's wife and was thrown in prison. We don't know from Scripture why he was thrown into the fire this time. He didn't seem to have any obvious character traits that needed to be pruned or pressed. But God knew.

God sees us when we're in the fire, knows why we are there, and is working something out for our good.

Maybe Joseph needed time to be alone before he was catapulted into a position of influence, maybe he needed to just really learn how to depend on God, maybe he needed to learn what it was like to be stripped of everything, and maybe God wanted to teach him appreciation and perspective. Or perhaps his fire was a result of someone else's bad choices; whatever the case, the fire is never wasted. There's always something for us to learn.

Even in prison, God's blessing was on Joseph and he prospered. While Joseph was in prison, two inmates had dreams that needed to be interpreted. And look who was there at just the right time with the right gift. The gift to interpret dreams may have gotten Joseph into trouble when he was younger, but now, it's something supernatural.

Friend, sometimes, in the fire, you get the opportunity to practice what you're going to do when you're walking in favor.

Did you get that? You might be in the middle of the fire, but you are learning and practicing something God wants to use in the future. You may be unnoticed to the world, but God sees you. God is lining things into place and setting you up for future favor.

You may be doing something that seems insignificant. Maybe it's changing diapers, or grading papers, or cleaning, or paper pushing, or serving behind the scenes. God wants you to learn how to be faithful first in little things before you're entrusted with bigger things (Luke 16:10). He wants to grow some gifts in your life while no one is watching, while there is no pressure, so if you fail, the stakes are not so high. Don't despise small beginnings; be content with where you are right now.

Joseph interpreted the dreams of his inmates and asked them to remember him and send help. But they forgot all about Joseph.

Two long years in a boring, unstimulating prison passed by. That's a long time to be in the fire. Why did it have to take so long? All we can know is that there was still more time needed to prepare Joseph. Time for God to set up other people and events. Remember, there's a fullness of time. The fire is never wasted space.

As Joseph's story continued, Pharaoh had two dreams and Joseph was summoned. Pharaoh relayed his dream and expected Joseph to interpret it. Without missing a beat, Joseph replied, "It is not in me. God shall give Pharaoh an answer of peace" (Gen 41:16 KJV). Joseph was not afraid of talking about the one true God in this deistic nation where pharaohs were seen as gods; rather, he quickly acknowledged God and gave Him glory.

This was a very different Joseph than the one we met thirteen years before. The once cocky, arrogant boy who took personal glory for God's positioning of his life now immediately gave God glory, even though the people around him gave him the credit.

The day had finally come when the secret gifts, having been refined and honed by the fire of aloneness, were to shine. But it wouldn't have happened without the time Joseph spent in prison where his gifts had the chance to grow. This was all necessary before he was catapulted to the next level.

Soon, Joseph was made second in command. His public favor was restored, although God's private favor had never left him. The rest is history. He led the people over the next fourteen years during feast and famine. During the first year of the famine, Joseph's brothers did, indeed, come and bow down before him, not just once, but twice. His family came to Egypt, settled in Goshen, and remained there for the next 400 years.

God turned around all that was intended for evil in Joseph's life!

It's Your Choice to Be Refined

Let's summarize a few principles on how to choose to be refined through fire and trials.

It's natural for us to be consumed with doubt, discouragement, and fear when we go through a challenging season. It's natural to let fear envelop us and dry up our faith. But it doesn't have to be that way. We can choose to either allow the fire to burn us or to refine us.

Jesus was able to go through His season of fire and trial because He fully understood what it was accomplishing. He was ready because He knew Father God was with Him.

For you and I to be ready in the fire, we, too, must look within, look up to God, and look beyond.

Look within.

When we're in the fire, God seeks to purify us and cleanse us and make us more like Him.

I walked through my own season of refining fire when George and I contracted Covid shortly after moving to Houston. I started going into a dark place with my thoughts after three weeks of exhaustion and frustration—bills were piling high with our newest ATC campus in Houston for which I was responsible, and the demands never stopped. I was overwhelmed by unpacked boxes and mounting responsibilities.

Like Judy Hopps, ready to conquer Zootopia, I felt eager to "go get 'em" in this new city and plunge ahead with launching the women's program. But when Covid struck, I felt stuck and interrupted. If you had asked me two weeks before the virus if I struggled with insecurity or feeling insignificant or pride or jealousy, I would have said no. However, I was moving too fast in life to notice myself. Thank God, He saw me. Through the fire, He halted me, and once I finally submitted to Him in confession and got out of my own pity-party, He showed me I had too much ambition. I had my own agenda, and He was stripping me so that He could use me.

A week after God allowed me to recover from Covid, I wound up tripping over a piece of furniture, breaking my finger, and needing surgery. This time, though, because I had just been through His refining, I saw God's hand and favor in it immediately. Yes, I wouldn't be able to type for a while, I had many medical visits, I couldn't meet all the people I needed to meet, and I was in pain. But I was at peace.

Right before surgery, my daughter Jadyn shared Isaiah 41:13 with me. "For I am the Lord your God who takes hold of your right hand and says to you, Do not fear; I will help you." Through my brokenness, I immediately saw how God was going to be lifted high. A finger on my left hand was broken, but His righteous right hand was enough. He was going to do supernatural things, and He was going to get all the glory and credit for it. In fact, a verse God showed me during the fire was John 4:38. "I sent you to reap that whereon ye bestowed no labour; other men labored, and ye have entered into their labours" (KJV). God revealed that He was going to get the glory and that I was sent to continue the work others worked hard for, to reap what they had sown. The journey has been hard, but supernatural, watching God provide finances and bring in co-laborers. And the scar on my left pinkie is a memorial to the amazing grace and favor of God in the fire.

Romans 5:3-5 states, "We can rejoice, too, when we run into problems and trials, for we know that they help us develop endurance. And endurance develops strength of character, and character strengthens our confident hope of salvation. And this hope will not lead to disappointment. For we know how dearly God loves us because he has given us the Holy Spirit to fill our hearts with his love" (NLT).

In other words, God, in His love for us, uses the tests of life to work out our character and hope. I imagine a trainer who pushes his client to his fitness goals, using a hard sequence of exercises to grow an area of muscles. The Lord, who has perfect plans for us, sees who we're becoming, knows what we're intended to fulfill in life, and uses our difficulties to exercise our faith and mature our character.

What about you? Can you look within? What is God wanting to strip from within you through the fire?

Look up.

No matter what changes around us, no matter how fickle the people in our lives seem, no matter how disappointing everything is, God does not change.

He is still good, He is still sovereign, and He is still capable and able. As Warren Wiersbe poignantly phrased it, "When God puts His own people into the furnace, He keeps His eye on the clock and His hand on the thermostat. He knows how long and how much."[56]

Our Lord is not an arsonist, but a Refiner! Isaiah 48:10 proclaims, "Behold, I have refined you, but not as silver; I have tried you in the furnace of affliction" (ESV).

When we walk through a fire, we need to remember that God is allowing it. "Beloved, do not be surprised at the fiery trial when it comes upon you to test you, as though something strange were happening to you" (1 Peter 4:12 ESV).

When we walk through the fire, we need to praise God. We are being transformed and made more beautiful and whole. He's lining things up for us, like he did for Joseph.

My son Luke and I were playing the other day. To his sisters' chagrin, he loves to go around the house singing a line from the animated movie *Joseph: King of Dreams* about being the best, brightest miracle child. I was tossing him onto the couch, pretending to be the prison guard throwing Joseph into prison. Of course, Luke is getting bigger and wouldn't let his mama just toss him onto the couch. So while he was resisting me, I admonished him: "Joseph, if you don't go into that prison, you will miss your destiny, young man."

The Holy Spirit spoke to me at that moment.

Friends, if we don't go through this difficult season, this trial we are suffering, we will miss what God has next for us. We may miss our promotion. We may not meet the people we are supposed to meet, people we would only meet because of this unique trial during the fire, people God has ordained for us to meet. If we miss this season, we will miss out on all the preparation God wants to do for the next chapter He has for us. If we don't go through the fire, we may miss His favor.

If Joseph hadn't gone to prison, he would not have met the baker and the cupbearer, whose dreams he interpreted. The help he gave to them in their time of need set the stage for him to meet the Pharaoh and go on to do what he was destined to do—save the Israelites and preserve God's holy people. God predetermined the refining fire of prison to prepare Joseph for His glory.

So look up, friend! We may not see it all right now. Our marriage is in pieces, our kids are affected; how can this be used for good? But God has a plan. God's ways are higher than ours.

"In this you rejoice, though now for a little while, if necessary, you have been grieved by various trials, so that the tested genuineness of your faith—more precious than gold that perishes though it is tested by fire—may be found to result in praise and glory and honor at the revelation of Jesus Christ" (1 Peter 1:6-7 ESV).

Look beyond.

Finally, we find victory in the fire by looking beyond. James 1:2 says, "My brethren, count it all joy when ye fall into divers temptations; knowing this, that the trying of your faith worketh patience" (KJV).

Count it all joy. It doesn't say: have joy in this trial, or enjoy this suffering. The fire is not easy. It's lonely and painful. But consider it all joy. We must look beyond the feelings of the fire and get the right focus, the right perspective. Look up and look beyond the circumstances. We get the opportunity to grow and become more like Jesus. C. H. Spurgeon said, "I owe more to the fire, and the hammer, and the file, than to anything else in my Lord's workshop."[57]

So don't resist the fire, the trial you are suffering. We don't know the next level God wants to take us to, but we will only get there if we first pass through this trial. Here's the bottom line, the good news—if we're still in the fire, it's not the end of the story. The Refiner's not finished yet. He's still working on us. We can choose to embrace the fire and the refining that comes by fire as much as we naturally embrace the favor because we know that God uses both sides.

Are you in a crucible today? Know that God loves you and has crafted this time to bring about His desired results. Make your thoughts plain before the Lord, then confess your sin and come into alignment with His truth. Trials are tryouts. You will experience a turn of events; your fire sets you up for your platform. Your fire puts things into focus. Your fire leads to favor.

Joseph named his two children Manasseh, which means "forgetting," and Ephraim, which means "fruitful." What a beautiful ending. In the place of his fire, in which Joseph was forgotten and rejected many times, God gave him favor and made him fruitful.

Joseph saw the value of the fire and learned how to walk in favor, keeping those secrets God had taught him in the fire. Because God is with us in the fire, we are highly favored. Isaiah 43 promises that when we walk through the fire, the Lord is with us and we will not be burned or consumed. The circumstances might feel overwhelming, but we are exactly where we need to be.

Jesus underwent His trial knowing the joy set before Him, knowing the great outcome of that fire—all the souls who would be saved as a result of His obedience and grace under fire. We may have a tendency to only rejoice when we are blessed and when it seems like we are blooming, but the reality is, God is with us and for us just as much when we are pressed and pruned. He loves us and will never leave us nor forsake us in the favor or in the fire!

Recap and Engage

Truths to Calm Mental Storms: God is behind the scenes in our trials and has given us a perfect example in Christ to help us walk through trials.

Lies to Refute: I am alone in my suffering. Nothing good can come out of what I'm walking through.

Take It to Heart: This chapter offers a reframe of the fire, a fresh way to look at your pain. Take a moment to see His favor in the midst of your fire. What miracles is He working out, around and within you? In the fire, it helps to pause and reflect on God's hand. Journal a different way He's providing for you through people and circumstances every day this week.

Sometimes our fire is caused by our negligence, poor choices, and disobedience. Our difficulties are a result of our own sin. If that is the case, we must confess our sins and make ourselves right with God. We can't expect favor in the fire when our choices are consistently separating us from God's blessing. Is there anything you are doing to contribute to the fire? Make it right with God and repent today.

Worshiping God brings freedom and prepares us for heaven. Praising God is probably the most effective thing you can do in the midst of fire. Will you commit to spending extra time every day this week worshiping God?

Prayer: *Lord, thank You for how You use the fire in my life to heal my mind and help me to know You more, trust in You, depend less on me, and see Your amazing hand in my life. I declare that You are for me in the fire; help my unbelief and fear. Strengthen me as I walk through this, and show me how to continue. I choose to be refined. In Jesus' name, amen.*

Choose to Forgive

Read: John 19

Never! Cyndi grimaced as the speaker continued. I will never be able to forgive him for what he did to me! She had been intrigued until the speaker stated that mental health requires forgiveness. That made her mad. How dare anyone ask her to forgive?

Lost in thought, Cyndi crumbled into herself as memories of the betrayal and deceit flooded her mind. He didn't deserve forgiveness. As if it were even possible to undo the damage he'd done. Not going to happen!

Ready to tune the speaker out, Cyndi suddenly caught words claiming forgiveness would bring freedom. Freedom? How could it be possible that offering something to someone who didn't deserve anything at all would actually free her? Cyndi leaned in to pay attention. The speaker expounded on the freedom that would come from letting God deal with the offender. Letting go and letting God.

When the speaker asked if anyone needed prayer, Cyndi hesitantly shuffled forward in the prayer line. Her heart pounded. The speaker approached her with a gentle greeting, and slowly, Cyndi began to unleash the years of pain and bitterness. It finally dawned on her how heavy the weight she carried was, and she agreed to ask for God's help to let it all go. She hadn't realized how much the pain and bitterness had infiltrated her life, notably, her relationships. Little did she know the gift she was giving herself as she let go.

"To forgive is to set a prisoner free and discover that the prisoner was you."[58]

The Impossible

My encounter with Cyndi marked me. Sensing the magnitude of her hurt, I recognized that the only way to help her even contemplate the impossible task of forgiving an undeserving offender was to point her to the One who made forgiveness possible. As she gazed on Him, there was hope because there was precedent. We forgive because Jesus forgave. We do the impossible because He did it first.

In John 19, the Storm Whisperer faced the greatest tempest of all time, the impossible sin problem of mankind, to be resolved and conquered at the cross. The reason for which He came to earth had unfolded, and His motivation remained focused on love and redemption. After all, there was no other hope for uniting creation to their Creator. No Plan B. Only the cross.

The chapter opens with Jesus' continued ministry to Pilate, the Roman governor of Judea who would eventually hand Him over to death. Jesus' encounters with individuals were always intentional.

Pilate had been given great authority but struggled with insecurity and fear. In love, Jesus offered him a chance to listen and discover truth. Pilate refused, although he was certainly struck by the fact that Jesus' actions and claims did not warrant death.

The irony is unreal. The Jews had waited centuries for their Messiah; He now stood before them, but they did not recognize Him. Pilate had Jesus flogged, hoping to satisfy the crowd and to possibly convince Jesus to lay low and be more discreet with His message. Ha! Jesus, lay low? His time had finally come to be "lifted high" for all the world to see.

The Power of Decision

God warned Pilate through his wife's dreams that Jesus was innocent. Pilate's own conscience nagged him as he interacted with the sinless Savior, but he chose to give in to the religious leaders' rage. Pilate had a choice. He could have freed Jesus and let Him go. But he felt trapped. He didn't want to give in to the leaders' demonic desire to murder the one who was truly their Messiah, but he also did not want to appear disloyal to Caesar. After all, the Jewish leaders said Jesus had claimed to be King. Secondly, Pilate realized that if he could not manage these religious leaders, Rome would take notice. His platform and the perks that came along with his position would be jeopardized.

Have you ever felt like you had to prove yourself? To show people you had what it took to fulfill a task, despite their doubts about you? Have you struggled with doing the right thing, even if it could cost you your job, your pleasures, your friendships, or your status? Pilate struggled with these issues—needing to prove himself and yet struggling to do the right thing. It was this struggle, in fact, that influenced Pilate to forfeit the chance to side with truth and stand for Jesus.

When Pilate heard the Jewish accusation that Jesus claimed to be the Son of God, he became even more afraid. Finding nothing wrong with Jesus, Pilate asked Him, "Don't you realize that I have power either to free you or to crucify you?" (John 19:10).

What Pilate didn't realize was that Jesus had already made up His mind to follow His Father to the cross. To wear all our guilt and shame. The agony of Gethsemane was behind Him; our Savior and hero had fully resolved to face man's fiercest foe: death itself.

"You would have no power over me if it were not given to you from above," Jesus retorted (John 19:11). Jesus was quite clear that both He and Pilate were only where they were because God set it up that way.

Amazing words: you have no power over me. When we make up our minds, no one else can influence or hold power over us.

When my children attended public schools, my girls would come home and describe how evil their school world seemed to be. Children cussed non-stop, showing little regard for life, morality, modesty, authority, and even themselves. We discussed that the only way to thrive in that environment and not be influenced by the world around us is to have a mind made up to follow Jesus.

Daniel, in the Old Testament, lived out this principle of not allowing popular culture or the opinions of others to change what you know is right to do. He "resolved not to defile himself" (Dan. 1:8). Taken as a refugee into the Persian royal court, he made up his mind not to pollute his body or his mind with the delicacies and sinful habits of the surrounding culture. Daniel allied himself with a few peers who were equally resolved. No leader or layperson had power over them.

There's nothing quite as unstoppable as a made-up mind. Some students come through Adult & Teen Challenge with minds clearly made up from the time they begin the program. *No matter what comes my way, I'm going to do this and get my life right!*

This kind of determination excites me. Personal resolve coupled with a mandate from God to accomplish something creates an unbeatable combination. This person will make it, come what may.

How resolved are you to keep following Jesus, no matter the costs? A made-up mind, focused and determined, can achieve goals that are otherwise impossible. A made-up mind, unafraid and willing to do what it takes leads to emotional and relational security. Rather than constantly second guessing yourself, you use the Word of God and the life and principles of Jesus as your basis for decisions and relationships.

With a made-up mind, Jesus forged ahead to the cross.

The irony of John 19:16 strikes me. "Finally Pilate handed him over to them to be crucified. So the soldiers took charge of Jesus." How do you take charge of the One who is in charge of everything, even up until His dying moments? How can you take charge of the One who created the world and was penultimately in charge?

Yet, despite His sovereignty, Jesus fulfilled His sole mission in obedience and submission. He came to earth to obey His Father and lived His life to fulfill Scripture.

Time and again, John 19 points out events that happened so Scripture might be fulfilled. Over three hundred Old Testament prophecies of the Messiah were fulfilled in the life and death of Jesus. He was conscious of every detail, even up until His final moments. He expressed thirst on the cross. He made sure His mother was taken care of. He communed with His Father until His final breath. Every word, every encounter, every last detail fulfilled a purpose.

Remember Me

Before His final words on the cross, Jesus had one more assignment. In the middle of the utmost human agony one can imagine, Jesus reached out to the two criminals hanging on crosses beside Him. Let that sink in. Jesus had one more soul to rescue. One more life to restore. Even in the middle of His deepest agony, His time was not yet over. He had one more storm on earth to calm.

One thief hurled insults at Jesus. The second boldly defended Jesus.

Let's pause to consider this unnamed bandit and his last-second act of bravery. By his own admission, this crook deserved execution. By his own admission, he was a nobody and no good. This thief was a perfect example of being poor in spirit.

But, oh, the wonder of the mercy of God! This thief had the greatest honor of his lifetime—he was privileged to die beside the King of the world, his very Creator. Though he did not deserve it, Jesus noticed him.

When we defend the Gospel, God sees us, too. He sees our risks and remains true to His promise. "Those who look to him are radiant, and their faces will never be ashamed" (Ps. 34:5 ESV). Jesus guaranteed the thief hope and a future. His bold defense of the Savior foreshadowed a principle Paul experienced in his encounter with Jesus.

"If you declare with your mouth, 'Jesus is Lord,' and believe in your heart that God raised him from the dead, you will be saved. For it is with your heart that you believe and are justified, and it is with your mouth that you profess your faith and are saved. As Scripture says, 'Anyone who believes in him will never be put to shame'" (Rom. 10:9-11).

The thief knew Jesus did not deserve His death sentence and asked Jesus for a great favor. Most likely he had heard of this Jesus of Nazareth, and he showed an uncommon belief in Christ's controversial words—offensive to the proud but medicinal to the pauper—the criminal asked, "Can you remember me?"

In other words . . . "Is it possible someone like You could actually forgive and accept someone like me? When You're doing Your King thing in Your new kingdom, could you somehow let me be part of that?"

That's pretty amazing faith. Jesus' prospects for doing anything else, much less accomplishing the bringing in of a new kingdom, would have seemed very grim to the naked, unbelieving eye at that time. He was hanging on a cross. But the thief chose to believe. God helped the thief recognize that Jesus would do what He said He would do.

The Messiah promised that the thief would come into His kingdom and that he would be with Him in paradise. Right then and there, the score was settled. The debts forgiven. The man now had the hope of eternal life and a bright future, quite literally, to look forward to in heaven. All because this man asked and Jesus chose to forgive.

THE POWER OF FORGIVENESS

When Jesus was nailed to the cross, He prayed one of the most tender prayers a loving Savior could pray for His children. Calling out to His Heavenly Father, He pleaded, "Father, forgive them, for they know not what they do." In the midst of people spitting on Him, cursing Him, beating the blood out of Him, abusing Him, stripping Him, and scarring Him, Jesus forgave and asked the Father to forgive.

"For they know not what they do," Jesus explained. Really? Did these people not know the pain they were causing? Did they not understand that Jesus really didn't deserve this torture?

Of course they were responsible, but Jesus saw something deeper. He understood how limited people are in the ability to perceive.

We don't know the depths of pain our sin causes our God and Lord. Although we might be aware we are doing wrong, many of us are blind to the gravity of our sin. We become deceived or complacent about the real enemy of our souls who works against us in the spiritual realm.

Of course, we're not off the hook. At some point, we come to the place of awareness and responsibility. The more we know, the more is expected of us. James warned that teachers will be judged more strictly because they have greater understanding.

The Romans who crucified Jesus and the Jewish leaders who got Him to that point were not absolved of their actions. They mercilessly crucified a man they knew deep down was innocent because they hated His claims. Despite that, Jesus petitioned His Father to forgive them.

How Could He Forgive Such Cruelty?

First, He knew the true mental, emotional, cognitive and spiritual state of His enemies. He understood their shortcomings and what led them to such a position of blindness.

In the same way, when we are deeply wronged, it's sometimes helpful to take a moment and consider the oppressor. How did he or she get to be the way they are? What were their parents like? How were they treated? Since it's true that hurting people hurt people, what struggles are they enduring currently or from the past?

Sometimes understanding our enemies helps us consider context and gain insight. This exercise does not excuse wrong actions. But we can understand that they may not have necessarily caused the trouble and pain because they thought we deserved it. It could be they are dealing with a deep inner struggle they allow to be converted into pain and aggression towards others. Again, their actions are still wrong, but when we recognize the other party really may not realize the pain they caused, it reminds us that we often find ourselves in the same position in terms of how we offend our Savior.

Second, Jesus called on the Father to forgive the people responsible for His mistreatment and death. In yet another act of fulfilling Scripture, by calling out to God, Jesus "made intercession for the transgressors," as Isaiah prophesied (Isa. 53:12).

As our intercessor, Jesus steps in for those who do wrong and stands between people and the judgment we deserve. Scripture teaches that He lives to intercede for us. "But because Jesus lives forever, he has a permanent priesthood. Therefore he is able to save completely those who come to God through him, because he always lives to intercede for them" (Heb. 7:24-25).

Jesus modeled how to offer forgiveness of those who curse us, persecute us, and seek to hurt us. He also showed us that He is praying for us, standing in the gap, in all our need. We certainly need His help to forgive our greatest offenders.

Sometimes our worst enemy can be our past choices and the way we let ourselves down. Do you find it difficult to forgive yourself?

Our Hero acted in consistency with His teachings and beliefs. Jesus taught His disciples to pray, "Forgive us our debts, as we also have forgiven our debtors . . . For if you forgive other people when they sin against you, your heavenly Father will also forgive you. But if you do not forgive others their sins, your Father will not forgive your sins" (Matt. 6:11, 14-15).

So, in order to be forgiven, I must forgive. It's not a suggestion; it's not optional. "And when you stand praying, if you hold anything against anyone, forgive them, so that your father in heaven may forgive you your sins" (Mark 11:25). Forgiveness of others is a prerequisite for our own forgiveness and right standing with God.

Sometimes it's helpful to understand that forgiveness may be given while pain and distrust may still be present. That is natural and okay. You may not feel like forgiving someone because you still feel hurt, but you can decide to forgive.

You can pray, "Lord, because I want to be forgiven by You, and it is only by Your mercy that I am forgiven, I choose to forgive and have Your heart for my offender. Just as You forgave me for hurting You, I choose to forgive those who have hurt me. I let them off the hook and give them over to You. I don't have the power to deal with the pain they caused me. Only You can handle that. So by forgiving them, I am trusting You."

Start with the decision; let the feelings follow. Your thoughts about that person and what they did will diminish over time. Your pain will subside, but you have to start with a made-up mind.

The Dangers of Unforgiveness

Cognitive forgiveness is choosing to not let the actions of the offender and the pain they caused continue to rob us of peace. Because that's what unforgiveness does—it steals, kills, and destroys.

Sound familiar?

Strikingly similar to the strategy of the thief Jesus warned about in John 10, unforgiveness interrupts peace, joy, and health. As someone once coined, "Unforgiveness is like drinking poison, hoping the other person is going to die."[59]

I believe that the root of much mental illness is often a pattern of unforgiveness. Thinking about an offender, overplaying hurtful conversations, and ruminating over the wrongs all lead to symptoms of anxiety and depression, including sleep interference, intrusive thoughts, poor concentration, and diminished self-esteem. Unforgiveness interferes with mental wellness and the abundant life Jesus came to give us. I liken it to a cancer that spreads within, at first unnoticed. But once the thoughts of hatred and hurt proliferate within the mind, unforgiveness begins to affect one's decisions, relationships, and even physical health.

I have witnessed the trap of unforgiveness, a reason for which many come to counseling, although they may not recognize it at first. Usually, it's joylessness and relationship issues that bring people in, but when we peel back the layers, unforgiveness surfaces as an underlying root and culprit to part of the pain.

I have also seen the joy of breakthrough that comes from choosing to pardon.

Catalina, a student at ATC, finally chose to forgive herself for actions she felt led to the death of her father. Although there was no way she could have caused the tragic accidental death of her dad who was, at the time, on his way to see her, the fact that she was involved haunted her and led to a downward spiral. Drugs numbed her pain but then enslaved her as she found herself doing things she would never have imagined for herself or her family.

Once the Lord helped her to forgive herself, to let herself off the hook, there was freedom. Releasing the pain and hurt was one of the greatest turning points of her life. She felt lighter as she chose to let God carry the burden of her mistakes and failures. It opened the door for a new future.

No wonder our Savior ministered to mankind, not just the thief on the cross, or His executioners, but to all who would believe. Forgiveness is a path to freedom.

Is there anyone in your life you need to forgive today? Is your mood and health affected by the things people have done to cause you pain? Forgiveness does not necessarily mean reconciliation with an offender, but it does mean letting them go so Jesus can do the work of reconciling that person to Himself. It's not our job, nor our cross to carry. Only God can handle that.

JESUS' POWERFUL LAST WORDS

The Gospels record that Jesus spoke seven statements while hanging on the cross. These words are significant because each came with severely labored breath and deep intention. Jesus meant for you and I to learn something with each word. In these words, we see Jesus' heart and a true model for how to live the abundant life. In each statement, our Savior ministers whole health and gives principles for a life of freedom, joy, and mental wellness.

"Father, forgive them."

We are forgiven! Despite our ignorance and foolishness, we have hope. As Colossians 2:13-14 says, "When you were dead in your sins and in the uncircumcision of your flesh, God made you alive with Christ. He forgave us all our sins, having canceled the charge of our legal indebtedness, which stood against us and condemned us; he has taken it away, nailing it to the cross." Our debt is paid.

Jesus' words also inspire us to forgive others. A life that refuses to stay offended by others and chooses forgiveness again and again is a blessed and abundant life. Offense is a joy stealer and leads to bitterness. Unforgiveness literally damages our minds and bodies. Choose to release your offenders and perpetrators and give them over to the Lord, as often as an offense comes to mind. As Jesus taught His disciples: "Forgive seventy times seven," a hyperbole to indicate that forgiveness should be often and constant and pervasive. Forgiveness leads to wholeness.

"Today you will be with Me in paradise."

Jesus said this to the thief on the cross beside Him. Jesus came to earth to seek and to save the lost so that we may have abundant life.

We are reminded to seek God today, while we still have breath. Salvation is the ticket to paradise. Jesus is the only way to heaven, for He is "the way and the truth and the life" (John 14:6).

"Truly, truly, I say to you, whoever hears my word and believes him who sent me has eternal life. He does not come into judgment, but has passed from death to life" (John 5:24).

"Woman, behold thy son! . . . Behold thy mother!"

In addressing His biological mother in John 19:26-27, Jesus provided for her in the midst of her greatest loss. She had known a sword would pierce her soul one day (Luke 2:35), and that moment had come. Jesus showed His compassion, humanity, and care for family relationships and emotional pain by setting up a plan for His own mom and entrusting John, His closest friend, to take care of her.

The Lord cares about our relationships and knows how important they are to our mental wellness. We must take our relationships to Him in prayer. True and healthy relationships with our family members don't just happen. Neither do friendships, so we must be seek God's help for relationships to be fruitful in our lives.

My God, why have You forsaken Me?

Feeling abandoned by His Father as He carried the weight of the world's sin, Jesus uttered words of spiritual suffering. All other pain He had endured to that point paled in comparison to His spiritual suffering in this moment. The Father could not look upon sin, and since Jesus was carrying it all as the unblemished Lamb of God, He felt the weight of aloneness.

How does this minister to our mental health? We don't ever have to endure this spiritual suffering because through Christ, we are never alone. We are never apart from God. His sacrifice paved the way for us to never be forsaken (Heb. 13:5). Oh, what a Savior! We don't ever have to feel alone or abandoned because Jesus endured that pain for us. Replace those feelings by accepting His presence in your life today!

I thirst.

Jesus showed His humanity as He endured physical suffering. Our Savior, both man and God, took the punishment for our sins. Yet in His physical suffering, He refused to sin or water down the pain. He refused the wine vinegar that was offered to Him on a stick.

Jesus fully endured every physical temptation known to man. "No temptation has overtaken you except what is common to mankind. And God is faithful; he will not let you be tempted beyond what you can bear. But when you are tempted, he will also provide a way out so that you can endure it" (1 Cor. 10:13). In our greatest temptation, there is a way out—calling on Jesus to help us, asking the Holy Spirit to fill us, and trusting God the Father to guide us into the right path.

It is finished!

Jesus set the perfect example when He fulfilled His mission to save all of humanity.

Purpose anxiety is a real phenomenon which comes from not knowing why we are here on earth. Praise God that, as His children, you and I know our purpose—to point others to Christ and in doing so, into eternity with God.

"Into Your hands I commit My spirit."

In these final words, after uttering, "It is finished!" Jesus surrendered His Spirit to His Father. Just moves me to tears as I think of our Savior considering you and me as He cried out on the cross.

Jesus trusted in Father God with His final breath. Hallelujah! I want to trust my Father with my last breath; what a perfect segue into eternity. I look forward to that, but for now, I will continue to observe Jesus' behavior to learn how to fulfill my God-given mission.

Do any of these seven statements resonate with you? If you choose not to follow Christ's example, you shortchange yourself and jeopardize your mental health. Let Jesus' final act of obedience on the cross inspire you to make up your mind to follow Him and to forgive others, including yourself.

RECAP AND ENGAGE

Truths to Calm Mental Storms: Make up your mind to do what is right, no matter how tempting it is to cave in to the world. A made-up mind leads to emotional security. God is merciful to forgive us no matter how incorrectly we have lived.

Lies to Refute: It's okay to have one foot in the world and one foot in Christ. I cannot be forgiven.

Take It to Heart: Do you struggle with a wishy washy mind? Who are you afraid of, who are you trying to please, who are you trying to impress? Ask yourself these questions and explore what motivates you to go back and forth in your mind. Then ask the Lord to help you be resolved to do what is right, no matter who you are around.

Are you moved to forgive someone today? You can't do this in your own strength. Ask God to show you how to love the unlovable and to forgive even when it seems impossible.

When you have been deeply wounded or betrayed by someone, the thought of letting that person off the hook can seem grossly unfair. Your natural feeling is anger, self-defense, and deep sadness. Acknowledge your pain and give these feelings to the Lord. Determine to not walk in unforgiveness that kills you, one thought at a time. Rather, choose forgiveness that affords you life, one thought at a time.

Prayer: *Father, thank You for the perfect example of Jesus' resolved mind. He did not let anything or anyone sway Him from the cross ahead of Him, and I praise You for that. Help me to live resolved in this world, despite the temptation around me to please and live like the world. Lord, I need Your help in forgiving those who have hurt me. Please help me to follow Your example. Thank You, Jesus, for constantly interceding for me and for being my Savior. I love you! In Jesus' name, amen.*

Choose to Stay Close to Jesus

Read: John 20

My friend Jana once told me about a mission trip she took as a teenager to the L. A. Dream Center. One day, while street evangelizing, she met a young man and began talking with him in hopes of sharing the gospel. His eyes were a pale blue, and she found herself unwittingly mesmerized by his charisma and presence.

In the course of the conversation, however, it seemed that this young man had an ulterior agenda besides simply getting to know my friend. He eventually tried to lure her to come with him and join a Satanic ritual he was organizing. Shaken up, Jana learned to never underestimate the charm of the devil. Nor would she forget the chill she experienced in the eerie presence of the enemy of our soul.

The well-loved Psalm 23 says that God, as our Good Shepherd, actually allows us to be in the presence of our enemies. In fact, He invites us to rest in places where the enemy might linger because He knows that His presence alone is all we need to supersede fear and unrest. His presence is enough; in fact, He is more than we need.

The devil wreaks havoc in people's minds and bring storms to trap people through negative thinking, unforgiveness, broken relationships, and trauma. His strategies are predictable, yet effective. It's impossible for a Christian to remove himself from wickedness; it's all around us.

Romans 12:2 offers counsel: "Do not be conformed to this world, but be transformed by the renewal of your mind, that by testing you may discern what is the will of God, what is good and acceptable and perfect." How do we do that? Jesus said, "I am the light of the world. Whoever follows me will not walk in darkness, but will have the light of life" (John 8:12).

John 20 details the amazing account of the resurrection of Jesus, His ultimate victory over death, and His fulfillment of the promise to come back after three days. Interestingly, His first appearance after He rose from the dead involved a very personal encounter with a woman who at one point in her life battled with the enemy and almost succumbed to his power. But God! After an encounter with Jesus, she began a friendship that changed her future.

Luke 8:1-3 tells the story of Mary Magdalene. The city of Magdala bordered the Sea of Galilee where Jesus miraculously calmed the furious storm—a picture of what Jesus would do for Mary.

Scripture gives no record of Mary's parentage, marital status, or age. People often assume that Mary was a harlot or had a dicey reputation, possibly because the Jewish Talmud states that the town of Magdala had a bad reputation for harlotry.

The Bible, however, describes Mary as a deeply afflicted woman whom Jesus set free. Every reference to her describes her as one of the most faithful and beautiful characters of the Bible, delivered from a dark past through her friendship with Jesus.

Luke describes Mary as having seven devils or demons. Revelation 12 teaches us there is only one Satan or devil, but there are legions of fallen angels or demons. Seven is a Biblical number that signifies completeness. Evil spirits wholly dominated Mary's life at one point.

Uncovering Satan's Strategies

We don't know how those evil spirits settled in Mary, but we know the enemy is constantly on attack with intent to destroy our thought life, family, marriage, and community at church. Satan's pursuit is relentless. Victims get trapped by "playing" with the occult, habitual sin, relationship bondage, unforgiveness, jealousy, unchecked anger, or belief in lies. We need to understand how the enemy afflicts people.

Possession

One way the enemy afflicts is through complete "possession." This cannot happen if you are saved because the Spirit of God cannot share space with the spirit of the enemy. As believers, we can be oppressed or attacked of the devil, but not possessed.

People *can* open themselves to these spirits by following occult practices like tarot cards, palm reading, witchcraft, Wikken, and the like. Their choice to follow the devil invites the enemy to take physical, mental, relational, and spiritual territory and authority in their lives.

Sadly, in my work with ATC, I have encountered many people who have dabbled in the occult and "given themselves" to possession by the enemy. While on drugs, they made a decision to worship Satan and follow his evil practices. Not realizing that they had been duped by something "masquerading in light," they declared allegiance to that which trapped them. As a result, they could not concentrate, their thoughts disturbed them, they were plagued with dark voices and thoughts, and they never slept well because demons haunted them.

It's difficult to have a conversation with someone so demonized. Their symptoms mirror psychosis, where thoughts are tangential, their affect is either catatonic or erratic, and their behavior is strange. Many have battled demonic voices after exposing themselves to evil incantations; many experience hallucinations and delusions. It's a horrible existence.

As Christians, we don't need to be afraid we might be possessed because the spirit of the enemy cannot cohabitate with the Spirit of God. That said, the Bible says we need to be "self controlled and alert" (1 Peter 5:8). "The devil prowls around like a roaring lion looking for someone to devour. Resist him, standing firm in the faith."

There are subtle ways of being exposed to the occult. I was at a class get-together once in graduate school when people started trying to levitate someone. Feeling uneasy, I said to myself, "Nah, I don't want to be part of this" and excused myself from the gathering.

Even a fascination with evil or evil plots like in movies or books can create a door for the enemy. I have read how an evil spirit would help an author write a mystery or detective story. Listen to that check in your spirit if it feels weird or strange. Be aware and alert!

STRONGHOLDS

Another way the enemy afflicts people is through strongholds or bondage. The word stronghold refers to an area in our thought life where we get stuck. It can lead to an addiction, a feeling of being enslaved or trapped.

We can be saved but still struggle with a stronghold. How does that happen? With salvation, our spirits are made new, but our soul (our mind, will, and emotions) and bodies are not new yet.

Our soul begins a process of sanctification at salvation. When this happens, our spirits are made free, but there can be an area in our thought life that is still under the captivity of the enemy. That's why 2 Corinthians 10:3-5, as we have already explored in our study of John 10, teaches us to fight against these strongholds with the Word of God.

> For though we live in the world, we do not wage war as the world does. The weapons we fight with are not the weapons of the world. On the contrary, they have divine power to demolish strongholds. We demolish arguments and every pretension that sets itself up against the knowledge of God, and we take captive every thought to make it obedient to Christ.

Maybe you've felt trapped by an addiction or a relationship like so many of my clients who have battled pornography or substance abuse. Even when you know you should stop, it feels impossible.

Maybe it wasn't a relationship; maybe it was drugs or alcohol. Maybe you have felt like a slave to fear or money or worry, so it's hard for you to trust. How will it all work out? Maybe it's a sin habit like pride or lust. God says His Word is our weapon against these strongholds. Mary Magdalene held on to the words of Jesus.

A Foothold

Another way the enemy bothers believers is by getting a foothold. My siblings and I used to play tag often, and we would chase each other all the way to our bedrooms. When I was "it," I would try to pry myself through their door, but of course, they were pushing with all their might on the other side. However, if I could somehow weasel my little foot into the door, I knew I had won. I had enough of a hold to be able to push the whole door open. The power of a foothold!

You may never have dabbled in the occult or had a life-controlling issue or relationship. There are subtle and perhaps more common ways we expose ourselves to the enemy and give him power in our lives.

As I studied Mary's life, the Lord reminded me of a Biblical passage. Jesus had driven out a demon who had made someone mute, and the people began to accuse Him of driving out demons by the power of the devil himself. Jesus said that was not possible and gave insight into the spiritual realm: when a demonic spirit is released, he is restless until he finds a place to land—someone in which to inhabit.

> When the unclean spirit has gone out of a person, it passes through waterless places seeking rest, and finding none it says, "I will return to my house from which I came." And when it comes, it finds the house swept and put in order. Then it goes and brings seven other spirits more evil than itself, and they enter and dwell there. And the last state of that person is worse than the first. (Luke 11:24-26)

The Greek word for waterless places is *topos* and means a foothold or a place.[60] The unclean spirit is searching for a place to rest. The image I get is one of the enemy setting up camp in our minds. Getting comfortable in our lives. Isn't that a sick thought?

When we stay in the habit of negative thinking, cognitive neuroscience suggests that those thoughts get mapped out like trails in our cerebral cortex. In a way, we are literally giving the enemy space in our minds.

Another way we grieve the Holy Spirit is with a habit of sin. For example, having a habit of unchecked and unresolved anger can give the devil an entry point in our lives. Ephesians 4:25-31 lists habitual behaviors that give the devil a foothold in our lives: lying, stealing, unwholesome talk or gossip, rage, slander, and every form of malice.

It's interesting that this list in Ephesians is very similar to the list of the seven deadly sins in Proverbs 6:16-19.

> There are six things the Lord hates, seven that are detestable to him: haughty eyes, a lying tongue, hands that shed innocent blood, a heart that devises wicked schemes, feet that are quick to rush

into evil, a false witness who pours out lies and a person who stirs up conflict in the community.

These are deadly sins that the devil himself committed and still orchestrates in the lives of others. As described in Isaiah 14:12-14 and Ezekiel 28:12-18, Satan exhibited a haughty I-don't-need-God attitude that led to his fall.

LIES WHICH BRING DIVISION

When I was younger, my older boy cousins loved to tease and torment me. We've become great friends in adulthood, but childhood was rough.

One day they convinced my friend that I was saying bad things about her. They also convinced me she was saying bad things about me. Gullibly, I found myself getting annoyed with my friend, who otherwise had never said an unkind word to me. The lies made us doubt each other; they affected our ability to see clearly. Finally, we talked and discovered the truth.

Much like my cousins' approach, the enemy lies and accuses with the intent of dividing and destroying.

A common way we allow the enemy to affect our lives is by listening to lies and accusations. If it's not God's truth, then it is a lie. Satan is a sneaky accuser and tries to divide people, families, and churches. The enemy uses lies and accusations to divide, to steal peace, to kill joy, and to destroy.

Whatever the strategy, the impact of the enemy's wicked schemes can be debilitating, so we must take up our stand. Strongholds and lies can lead to severe anxiety, depression, and other types of mental illness. Personality disorders, which take years to develop, abound when there has been a longstanding history of spiritual, emotional, and relational struggles.

Ephesians 6:12 spells out clearly that our day-to-day "struggle is not against flesh and blood, but against the principalities, against powers, against the rulers of the darkness of this world, against spiritual wickedness in high places" (KJV).

We have to see our situations for what they really are. This does not mean that everything is the enemy's fault; we, too, play a significant role in our struggles. The truth is that we can only do life one way. We can let the enemy rule, or we can walk in victory.

A Hellish Hurricane Hushed

We don't know the root of her pain, but it's safe to say that Mary's life before Christ was utter agony. She was possessed, not in her right mind, and unable to make a good choice even if she so desired. She was a slave to the enemy and living a very scary life devoid of any peace.

Can you imagine the moment Jesus encountered Mary in her desperation? Perhaps she was revolting to look at—crazy hair, wild eyes, scary voice. All we know for sure was that in one moment she was completely ridden with evil, shame, hate, and darkness.

But in the next instant, Jesus spoke the Word and set her free! He rebuked the devil, those seven strong demons, and they left her. That anguish—gone! That hellish hurricane—hushed. That torment—destroyed. Oh, the power of the name of Jesus that can break any stronghold and set any captive free!

When Jesus delivered Mary, her freedom was as complete and whole as the imprisonment by the enemy had been. This was depicted well in the following commentary about Mary's life:

> In His authoritative voice He commanded the tormenting demons to come out—and stay out—of her. "Back! back! To your native hell, ye foul spirits of the pit," and the miracle happened. Her deranged and nerve-racked mind became as tranquil as the troubled lake Jesus calmed. Sanity returned, the rosy tint was restored to her cheeks, and she was made whole. Now, "clothed and in her right mind," she was ready to become one of the most devoted followers of Him to whom she owed so much.[61]

What happened to Mary? The Bible says, "Submit yourselves, then, to God. Resist the devil, and he will flee from you" (James 4:7). Mary let Jesus into her life and heart. The Holy Spirit came to dwell within her. The demons had to flee, and Mary was returned to her right mind.

And then, Mary made a choice that would change the trajectory of her future. She chose to stay close to Jesus.

What a Friend She Found in Jesus

What was the secret to Mary's long-lasting freedom from the enemy? She valued her friendship with Jesus over everything else. She left her home in Magdala and traveled everywhere with the disciples who followed Jesus. She and her girlfriends aided Jesus in His missionary activities. Quietly and effectively, these women did whatever Jesus asked.

Even when life got super confusing, Mary stayed close to Jesus. She identified with Jesus in His death and burial even though others deserted Him, denied Him, or betrayed Him.

Mary was close at Pilate's hall when the religious leaders demanded Jesus' blood. She was close when Pontius Pilate pronounced His sentence of crucifixion. She was close when He was led to Calvary. She was close, with the other sorrowful women, as He died the agonizing death on the cross. She followed Joseph to the tomb into which He would be laid. She was there, preparing spices and perfumes. Mary was there. Last at the cross, first at the tomb.

In our times of difficulty and pain, how closely do we follow Jesus? Do we stay by Jesus' side even when we don't understand how it's all going to work out? Are we willing to risk all we have for Him? Do we display devotion even when our lives are not going according to plan? Do we realize that waking up in the morning to spend a few moments with God is a way for us to stay close to Jesus?

He waits, hoping to spend that time with us. He knows we have a million things to do, but He longs to whisper His infinite secrets to us.

I'm sure that staying near Jesus would have comforted Mary in the midst of her confusion. Staying near the Lord will bring us that same comfort. James 4:8 offers such a promise: "Come near to God and he will come near to you."

Seek and You Will Find

Let's pause for a moment to reflect on why Mary stayed so persistently close, seeking Jesus. What was she looking for? What did she expect?

Perhaps she kept pondering His words about the time being close for Him to go to the Father and the Holy Spirit to come, and she didn't want to miss anything. She stuck like glue, and her tenacity did not disappoint. Her relentless pursuit of God resulted in Jesus speaking to her and giving her direction.

When we hang close to Jesus, things change. Mountains move. God speaks. We find direction and breakthrough comes. But, we must keep seeking. We must keep pushing through until we sense His presence and His gentle whisper.

Mary of Magdala was distraught, but in the middle of her tears, Jesus came. At first, He was unrecognizable. Sometimes, when we're caught up in our emotions, we can also get too clouded by the here and now to see our Savior.

But God understands. He saw Mary and asked her, "What are you looking for?" In other words, Jesus asked Mary, "What is the greatest desire of your heart? Who do you want, meditate on, and strive after more than anything else?" Strangely enough, He asked the same question to the first disciples He chose in John 1:38, as we have already explored. Jesus always ministered to the deepest need of every soul.

Mary responded to Jesus, assuming He was a gardener who knew where Jesus was.

Recognizing the laser focus Mary had on Him, her endless pursuit and tenacity to stay close, Jesus did something remarkable. He showed up and showed Himself to her in a unique way. Mary Magdalene, a formerly demonized soul, rejected by the world, a torment to herself, became the first messenger of Christ's resurrection!

Called in the Confusion

In the moment of her gravest pain, there it was. The gentle whisper. The voice of the Master. The call in the midst of chaos, or maybe because of it. Jesus entrusted her with the greatest assignment of her life. Go, tell others. Jesus is alive! The Savior has risen!

Perhaps the storm you face today in your mind is a set up for you to do something. Your pain is never in vain. However, a healed perspective comes only as we stay close to the Lord.

Mary stayed close to Jesus during the tough times, and Jesus entrusted His calling on her life, making her His ambassador.

What could you and I be missing because we are not relentlessly pursuing Him? What direction might He want to give us if only we were close enough to Him to hear it?

I think of the summer several years ago when the Lord spoke to me in my prayer time about starting a counseling center. I never planned to do that. I'm not business savvy, and I didn't know the slightest thing about incorporating or creating a website.

But I was challenged to draw closer to the Lord, and as I sought Him, He spoke to me. He confirmed it to me in His Word, and step by step, He led me.

Within two short months, it was all set. Incorporated, website, and an office—all totally God because I did not have a clue on my own. But the Spirit of God spoke something to me. One day, when I was reading in the Bible about Abigail wasting no time (1 Sam. 25:18), the words came alive to me and stirred my spirit. I sensed God instructing me: "Waste no time."

Could we be missing a calling on our lives, blinded to a path or direction He's placing before us because we are not spending time with Him? I love the Scripture, "Call to me and I will answer you and tell you great and unsearchable things you do not know" (Jer. 33:3).

Staying Close Leads to Greater Things

Mary chose to stay close to God even when she could not see Him. According to Acts 1:14, she remained with the disciples after Jesus ascended into heaven and was most likely with the other women in the Upper Room when the Holy Spirit descended upon them all.

With a gap in her heart, Mary kept seeking the Lord even after He ascended and she could not see Him. Jeremiah 29:13 gives us a principle. "You will seek me and find me when you seek me with all your heart." She watched and waited, eager for Him to return. In this position, she was ready to be filled and refilled by the Holy Spirit.

"Suddenly a sound like the blowing of a violent wind came from heaven and filled the whole house where they were sitting. They saw what seemed to be tongues of fire that separated and came to rest on each of them. All of them were filled with the Holy Spirit and began to speak in other tongues as the Spirit enabled them" (Acts 2:2-4).

Imagine what it would have been like for her to be completely filled. What joy! What power the Lord would have given her to keep witnessing, to keep sharing the Gospel, to keep knowing His freedom.

There's so much for us to learn in that. We need to patiently stay close to God even if we do not see Him moving or speaking or calling us or doing anything exciting. We just need to stay close. He wants us to know Him more. We must seek to know all of Him and experience all of what He has to give us.

Think of the healing and freedom that comes from making the choice to read the Word of God daily and live by His principles.

Do you need freedom today? Maybe you realize that the enemy still has a foothold in your life because you are dabbling in some pattern of habitual sin. Unforgiveness, unchecked anger, lying, cheating, stealing. God loves you, sees you, and wants to help you. Confess your sin to Him. Repent of those habits and replace them.

Maybe you recognize a need to start a real friendship with the Lord. Maybe you have strayed from the Lord. He's beckoning you to come back to Him, to stay by His side now, more than ever.

The psalmist prayed, "Save by your right hand those who take refuge in you from their foes. Keep me as the apple of your eye; hide me in the shadow of your wings from the wicked who are out to destroy me" (Ps. 17:7-9). We might have a real enemy who attacks our mental wellness, but staying in the presence of the Lord is a forcefield and wall of protection. Go spend time with Him today!

Recap and Engage

Truths to Calm Mental Storms: Choosing to stay closely connected with Jesus will protect me from going back to my past hurts and hang-ups.

Lies to Refute: I will never get over my issues. I can have victory over my issues without being in the presence of God daily.

Take It to Heart: Have you entertained the occult or any other wicked practices? Now is the time to renounce all evil and confess Jesus as your Lord!

Do you have any strongholds or life-controlling habits? Look up Scripture that gives you insight on how to overcome, and courageously seek help from your pastor or godly friends.

Is there an area of your thought life you need to expose? Maintain a level of vulnerability with others so you can expose lies and ways the enemy is trying to stifle or distract you. Walk in freedom.

Give Him every concern you have. Literally, everything. Nothing is too big or too small. Do you feel distant from someone you love? Do you feel like you're not performing well at work or school or home? Do you feel inferior? Are you having a hard time with the aging process? Is there a loved one whose issues keep you up at night? Decide to talk to God about it, stay close to Him, and let Him do something about it.

Prayer: *Lord, thank You that You will bless my life as I choose to stay close to You by being in Your Word, spending time in prayer every day, thinking Your thoughts, surrounding myself with godly friends, and preventing myself from engaging in spiritually draining media and entertainment. Thank You for what happens as I stay close to You. I am free from the past grips of the enemy. I need You to help me stay close. In Jesus' name, amen.*

Choose to Get Back Up Again

Read: John 21

Seventy-eight year-old Harold slurred when he spoke and slobbered when he ate. A stroke had stolen his primary capacities; he was bedridden and sentenced to a long-term rehabilitation facility. He demonstrated signs of depression, and as the psychologist for the building, I was given the joy of meeting with him once a week. Whenever the weather was nice, I would wheel him outside, and we would "walk" and talk. I loved getting him into the sunlight and letting him smell the flowers. He said it helped him feel human again.

During our conversations, he expressed much pain over past mistakes as well as things he'd left undone. "I should have been a better dad. I should have been more faithful. Why did I throw my life away?" One day he sobbed heavily and asked, "Can God ever forgive me?"

I realized that Harold's motivation to heal physically was stunted by his emotional regret. Whole healing would come only with his willingness to accept His Creator's mercy and grace.

What about you? Is there anything you regret doing? A moment you wish you could erase? An impulsive move, a missed opportunity? Fear gripped you so you panicked and did the wrong thing. Maybe you were provoked by lust and acted against your morals. Maybe you betrayed someone. Or you wanted to win or get in so badly, you cheated. You behaved in such a way that you didn't even recognize yourself. Or maybe it was who you were back then, but so far from who you have become. The pain still haunts you.

We all have regrets, whether it's little moments of saying the wrong thing or more significant lapses in judgment and character that we wish we could undo. I've had many mom fails and several moments in marriage and in life that I wish I could undo. Regret. It's why I believe coming in second place is harder than coming in third, or any other place in a competition. Second-place Olympians, for example, have been found to be less happy and satisfied than bronze medalists. When you get silver, you tend to replay every aspect of how you performed and regret fumbling something that cost you the win.

Regret has been defined as feeling "sad, repentant, or disappointed over something that has happened or been done, especially a loss or missed opportunity."[62] According to Dr. Greenberg in *Psychology Today*, regret is a cognitive state in which we blame ourselves for a bad outcome and experience loss and sorrow over what might have been.[63] While regret can help you become more insightful and avoid future negative outcomes, a pattern of ruminating over your past mistakes can lead to depression.

Jesus understood the impact of living in our past failures and sins. He ministered to the heart of a broken, dejected soul in a way that gives us hope today. In the final chapter of John, we witness a tender conversation between Jesus and His zealous disciple, Peter. Although he had walked on water, Peter was notorious for having denied Jesus three times. But Jesus went out of His way to restore and transform this same Peter, who was full of regret.

Do You Still Love Me?

Life had been a whirlwind for the disciples; they felt like they lost Jesus to the tragedy of the cross. Though they heard Jesus had come back to life, Peter chose to go fishing. Six other disciples followed the natural-born leader. Can you imagine what Peter must have been thinking that night when he caught nothing? The accuser of his soul would have seized the moment of defeat to throw lies in his face. "You messed up your chance to follow Jesus. You can't even catch any fish. You can't even do what you were born to do. What good are you?"

Jesus interrupted Peter's distressed thoughts with a call from the shore. It was early in the morning when Jesus confidently invited the disciples to throw their nets onto the other side, into the shallow part of the water. After a failed attempt in a domain at which he used to be successful, Peter decided to give it a shot, and voila! A miraculous catch of big fish in the shallow Sea of Tiberias.

When Peter realized it was Jesus, he jumped in the water and swam over to his Savior; the others pulled the boat to shore.

After feeding the disciples physically and providing for them financially through the supernatural catch, Jesus ministered to Peter's deepest pain. Interestingly, He addressed Peter three times using his formal name, Simon, son of John. Although Jesus had renamed Peter earlier, calling him Cephas, the Greek word for rock, Jesus now used Peter's old name. Jesus did not assume that Peter was done with the old Peter. He used this opportunity to reinstate Peter and allow him to truly embrace the new man he was called to be.

In *The NIV Application Commentary of John*, Gary Burge wrote that Jesus' query of Peter is one of the most celebrated exchanges in the Bible. To appreciate the subtleties in the transaction, it's important to understand the specific Greek meanings of the word love.

Phileo is a brotherly love of friendship. *Agapao* love goes much deeper—an unconditional love, deep and fervent—which we discussed in John 13. Burge describes the distinction:

Take 1: Jesus said, "Do you love (agapao) me?" Peter answered, "I love (phileo) you."

Take 2: Jesus said, "Do you love (agapao) me?" Peter answered, "I love (phileo) you."

Take 3: Jesus asked, "Do you love (phileo) me?" Peter responded, "I love (phileo) you."[64]

Whether or not the Aramaic exchange between Jesus and Peter reflected the differences in the word for love that was used, we can note one thing. Peter was being very careful about how he spoke, maybe for the first time. He wasn't saying, "Yes, God, I love you unconditionally. I am sold out, all the way." His cautious honesty paid off. The third time Jesus reinstated Peter, He met him where his love was at and asked if Peter was willing to *phileo* love Him by feeding His sheep.

Too often we are tempted to believe we must become a *better* person before Jesus can really love us or before we *deserve* to walk in His love. That's just not true! Jesus came down to Peter's level. He will meet us right where we are. That takes off so much pressure to achieve.

Jesus saw what Peter was able to commit to in that moment. He worked with Peter, giving him a chance to be restored to God and His purpose for him. Even allowing Peter to be the one to bring in the net was an act of mercy, encouraging Peter to step once again into his calling of catching men.

Jesus' conversation with Peter shows us that as long as we come to Jesus, there is still hope. As long as we can breathe, there is still a chance to be forgiven. There is still a chance for a bright future ahead.

A Deeper Love

Even though he couldn't unconditionally, wholeheartedly love Jesus that day on the shore, Peter would soon be able to rise to a higher *agapao* love with the power of the Holy Spirit in his life.

After waiting for the Holy Spirit as Jesus instructed, Peter was filled with the Holy Spirit in the Upper Room, as recorded in Acts 1-2. He was set on fire and went on to start the church. In his epistles, Peter challenges believers to love God and love others; in each of seven verses about love, he refers to *agapao* love.

For example, he wrote in 1 Peter 1:22, "Now that you have purified yourselves by obeying the truth so that you have sincere love (*phileo*) for each other, love (*agapao*) one another deeply, from the heart." This verse could represent the transformation of Peter's own heart and love. He challenged believers to move from *phileo* to *agapao*, just as he had been able to do through the power of the Holy Spirit. Again, he stated in 1 Peter 4:8, "Above all, love (*agapao*) each other deeply, because love (*agapao*) covers a multitude of sins."

Who made the difference? The Holy Spirit. He brought Peter to a place of *agapao*, where he desired to meet Jesus. Peter needed the power of the Holy Spirit to help him truly love and act in accordance with God's will.

I can relate. I grew up in church learning about the Holy Spirit, but while on our honeymoon, George told me about the baptism of the Holy Spirit—being filled with the Spirit as a subsequent experience after salvation. I had no idea what he was talking about. Rather than try to convince me himself, my wise husband encouraged me to read the Scriptures. I sought the Lord and told Him genuinely, "I want more of You, Lord. I want everything of You that there is to have."

I poured over the Bible. I noticed a difference in the disciples from the time Jesus breathed on them for their salvation (John 20:22) and when they were baptized in the Holy Spirit (Acts 1-2). The disciples were empowered in a new way when the Holy Spirit filled them. They spoke in languages they did not understand. I began to pray and seek God for the Holy Spirit to move in my life more powerfully.

One day I noticed a pamphlet called "The Holy Spirit" at a Christian book store. I paged through it. The clerk must have seen the desperation on my face because to my surprise, he asked, "Do you want to be filled with the Spirit?"

"Um, yes. Actually, I've been praying for that for a long time."

When he offered to pray for me, I looked around. "Here?"

With caution, I followed the man to the back of the store. He put his hands on my head and prayed a simple prayer for me to be filled with the Holy Spirit. After he prayed, I opened my eyes, and he asked, "Did any new words or syllables come to you?"

"Maybe," I said.

"Don't be embarrassed. Just keep praying in the Spirit. Sing in the language He gives you in your car. Don't be afraid. God loves you."

And that was that. I took his advice. I continued to pray with the new sounds He put into my heart and mouth. I put the music on really loud so I wouldn't feel self-conscious. As I continued to pray, God began to give me more of a hunger for Him, more of a love for Him.

Naturally, I questioned if anything had changed or if this was real. But two things were happening that were undeniable.

First, I had more joy. I had battled disordered eating since I was thirteen years old. Now, as I began to pray in the Spirit, God healed me of this stronghold. I had victory to overcome through the Spirit of God!

Prior to the baptism of the Holy Spirit in my life, I thought that obsessing over food would be my life-long struggle, but now He broke me of something I couldn't overcome on my own.

Second, I felt a desire to share the gospel. In the next month at my hospital, affiliated with Yale School of Medicine, I felt compelled to share Christ with three different people. Each one got saved.

Prior to that, I think I had maybe led three people to the Lord in my lifetime. In just a couple of months after I received the baptism of the Holy Spirit, three souls were added to the Kingdom of God.

And this was just the beginning. God began to fill me with His love and the power to love in the deep way He had called me to love. I was becoming new.

The difference was the Baptism of the Holy Spirit.

The truth is that a deepening love for God and others was not just for Peter and certainly not just for me. The Holy Spirit can move in your life, too, to bring you to a deeper love for God, others, and yourself. I encourage you to pray this Scripture daily if you have never experienced the power of the baptism of the Holy Spirit: "He who did not spare his own Son, but gave him up for us all—how will he not also, along with him, graciously give us all things?" (Rom. 8:32).

Ask God, who has graciously given you salvation to graciously baptize you in the Holy Spirit.

The Greater Good

Jesus gave Peter a new purpose. He invited Peter to feed His lambs, take care of His sheep, and feed His sheep. He was asking him to tend to His flocks and watch over them like a shepherd would, to love them, care for them sacrificially, and help them in need. He was calling Peter to a life of feeding His lambs with the Word of God.

Peter's future would be more than fishing; it now included shepherding. The miraculous catch of fish became a reminder, a picture for the disciples to keep in their minds. In their own striving, they could not succeed, but with Jesus, success was guaranteed. With Him, failures could be erased.

Peter was called to embrace a greater good of loving the body of Christ, and his writings reflect it. You and I are called to do the same. We are to make our lives about more than ourselves.

Jesus could have said, "Peter, do you love Me? I love you too. Peter, do you love Me? You are great. Peter, do you love Me? You aren't a failure."

Those truths would have ministered to Peter, but Jesus took it a step further and defined Peter's purpose.

Jesus wasn't trying to stroke Peter's ego and make him feel better about himself. This is the problem with humanistic approaches to psychology, like positive psychology. In and of ourselves, we don't have what it takes to make others feel better or to heal ourselves. We must follow our Savior's example, for true satisfaction and healing from the past comes only by looking beyond our own interests and loving others (Phil. 2:4). The only way Peter was able to move beyond regret and failure was to look beyond himself and love others. A life spent in service to others, taking care of God's interests, will defeat every past failure and selfish interest.

Jesus told Peter how he would die by crucifixion, then invited him again to follow Him—not just in life, but even in death.

If we give our lives to Christ, He will take care of us. When we live crucified with Christ, we no longer live, but Christ lives in us (Gal. 2:20, author's paraphrase). Because of that, we don't have to worry about this life. God will see to it that our lives hold meaning and purpose and allow us a legacy beyond ourselves.

Beauty From Ashes

While the enemy wants to destroy and disqualify us, God uses our failures and flaws for His glory. He is able to turn around anything we go through and make it into something good.

Peter's downfall allowed him to be understanding when the people he served were tempted to fall away. Failure could have sent him into despair, like it did for Judas. What a contrast we see between Peter and Judas in the pages of history. Both fell short, but Peter chose to come back to Jesus and not remain in a state of self-criticism, depression, or pessimism. I've always wondered if it could have been different for Judas Iscariot if he had confessed to Jesus and sought His forgiveness and restoration.

Jesus reinstated Peter from his failures and deepest moment of regret. Peter realized only Jesus could restore him, so he hurried to the shore. I love the way theologian Gary Burge put this:

> He ran to the only one who could heal his memories; who could rewrite the terrible pictures and sounds of his recent past—the courtyard, the charcoal fire, the young man. The miracle demonstrated that despite Peter's failings, Jesus was still on his side, cooking a good meal for friends, having fun filling nets with fish. Then the invitation to affirm his love three times drowned out the echoes of his betrayal that haunted him. The last time Peter stood over a charcoal fire, he denied Jesus (John 18:18). Now Jesus invited Peter to stand over another charcoal fire (John 21:9), and with it, review old memories and remove them.

Burge goes on to say, "The work of the church can only go forward when we are unburdened of our destructive memories through the gracious forgiveness of God."[65]

Do you have destructive memories that hold you back, paralyze you, and remind you of everything you should be but cannot be?

How do we let these memories affect us? Do we write our personal narrative in a way that highlights our misses and mistakes? Or does our life story feature God's ability to redeem and turn those ashes into something beautiful? How do you view yourself today?

Overcoming our guilt and regret involves believing we can be forgiven, even for that one thing we did that seems unforgivable. Nothing is too hard for God, and nothing can separate you from His love. So humble yourself and let God forgive you and heal that wound in your heart.

Are you willing to let your life be used? Feeding others feeds your soul and heals your pain more than anything else can. Tending to the needs of others gives you the opportunity to make something beautiful even of your losses. Are there people in your life who are broken and need the love of Christ? Nurture them with the Word of God.

Science supports the truth that helping others helps us.[66] Many self-help articles cite evidence that helping others can benefit our own mental well-being. Some of the perks include: reduction of stress, improved mood, increased self-esteem, and a happier outlook.[67]

People experience a better quality of life when it is spent for others. Has God given you a dream about how He might use your life?

Have you let your regrets define you in such a way that you feel disqualified from your dreams? You might have been in jail, but God could call you to become a prison chaplain and minister in an effective way others could not without the experience. You may have had an abortion, but God may use you to minister uniquely to others with that kind of grief.

Your pain can become your platform.

I have many friends healed of addiction through the ministry of ATC who have decided to give their lives with great passion and commitment to the cause of seeing the addicted set free. Let yourself dream about how God could use you. There is no limit; just let your heart be open to tending to His sheep.

Recap and Engage

Truths to Calm Mental Storms: I can be forgiven of all my mistakes and live life beyond my regrets. A life of service to others is the most meaningful life!

Lies to Refute: My failures disqualify me from being used for God.

Take it to Heart: Is there a regret you need to give to the Lord today and receive His forgiveness? Take time to talk to Him and listen to His response. He will take care of you as you take care of His interests.

I encourage you to share with a friend about how God has healed you and ministered to you through this study.

Prayer: *Father, thank You that in Christ, I am forgiven, made new, and given the opportunity to start over and forge ahead. I'm not defined by my past; I am not imprisoned to regret. I am free to move on and shine like a star as I hold out the Word of life to others (Phil. 2:14-16). Help me declare Your truth boldly, for Your glory. In Jesus' name, amen.*

Epilogue: The Hush After the Storm

A little girl I'd just met pointed to the scar on my face. "What's that mark?"

I smiled at the bluntness of a child. Sometimes I forget about the scar left on my chin from that fiery night, but children occasionally point it out, sensing that it seems out of place with the rest of my face. Yet, the scar belongs.

Several months after the accident, my mom lovingly asked if I wanted to have plastic surgery to hide my scar. Somehow, I balked at the idea, and I'm so glad I kept it.

The scar tells the story of a day that would be forever etched in my mind: August 14, 1988, when my Dad went home.

It has become a keepsake of the goodness of God, His presence in the fire, and His lovingkindness in the storm.

It captures the journey of redemption, of Jesus doing what only God can do: take our worst nightmare and make something beautiful and meaningful out of it.

What about you, friend? What are your scars?

How I wish I could know you and your story! I'd love to learn about your struggles and victories and hear how Jesus, the Storm Whisperer, has worked in your life to bring you peace and perspective.

As I wrote and thought of you, the Lord inspired me daily with a theme verse to anchor every chapter: "He calmed the storm to a whisper, and the waves of the sea were hushed" (Ps. 107:29 BSB).

Have you ever beheld the wonder of the hush after a storm? I visited my family in South India every few years during my childhood, often during monsoon season. A storm would come out of nowhere and ransack the earth with a torrential downpour and then vanish with an eerie whisper that left the air thick and slightly cooled. I loved sitting on the patio of my grandparents' farm and watching the earth recover, the waterlogged flowers slowly straighten, and animals come out of hiding.

Can you imagine the greatest storm that ever hit the earth and the holy hush that would have followed? In Genesis 9, the Bible recounts that God sent forty days of rain to judge humankind. The flood changed the face of the planet and wiped out all life except for the eight people and diverse pairs of animals that were saved on the ark. The Creator made a covenant with Noah that the earth would never again be destroyed by a flood (Gen. 9:8-11). To prove that He would never forget His promise, God sent Noah a sign.

After commanding the epic storm to stop, the Storm Whisperer kissed the sky with a rainbow. What splendor! An optical phenomenon with its shimmering array of color, the rainbow is one of my favorites in nature, especially because of what it was designed to symbolize. This is God talking to us! This is God reminding Himself of a promise He made to all creation. He hushed the storm, then touched the sky with a symbol of His presence (Rev. 4:3, Eze. 1:28).

We may be storm-averse, but it often takes a storm for us to see a rainbow, a principle echoed throughout Scripture. The Lord makes beauty from ashes (Isa. 61:3), gladness from mourning (Isa. 61:3), and life from death (John 12:25). Your scars testify of this divine reversal. The Storm Whisperer shows Himself to us in undeniable ways amid great difficulty. This truth applies to the chaos in our minds.

As I wrote, I prayed the Lord would miraculously calm your mental storms and give you His peace and freedom. After working through the chapters of John, I pray you feel refreshed—like life has been breathed into your soul through the power of His Word, that you feel equipped to live the blessed, abundant life God sent His Son for you to have, and that you are ready to experience whole health through the presence of the Holy Spirit. This doesn't mean all your old memories are erased or that your pain is forgotten; rather, the Lord has given you tools to walk out a wholly healthy life. I hope you have grown to love God, who came down to earth to save you, more intimately.

That's how I feel after writing this text—totally grateful for the life and ministry of Jesus and how He saved my soul. I love how He personally healed the inner storms of every person He encountered and how He leaves rainbows in the wake of life's storms. That is the way I want to live!

You may find you take a couple steps back, even as you are transforming. This happens. Don't be discouraged or live in regret. Confess your failures and mistakes to God. Onward, Christian soldier!

A life focused on worshipping the one true God is a life that will always be successful and blessed, both in this life and in the one to come. Take care of your body—it is the temple of the Holy Spirit. Don't go overboard; but you can't neglect your physical health either.

Continue to walk in the soul-breathing affirmations we've navigated together. You are loved and important, my friend. Your life has tremendous purpose, and you don't need anyone's affirmation or approval to prove it. Jesus already said so! You don't have to perform to be of value. Jesus wants to take your shame, grief, and pain and help you walk in healing. Remember how He encountered Nicodemus, Mary and Martha, Mary Magdalene, and Peter? If you fail, He is there to pick you up; but cling to Him. Abiding in Christ is the key to abundance in every way.

Listen to His voice more than those ugly lies of the evil one. Confess your sins, forgive others, and replace anxious thoughts with affirmations of trust. Take these truths like medicine for your weary soul; these principles will invigorate your life.

It's been such a privilege to travel with you on this journey. I "ask God to fill you with the knowledge of his will through all the wisdom and understanding that the Spirit gives, so that you may live a life worthy of the Lord and please him in every way: bearing fruit in every good work, growing in the knowledge of God, being strengthened with all power according to his glorious might so that you may have great endurance and patience, and giving joyful thanks to the Father, who has qualified you to share in the inheritance of his holy people in the kingdom of light" (Col. 1:9-12).

Peace and love!

dolly

VERSES TO ANCHOR YOU IN THE STORM

May He equip you with all you need for doing his will. May he produce in you, through the power of Jesus Christ, every good thing that is pleasing to him. All glory to him forever and ever! Amen.
Hebrews 13:21 (NLT)

So do not fear, for I am with you; do not be dismayed, for I am your God. I will strengthen you and help you; I will uphold you with my righteous right hand. "All who rage against you will surely be ashamed and disgraced; those who oppose you will be as nothing and perish."
Isaiah 41:10-11

For we are God's handiwork, created in Christ Jesus to do good works, which God prepared in advance for us to do.
Ephesians 2:10

I can do all things through Christ who gives me strength.
Philippians 4:13 (NKJV)

Therefore, my dear brothers and sisters, stand firm. Let nothing move you. Always give yourselves fully to the work of the Lord, because you know that your labor in the Lord is not in vain.
1 Corinthians 15:58

I have loved you with an everlasting love; I have drawn you with unfailing kindness.
Jeremiah 31:3

"Can a mother forget the baby at her breast and have no compassion on the child she has borne? Though she may forget, I will not forget you! See, I have engraved you on the palms of my hands."
Isaiah 49:15-16

When you pass through the waters, I will be with you; and when you pass through the rivers, they will not sweep over you. When you walk through the fire, you will not be burned; the flames will not set you ablaze.
Isaiah 43:2

For the eyes of the Lord range throughout the earth to strengthen those whose hearts are fully committed to him.
2 Chronicles 16:9

If you remain in me and my words remain in you, ask whatever you wish, and it will be done for you. This is to my Father's glory, that you bear much fruit, showing yourselves to be my disciples.
John 15:7-8

"I will restore you to health and heal your wounds" declares the Lord.
Jeremiah 30:17

Praise the Lord, O my soul, and forget not all his benefits—who forgives all your sins and heals all your diseases.
Psalm 103:2-3

Beloved, I pray that you may prosper in all things and be in health, just as your soul prospers.
3 John 2 (NKJV)

For though we live in the world, we do not wage war as the world does. The weapons we fight with are not the weapons of the world. On the contrary, they have divine power to demolish strongholds. We demolish arguments and every pretension that sets itself up against the knowledge of God, and we take captive every thought to make it obedient to Christ
2 Corinthians 10:3-5

And surely I am with you always, to the very end of the age.
Matthew 28:20

Finally, brothers, whatever is true, whatever is honorable, whatever is just, whatever is pure, whatever is lovely, whatever is commendable, if there is any excellence, if there is anything worthy of praise, think about these things.
Philippians 4:8 (ESV)

No weapon that is fashioned against you shall succeed, and you shall refute every tongue that rises against you in judgment. This is the heritage of the servants of the Lord and their vindication from me, declares the Lord."
Isaiah 54:17 (ESV)

Faith

AUTHOR PAGE

Dr. Dolly Thomas is a wife, mom, licensed psychologist, writer, and speaker. Since 2009, she has ministered to the staff and students of Adult and Teen Challenge of Texas, where she currently serves as the Director of Counseling for the organization and the Director of the Houston Women's Program. In 2013, she founded Transform Counseling to bring God's love, truth, and healing to the broken and hurting. Her call to counsel came after the tragic death of her father during early adolescence. Dolly completed post-doctoral training at Yale Medical School and holds undergraduate and graduate degrees from the University of Pennsylvania and Fordham University, respectively. She and her husband George, President of ATCOT, enjoy raising together their four incredible children, Jadyn, Liana, Caris, and Luke, in Houston. An avid jogger and hobby artist, Dolly loves rainbows, reading her Bible, and seeing a soul added to the Kingdom of God.

If while reading *The Storm Whisperer*, you have made the decision to ask Jesus to be your Savior, or if you have experienced healing in your thought life in some way, Dolly would love to hear from you.

Connect with her via email at transformcounseling@gmail.com or on social media.

For additional resources, visit her counseling website at www.transformcounselingcenter.com.

If anyone you know is struggling with addiction and needs help, please visit www.tctexas.org.

ENDNOTES

1 May, J. (2019, October 14). Nationwide study confirms Adult & Teen Challenge Program Success. Adult & Teen Challenge. https://teenchallengeusa.org/news/nationwide-study-confirms-adult-teen-challenge-program-success/

2 G4053 – Perissos – Strong's Greek lexicon (KJV). Blue Letter Bible. (n.d.) https://www.blueletterbible.org/lexicon/g4053/kjv/tr/0-1/

3 Leaf, Caroline. (2018) Switch On Your Brain: The Key to Peak Happiness, Thinking, and Health. Baker Book House.

4 KJV dictionary definition: Choice. AV1611.com (n.d.). https://av1611.com/kjbp/kjv-dictionary/choice.html

5 (2016, December 26). Retrieved from https://twitter.com/timkellernyc/status/813466973057220609?lang=en

6 Shaw, M. E. (2018) The Heart of Addiction: A Biblical Perspective. Focus Publishing

7 G2212 – zeteo – Strong's Greek lexicon (KJV). Blue Letter Bible. (n.d.) https://www.blueletterbible.org/lexicon/g2212/kjv/tr/0-1/

8 Tripp, P. D. (2022). Age of Opportunity: A Biblical Guide to Parenting Teens. P&R Publishing.

9 Blog. Dr. Leslie Korn. (n.d.). Retrieved July 9, 2022, from https://drlesliekorn.com/blog/

10 Ahlskog, J. E., Geda, Y. E., Graff-Radford, N. R., & Petersen, R. C. (2011, September 1). Physical exercise as a preventatitve of disease-modifying treatment of dementia and brain aging. Mayo Clinic Proceedings. http://www.mayoclinicalproceedings.org/article/S0025-6196(11)65219-1/fulltext

11 Salmon, P. (2001). Effects of physical exercise on anxiety, depression, and sensitivity to stress. Clinical Psychology Review, 21(1), 33-61. https://doi.org/10.1016/s0272-7358(99)00032-2

12 Nittle, N. (2021, July1). Can social media cause depression? Verywell Mind. https://www.verywellmind.com/social-media-and-depression-5085354

13 Burge, G. The NIV Application Commentary: John, p. 114)

14 van Rosmalen, L., van der Veer, R., & van der Horst, F. C. (2020, June). The Nature of Love: Harlow, Bowlby and Bettelheim on affectionless mothers. History of psychiatry. https://www.ncbi.nlm.nih.gov/pmc/articles/PMC7433398/

15 McLeod, S. (2020, September 18). Harry Harlow, Monkey Love Experiments. Harry Harlow, Monkey Love Experiments Simply Psychology. https://www.simplypsychology.org/harlow-monkey.html

16 McLeod, S. (1970, January 1). Saul McLeod. Strange Situation/Simply Psychology. https:www/simplypsychology.org/mary-ainsworth.html

17 The ultimate journey. Christ-Life Ministries. (n.d.). https://www.theultimatejourney.org/store/phase-1/phase-1-program/version1

18 Holland, P.S. (n.d.). The Samaritan Woman, equal to the apostles, St Photina. Samaritan woman, Equal to the apostles, St Photina. Questions & answer https://www.orthodox.net/questions/samaritan_woman_1.html.

19 Cloud, H., & Townsend, J. S. (2004) Boundaries. Zondervan.

20 DiMaria, L. (2020, September 17). Learned helplessness in children. Verywell Mind. https://www.verywellmind.com/learned-helplessness-in-children-1066762

21 What are attributional and explanatory styles in psychology? PositivePsychology.com (2022, May 27). https://positivepsychology.com/explanatory-styles-optimism.

22 Guzik, D. (1970, February 21). Study guide for John 5 by David Guzik. Blue Letter Bible. https://www.blueletterbible.org/Comm/guzik_david/StudyGuide2017-Jhn-5.cfm?a=1002001

23 G2309 – thelo – Strong's Greek lexicon (NIV). Blue Letter Bible. (n.d.) https://www.blueletterbible.org/lexicon/g2309/niv/mgnt/0-1/

24 G5199 – hygies – Strong's Greek lexicon (NIV). Blue Letter Bible. (n.d.) https://www.blueletterbible.org/lexicon/g5199/mgnt/tr/0-1/
25 G1453 – egeioro – Strong's Greek lexicon (NIV). Blue Letter Bible. (n.d.) https://www.blueletterbible.org/lexicon/g1453/niv/mgnt/0-1/
26 G5281 – hypomone – Strong's Greek lexicon (NIV). Blue Letter Bible. (n.d.) https://www.blueletterbible.org/lexicon/g5281/esv/mgnt/0-1/
27 Duckworth, A., 2022. Grit: The power of passion and perseverance. [online] Ted.com. Available at https//www.ted.com/talks/angela_lee_duckworth_grit_the_power_of_passion_and_perseverance?language=en
28 Schimelpfening, N. (2021, January 29). Do you know the signs of clinical depression? Verywell Mind. https://www.verywellmind.com/top-depression-symptoms-1066910
29 Brene Brown. (2021, October 28). Shame vs. Guilt. Brene Brown. https://brenebrown.com/articles/2013/01/15/shame-v-guilt/
30 G225 – aletheia – Strong's Greek lexicon (NIV). Blue Letter Bible. (n.d.) https://www.blueletterbible.org/lexicon/g225/kjv/tr/0-1/
31 The ultimate journey. Christ-Life Ministries. (n.d.). https://www.theultimatejourney.org/store/phase-1/phase-1-program/version1
32 Psychiatric & Mental Health Services: Achieve Medical Center. Achieve Medical. (n.d.) https://www.achievemedicalcenter.com.
33 Lewis, C. S. (1996). The Screwtape Letters, p.16. Harper San Franciso.
34 Chand, S. R. (2015). Leadership Pain: The Classroom for Growth. Thomas Nelson
35 G2008 – epitimao – Strong's Greek lexicon (KJV). Blue Letter Bible. (n.d.) https://www.blueletterbible.org/lexicon/g2008/kjv/tr/0-1?
36 Murray, Andrew. (2019). Absolute surrender and other addresses. Digireads. com.
37 G5015 – tarasso – Strong's Greek lexicon (NIV). Blue Letter Bible. (n.d.) https://www.blueletterbible.org/lexicon/g5015/kjv/tr/0-1/
38 Cherry, K. (2021, April 26). Why we risk our own well-being to help others. Verywell Mind. https://www.verywellmind.com/what-is-altruism-2794828
39 Lewis, C.S. (2017). *The Four Loves.* HarperOne.
40 G5015 – tarasso – Strong's Greek lexicon (NIV). Blue Letter Bible. (n.d.) https://www.blueletterbible.org/lexicon/g5015/kjv/tr/0-1/
41 G4100 – pisteuo – Strong's Greek lexicon (NIV). Blue Letter Bible. (n.d.) https://www.blueletterbible.org/lexicon/g4100/kjv/tr/0-1/
42 Gaither, Bill and Gloria. "Because He Lives." Amazing Hymns. https://amazinghymns.com/because-he-lives/
43 G3134 – maranatha – Strong's Greek lexicon (NIV). Blue Letter Bible. (n.d.) https://www.blueletterbible.org/lexicon/g3134/kjv/tr/0-1/
44 Guzik, D. (1970, February 21). Study guide for 1 Corinthians 16 by David Guzik. Blue Letter Bible https://www.blueletterbible.org/Comm/guzik_david/StudyGuide2017 -1Cr/1Cr16.cfm?a=1078022
45 Thomas, G., & Thomas, G. (2018) Sacred Marriage. Zondervan.
46 G3306 – meno – Strong's Greek lexicon (NIV). Blue Letter Bible. (n.d.) https://www.blueletterbible.org/lexicon/g3306/kjv/tr/0-1/
47 Topical bible: Prune. (n.d.). https://biblehub.com/topical/p/prune.htm.
48 ABC News Network (n.d.). ABC News. https://abcnews.go.com/GMA/Healthy/story?id=1014636.
49 Morris, Robert. (2019). God I Never Knew. Gateway Create Pub.
50 G1651 – elegcho – Strong's Greek lexicon (NIV). Blue Letter Bible. (n.d.) https://www.blueletterbible.org/lexicon/g1651/kjv/tr/0-1/

51 H5162 – naham – Strong's Greek lexicon (NIV). Blue Letter Bible. (n.d.) https://www.blueletterbible.org/lexicon/H5162/kjv/wic/0-1/
52 NBCUniversal news Group, (2018,February 16). This is your brain on prayer and meditation. NBCNews.com. https://www.nbcnews.com/better/health/your-brain-pryaer-meditation-ncna812376
53 "Brain Images Reveal First Physical Evidence That AA Prayers Reduce Cravings." ScienceDaily, ScienceDaily, 12 May 2016, https://www.sciencedaily.com/releases/2016/05/160512142925.htm.
54 "Get Kids into the Bible-the Fun Way!" Pak, https://biblefactpak.com/.
55 Elizabeth. S. J. and. (1971). The Hiding Place – The Triumphant True Story of Corrie Ten Boom. Bantam Book.
56 Wiersbe, W. W. (1991). Be Patient. Chariot Victor Pub.
57 Spurgeon, C. (2015, December 22). I owe more to the fire, and the hammer, and the file, than to anything else in my lord's workshop – spurgeon. Twitter. https://twitter.com/spurgeon_/status/679153725865336832
58 Smedes, Lewis B. Forive and Forget – Healing the Hurts We don't Deserve. Harpercollins Publishers Inc, 2007.
59 Marianne Williamson Quotes. BrainyQuote.com, BrainyMedia Inc, 2022. https://www.brainyquote.com/quotes/marianne_williamson_635346.
60 G5117 – topos – Strong's Greek lexicon (KJV). Blue Letter Bible. (n.d.) https://www.blueletterbible.org/lexicon/g5117/kjv/tr/0-1/
61 Sermon: What Mary and John Saw John 20:1-18. Sovereign Grace Church/Chillicothe, OH. (2017, November 7). https://gccwaverly.net/2017/11/07/sermon-what-mary-and-john-saw-john.
62 "Regret English Definition and Meaning." Lexico Dictionaries/English, Lexico Diectionaries, https://www.lexico.com/en/definition/regret.
63 Sussex Publishers. (n.d.) The Psychology of Regret. Psychology Today. https://www.psychologytoday.com/us/blog/the-mindful-self-express/201205/the-psychology-regret
64 Burge, Gary. (2019). John (Vol. 978-0310452836), p. 587. Zondervan Pub. House.
65 Ibid., 684.
66 The Science of Kindness. Cedars. (n.d.). https://www.cedars-sinai.org/blog/science-of-kindness.html.
67 Giving. Action For Happiness. (n.d.) https://actionsforhappiness.org/10-keys/giving.

Made in the USA
Middletown, DE
27 February 2025

71913024R00157